Telling Truths

Storying Motherhood

Telling Truths
Storying Motherhood

EDITED BY
SHEENA WILSON AND DIANA DAVIDSON

DEMETER

DEMETER PRESS

Canada Council **Conseil des Arts**
for the Arts **du Canada**

The publisher gratefully acknowledges the support of the Canada Council for the Arts for its publishing program.

Demeter Press logo based on the sculpture "Demeter" by Maria-Luise Bodirsky <www.keramik-atelier.bodirsky.de>

Front cover artwork: "Phantom Vessel," ©Laura Endacott

Printed and Bound in Canada

Library and Archives Canada Cataloguing in Publication

Telling truths : storying motherhood / edited by Sheena Wilson and Diana Davidson.

Includes bibliographical references.
ISBN 978-1-927335-42-0 (pbk.)

1. Motherhood. 2. Mothers--Canada--Social conditions.
I. Davidson, Diana, 1976–, editor II. Wilson, Sheena, 1974–, editor

HQ759.T44 2014   306.874'3   C2014-902853-9

Demeter Press
140 Holland Street West
P. O. Box 13022
Bradford, ON L3Z 2Y5
Tel: (905) 775-9089
Email: info@demeterpress.org
Website: www.demeterpress.org

To our children:
Ewan, Roshan, Xander, Tejas and Viveka

Table of Contents

Acknowledgements

No one can really tell you how much you will change when you become or want to become a mother. That fierce love and almost manic need to protect your child can overwhelm you, save you, and push out room for nearly anything else in your life. And yet *Telling Truths* was born out of a desire to document this experience and also to create something about motherhood that is outside of motherhood itself.

We met in 2010, during a class called "Writing Motherhood" at "Women's Words: Summer Writing Week." "Women's Words" is a program that has been offered through the University of Alberta to support women's writing. It is a twenty-year tradition. In that time it has become a destination for women writers, published and unpublished, from across Canada and as far away as the United States, Mexico, and Australia, every June. Many of the two hundred abstracts from around the world that we received for *Telling Truths* came from women who had taken part in the program at some point over the past two decades. This year, "Women's Words" is on hiatus and we hope that the program continues in the near-future as it obviously inspires and supports women telling their stories.

Many writing groups have come out of "Women's Words" including the one that generated the seeds of this collection. The group has shifted and evolved over the past few years into a network of writers and friends who celebrated new babies, weathered marital woes and job changes, and commiserated over loss. We decided to try and publish some of the pieces. What you hold in your hands started off with that idea. Now we have an anthology with thirty-eight pieces by both well-known writers and writers publishing for the first-time. We are also proud that this book showcases diverse voices: there are women, and one man, of different ethnicities, classes, sexualities, and religions, all of whom have had wildly divergent experiences of motherhood.

In this book you'll find stories about pregnancy and giving birth, adoption, stepmothering, co-parenting and mothering through divorce, balancing the pressures of academic and writing lives, reconciling racial and cultural identities in a multicultural country, grandmothers who find themselves parenting, loss and death.

And since we decided to put the call out for this anthology of *Telling Truths*, as editors we have also had to challenge our own assumptions and truths. We have weathered the extreme highs and lows of being women who write and mother. Collectively we have experienced a new baby, divorce and navigating co-parenting, raising preschoolers and early-schoolers, supporting a friend who lost a child, mourning a friend who died of breast cancer leaving two toddlers motherless, and putting other writing and books out into the world. And in doing so, we discovered a whole community of other mothers who have been brave enough to write about their lives and experiences. We are thankful.

Telling Truths could not have come together without the support of many people. We would like to thank all the writers who contributed and worked with us on edits and rewrites, as well as Laura Endacott, who provided the cover image. Thank you to the women in our writing groups, and to our many generous colleagues. Thank you to Adam Carlson for helping us copy-edit the final manuscript.

We'd also like to note our appreciation to the following organizations for granting us republication permissions: The Sunday Edition, CBC Radio, for Fiona Tinwei Lam's "The Front of the Bus;" Freehand Books for Susan Olding's "Push-Me-Pull-You;" and Brindle & Glass for Jessica Kluthe's "Traces."

We are also thankful to Andrea O'Reilly for her commitment to scholarship that has created a space for research on motherhood to exist within Canadian academe. Without her dedication, this work would not have a place to exist and be in dialogue with other feminist discourses of motherhood. We also want to thank

Demeter Press for giving this collection a home. We are honoured that *Telling Truths* is being celebrated at the Mother's Day 2014 book launch as Demeter's fiftieth book—a milestone and a commendable achievement. Congratulations, Demeter!

We also wish to acknowledge our parents, our families, and our friends. We are grateful to all of you, especially those of you who took care of our children while we worked on a collection about motherhood. And Ajay, thank you for forging and negotiating with me our own version of empowered mothering and parenting informed by multiple cultures and languages.

Thank you to all the women in our lives who sustain us and all the mothers among you who inspire us: our sisters, cousins, aunts and friends. Thank you to our grandmothers, mothers, and mothers-in-law: Emilie, Katja, and Shirley; Phyllis, Bessie, Sharon, and Florence. Special thanks go to our children: Ewan, Roshan, Xander, Tejas, and Viveka.

To our readers, we hope you find your common ground in these pages.

—Sheena Wilson and Diana Davidson

Networks of Relations

Introduction to Writing Motherhood

SHEENA WILSON

AS MOTHERS we summon the depths of our personal power to bear our children into the world, literally and figuratively, and in so doing we are left bare. Exposed. The place we negotiate somewhere between our sense of self, our children, and society, is the liminal space of motherhood out of which our stories emerge. These stories are not always easy to share. Often it is hard to find the words to express the complexity of what happens when our socially constructed dreams of ourselves as mothers and our aspirations for our children intersect with our everyday lived realities: mothering through separation, divorce, combined family scenarios, and step-mothering; fostering; adopting; parenting through post-traumatic stress; mothering through child behaviour disorders, learning disabilities, physical disabilities; parenting through, and parenting children with, mental health issues; parenting through poverty; parenting across cultures; parenting in the face of racial discrimination; navigating heteronormativity as LGBT mothers; surviving the death of a child, the death of a spouse, and continuing to parent; surviving the betrayals and deceptions of our womanly bodies, of infertility, of miscarriages, of eating disorders; parenting through political and environmental crises; and ultimately, if our dreams go as planned, of having the privilege to learn to mother all over again—as we love, let go, and mother our adult children.

The moment of transformation from woman to mother is different for us all. Some of us morph into mothers at the inception of the idea, the knowledge we want to or will soon become mothers.

Others of us become mothers only once we have travailed in childbirth or after we have been handed our babies by surgically scrubbed OBGYNs. Some of us become mothers when we see our child in a photograph for the first time, or once we have flown the world over to meet our infant, or toddler or teenager in a foreign orphanage, or when a social worker knocks on the door holding the hand of a child who will become our own. For some of us the transformation to mother is less immediate. Even while we labour to perform the duties of motherwork and childcare, some of us still struggle to accept ourselves as mothers. This can occur due to postpartum depression, but it also happens for many other complicated reasons. Sometimes it is because we still walk unrecognized as mothers among our family and friends: perhaps while we struggle through fertility treatments, secret pregnancies, multiple miscarriages and even stillbirths. Then there are those of us who still go unrecognized because we have passed our children to other mothers through adoption or foster care. And then there are still others who feel unable to claim our status as mothers because our mothering is linked to some adjectival descriptor—a linguistic hint—that our version of mothering is somehow occurring in the shadow of genuine mothering, perhaps because we are birth-mothers or surrogate-mothers or foster-mothers or adoptive-mothers or step-mothers or single-mothers, or divorced-mothers or depressed-mothers or transgender-mothers or lesbian-mothers or poor-mothers or welfare-mothers or some other-mother. And finally, there is the plight of almost all mothers who parent in the shadow of imagined and imposed social dictates around how mothering should be practiced; and these notions of motherhood engender shame and confusion, and create fractures amongst communities of women based on false visions of what defines motherhood.

These are the stories the contributors to this collection are authoring—bearing into being and in so doing baring themselves to us, their readers, their community, other mothers and parents. Collectively, they are telling some of the truths of mothering in the late twentieth and early twenty-first centuries. This is their contribution to the body of published and publicly acknowledged women's writing, and motherwriting. Together we are resisting imposed definitions of motherhood and writing ourselves into the world.

MOTHERHOOD WRITES: RESISTANCE

The stories in *Telling Truths* contribute to an ongoing dialogue of rupture aimed at displacing patriarchal motherhood and ultimately at disrupting existing narratives of what it means to be a woman and mother. Motherhood, like marriage or any other institution, is subject to regulation and discipline—largely social but also legal and criminal. Versions of motherhood condoned by patriarchy limit and contain women's potentialities, often denying our subjectivity as thinking, acting, becoming women who exceed our roles as mothers.

Using literary license, contributing authors explore their lived realities and personal mothering experiences in ways that, when considered collectively, have the potential to expose falsely restrictive definitions of motherhood. Not every contributing writer is consciously acting according to or against particular definitions of mothering, but all of these stories complicate and break open constraining ideals of motherhood to which none of us can, and many of us don't want to, conform.

To write is to resist being restricted into predetermined roles. It is to experiment with what in the 1970s Adrienne Rich called being a courageous mother.[1] What, in the 1980s, Baba Cooper called radical mothering.[2] What Ariel Gore called hip mothering at the turn of the new millennium. What Susan Douglas and Meredith Michaels term rebellious mothering in 2004.[3] And what Andrea O'Reilly has described in great detail as mother outlaw (as Rich had before her), and empowered mothering, in all its modes, including feminist mothering, which Fiona Joy Green has written about extensively.[4] Ultimately, empowered mothers, according to O'Reilly, express their identity through "work, activism, friendships, relationships, hobbies and motherhood. These mothers insist on their own authority as mothers and refuse the relinquishment of their power as mandated in the patriarchal institution of motherhood" (*Feminist Mothering* 7). Empowered motherhood leaves a space for all of us to mother as an extension of ourselves and not as the fulfillment of a prescribed mandate.

Even to write our stories is considered, by some, a transgression. In particular, to write motherhood as creative non-fiction, the genre of this collection, might be judged a moral lapse. For creative non-fiction is a form based in experience and while its writers are empowered to use creative techniques associated with fiction to push the boundaries of how we tell truths, ultimately it is a truth-telling genre aimed at unveiling the "real." The edges of the stories of mothers are amorphous and jagged, infringing into territories inhabited by our children. For where do our stories end and the stories of our children begin? Where do we, as mothers, end and where do our children begin? A critique that we do not adhere to in this collection demarcates territory: these stories are not our stories, they do not belong to us because by writing about our children—minors for whom we are responsible—we are somehow profiteering or robbing or damaging them. However, this critical stance is part of a long silencing tradition that removes mothers from the spotlight, denying our own central role in the narrative of family. Of course, many contributors to this collection are writing their truths under pseudonyms to protect their children and their own identities. Yet, they are still driven to share these experiences, to contribute to a collective story of motherhood that is as complex and difficult as it is rewarding and empowering. And in so doing, we build a repertoire of new or familiar choreographies.

Women's tradition of storytelling is as long as that of men's stories and male authors. However, the oral and unpublished and private nature of these stories has meant that we have not been able to preserve large quantities of this female knowledge and transmit it through the generations. Little of the practical realities or the more sophisticated contemplations of women's lives have been preserved—fewer still in literary forms. Historically, if women were literate, much of what they wrote remained unpublished, private endeavours recorded in epistolary and diary writing forms. Writing—a practice seen as unfit for women was an alleged cause for madness. A writing woman: at one time, the very definition of an untamed and unruly female, and yet, women still had a need to tell their stories. Hidden stories. Private poems. Circulating unofficially, if they were shared at all. We can only imagine the

4

rich her-stories of the oral tradition that have been lost to us. Even from what was written, much has been lost to the archive, despite the valiant and ongoing efforts of literary historians. That said, over the last four decades, women and mothers have increasingly had the social place and privilege to write their stories.

WRITING MOTHERHOOD INTO THE CENTRE

We are the stories we tell about ourselves. The writers in this collection are writing to create knowledge—to know themselves—as mothers. They are writing to record their mother-knowledge and mother-experiences. They write to share this knowledge with women across time and space. Their writings have the potential to disrupt what has been written about women and mothers. These women contribute to the stories already told, already written, already shared: they contribute to writing away our absence. Stories of motherhood are scant in the recorded history of world literature, where men have historically been the protagonists, and women maintained peripheral roles. To write motherhood is to reposition existing daughter-centred cultural narratives.[5] To write motherhood is to write ourselves into the centre of the story.

The cover image, by Montreal artist Laura Endacott, which is part of a larger project titled *Phantom Vessel*, works to re-imagine maternal space. The design of this installation piece limits movement, symbolic of the restrictions of motherhood, but it also transitions mothering from the domestic to the public sphere, where participants in the project can engage in discussion and (re)articulate the place and agency of motherhood, and parenting, in contemporary cultural life. (For more details see "Notes on the Cover Image.") Much like Endacott's installation project, the stories in this book explore the limits of mother-identities undergoing transition.

In "Not my Children," Kat Wiebe, must reconsider her relationship to her very young children as a result of divorce. Wiebe explores her grief at the imposed transformation to her attachment-mothering practices as she learns to temporarily but continuously separate from her very young boys, in order to co-parent with their father.

Chris Bobel, in "The End of When," flounders as she attempts to parent one child while drowning in the agony of losing another. Her story of Gracie's unexpected death in a car accident on a school trip exposes her "searing grief" that never subsides and which leaves her angry and behaving in ways that cut "permanent holes" into Zoe, her surviving daughter.

Garrett Riggs, in "Changing Terms," tells of what it is like to transition from a mother to a father, to undergo hormone treatments, and to have family and friends and colleagues make the transition from female to male pronouns, to a new name, to new terms on school forms, no longer filling in the blank next to "mother," but identifying as "father" instead, while knowing that his ability to parent has been enriched by having lived as both sexes. He is mother and father to his boys.

Janice Williamson's collage essay, "Pivot: Fragments from Mothering Through Time," speaks to the daily morphability required of her: of what it has meant to be an academic woman whose own infertility led her to adopt and parent as a single mother and whose motherlove and motherwork is paralleled by the work she engages in as a public intellectual committed to many human rights and environmental issues. And through it all, the bonds between her own mother, herself and her-now teenage daughter resonate with the possibilities of genealogies forged by love and devotion and commitment to family and friends and community that encompass and exceed the limits of biologically determined networks.

Fiona Tinwei Lam's "The Front of the Bus," tells the story of an encounter on Vancouver city transit. She poignantly reveals what it means to mother in the face of racism and to be confronted by vicious ignorance in a public setting. In writing this essay, she calls all Canadians to account for the many silences—ongoing and historical—in this country.

Several contributing mothers to the collection explore what it means to have a child who struggles to conform to social and institutional expectations of the good child for any number of reasons, including developmental disabilities and past trauma. Janine Alcott and Karen Grove explore these issues from the perspective of biological mothers, while Susan Olding, Martha Marinara, and P. R. Newton share similar experiences as adoptive mothers.

In "Constellation," Alcott employs the configurations of the stars and the myths of ancient Greece to provide shape to her story and that of her youngest son, as the two of them attempt to navigate a world in which they are both warriors and he, in particular, is dislocated from another time and place: a "bright but tempestuous" child who struggled to navigate the transitions between his divorced mother and father, and who even later in life flails in his attempts to conform to the high-achieving expectations of his parents and grandparents.

Grove, in "Crazy Too," tells of being judged, along the lines of a "refrigerator mother[6]"; her parenting is considered to be a cause of her son's behaviour, later diagnosed as autism. Crazy, in this story, becomes the catchall for an inability to conform to the institution of motherhood, to the educational institution, and even to the institutional demands of the child psychiatric hospital in the 1990s.

Olding's "Push-Me-Pull-You," Marinara's "You Don't Know What It's Like," and Newton's "Ethiopian Incense," all expose the challenges of mothering children with reactions and coping mechanisms as complex, unexpected and unknown as their histories—biographical and medical. Whether it is autism and other medical diagnoses, or traumas of abandonment and violence, all of these mothers share how these issues express in ongoing everyday ways, hinting at other stories about what this means for spouses and siblings and marriages and family life.

Kate Greenway writes "Ephemera" from the perspective of an adoptee, whose thirty-five-year-old unwed mother—a career woman—was still forced by the social mores of 1960s-era Canada to relinquish her baby girl. Greenway makes explicit the constraints her mother's generation faced—not having the options other twenty-first-century single mothers write about elsewhere in this collection—as she renders explicit the fundamental losses of the adoption process: "the loss of the child, loss of the mother, of agency, biological connection, familial identity, ritual, and story."

Lynn Gidluck, by contrast, writes of the positive gains of adoptive mothering in "Reflections on Becoming a 'Real' Mother." After having adopted two daughters from China, Gidluck recounts her experiences of pregnancy and natural childbirth: her own reactions, as well as other people's thoughtless commentary about how she will now become a "real" mother, throwing into question her status as mother to her older daughters, and making her worry for their sense of security and place.

Eating disorders also factor into mothering and becoming a mother. Melissa Morelli Lacroix in "Nine Months to a New Me" illustrates the mental and emotional gymnastics required to healthfully nourish her pregnant body and her baby, gaining weight month after month, after only just in the previous five years having managed to lose the weight associated with compulsive eating—a personal history that leaves her body and her body image scarred.

Anne Cameron Sadava in "The Lucky Ones" tells of being re-confronted with the eating-disorders of her own youth as she is forced to watch her daughter struggle with anorexia. Cameron Sadava tells of her self-doubt and multi-layered guilt, and shares how this experience also leads to greater empathy for her own mother, who must have suffered in similar ways years earlier. Furthermore, all of this takes place just as her daughter transitions to adulthood and Cameron Sadava must negotiate and learn to parent her in new ways.

Parenting adult children is also the subject of Leslie Vryenhoek's "Goodbye, Girl." Vryenhoek tells of the very different relationships she has with her two now-grown daughters and she explores the difficulties inherent in transitioning from being the mother-nucleus of her family, to mothering from the sidelines—"adjunct" to the lives of her daughters, as she terms it.

For different reasons and at a different stage in her children's lives, Sandra McEnhill too must learn to parent her daughters under shifting conditions. In "Let's Make Glitter Cards" she takes readers on her journey through quite a different story, one of parenting after divorce, and the all-too-common but more rarely disclosed realities of parental alienation.

Mother love is forever accompanied by the fear that we will not be able to keep our children safe. Ann Sutherland in "Behind the Gate" tells of how she very nearly ran over her son as a toddler, and she explores the element of fear in our practices of motherhood— our terror at what can happen if we cannot keep our children safe.

By contrast, Bobbi Junior tells the hard story of what does happen. In "Tell Me About Today…" her teenage daughter survives a terrible car crash, paralyzed by a spinal cord injury. Junior illustrates the complexities of surviving those first few years after the accident, and exposes how she was forced to transform her mothering if her daughter was ever to achieve maturity by making the mistakes that any teenager would, despite lacking the independence to do so without her mother's knowledge.

Genealogical ties are explored in several of these pieces. Allison Akgungor's "Needing Mom" celebrates her own mother and the role she played in supporting Akgungor and her young husband, virtual newlyweds, as they were confronted with his palliative brain cancer diagnosis. Through a genealogy of caring, Akgungor now passes on this same motherlove to her own adult daughter struggling with the challenges of a working twenty-first-century mother.

In "Nesting Dolls," Nancy Slukynski writes a generative story that explores and celebrates the women in her family: namely, her matrilineal grandmother and mother. On the way to the hospital her friend says to her over the phone, "You birth like the person you are." But, who Slukynski is—as the story reveals—is strongly linked to the stories of her foremothers that empower her as she births her eldest daughter.

In "Traces," Jessica Kluthe, too, tells of how at the moment she suspects that she is pregnant, she begins to trace back her matrilineal line to her great-great-grandmother Rosina, who was a midwife in Italy and who had delivered hundreds of babies.

In "Me, Myself and My Mother," Sonia Nijjar explores the intricate weaving of her self into her mother's self, raising questions about where the boundaries between the two have melded into one. As the Canadian-born daughter of a mother whose own childhood in India was so different from her own, Nijjar struggles to understand—to "see"—her mother, to know who she once was and who she has now become. Through this "seeing" Nijjar attempts to find some happiness in the spaces of overlap, where her mother's being intertwines with her own sense of belonging. And as these genealogies are explored, so too are ethno-cultural roots. In the case of Stephanie Werner's "Voice," these go back to the French Canadian and German matriarchs in her family, who now resonate through her and her sister's own lives and can be heard in serious and more lighthearted ways through her three daughters. In M. Elizabeth Sargent's piece, "Our Dead Fish," she explores how humour and motherlove factor into her daughters' early encounter with the death of their pet.

Faye Hansen explores what it means to mother as an older woman, drawing parallels between another woman who made this choice, and her own situation where she is unexpectedly required to take over the custody of her grandchildren. In "Late Born: Motherhood at Sixty-Two," Hansen touches on those hard truths about what it means to have taken on her granddaughter and her granddaughter's brother; the story also makes tentative forays into the complicated feelings around what it means to be mothering your grandchildren because your own child is unable to parent.

Naomi McIlwraith celebrates her biological mother for the love and knowledge that she has shown all the children that she has helped raise—both those babies she birthed and the many she has fostered. "Sleep Little One, Sleep" celebrates McIlwraith's Métis mother as an Indigenous wise woman, a powerful matriarch in her family and community. Likewise, in telling her mother's story, McIlwraith shares the story of her foster-sister Jill, another Indigenous woman whose legacy is to live "at the very margins of an affluent society where bitumen and banknotes lubricate the ball bearings of a global economy, and yet she and her children—her family—are left struggling for minimum subsistence." And in all of this McIlwraith invokes the injustices enacted by historical Canadian governments as well as the ongoing polemics of government legislation and the foster care system in Canada.

"The Estrangement," by contrast, tells quite another story of what it is to be the child of neglect and to dislike your own mother. Now a mother herself, Natasha Clark chooses to block her mother on Facebook not because of "resentment or grudges" but because she doesn't like her: "without an umbilical cord bridge, our paths would never have crossed."

Beth Osnes' "Mud Bath" tells of the beauty and the trials of foster mothering, as she reflects back on a special shared trip taken with her then teen-aged foster-daughter who had been cutting herself. As Osnes brings her daughter to life through story, she also exquisitely illustrates that all our children are complicated human beings, none of whom can be captured by one moment or tragedy. None of us are merely one story.

Julie Gosselin, in "Nevermom," examines the role of step-mother, a social role that is historically linked to very negative attitudes and images of motherhood, but is increasingly common in our twenty-first-century North American context, where blended families are part of the new normal. Gosselin tells of the joys and pain of forging relationships with her step-daughters over many years, of loving them, and of mothering them as step-mother—a type of motherhood that even at its best goes largely unacknowledged. And then, she pushes this story one step further by sharing what happens when a woman mothers children to whom she has no biological or legal link and then her relationship with their father ends in divorce.

In "What I Need is a Wife," Marita Dachsel takes up this oft-reiterated punchline and explores both what it might mean to live in a polygamous relationship and what it says about our culture that in the twenty-first century we still associate the burden of domestic labour with the role of wife.

Pam Klassen-Dueck's "(Mis)Conceptions: A Meditation on Red" artfully explores the complexities of being a Manitoba Mennonite farm girl cum academic woman studying feminist history and motherhood. She writes of bell hooks and Adrienne Rich and Sara Ruddick and Madeleine Grumet and Hélène Cixous and confesses to feeling guilty for wishing she could be "in the mommy club." She writes of ART (Assisted Reproductive Technology) and splendour and agony and longing: "It's all so much beauty for a Manitoba Mennonite farm girl."

Sara Graefe's "Out in Mommyland" illustrates how the possibilities of reproductive technology have changed her life and the lesbian community. She shares how she is paradoxically both outed and invisible, "abruptly plucked from my tight-knit social circle in the queer community, and unceremoniously dumped onto the strange, other-worldly planet of Mommyland."

In "Snow Day," Robin Silbergleid writes of mothering as a single parent and an academic woman, choices that would not always have been technologically, economically or socially available to her. She writes about how "snow days ask you to stop and take notice. As a woman trying to get pregnant, I live too often in the future rather than the present, the blank screen of the negative test." And on the particular snow day in question, she contemplates both the current complexities and all the potentialities of mothering on her own.

Diana Davidson, in "Traps, Stars and Raising Men," considers what it means to suddenly find herself co-parenting through divorce, with new and unexpected responsibilities. Pushing beyond her grief and loss to build a leprechaun trap with her son, she navigates other traps—actual and rhetorical—as she answers his hard questions about love and divorce in ways that will best allow him to become the type of caring, thoughtful, feminist man she dreams for him to be. Building something with her son also includes freeing herself to build a new independent life while she mothers him.

Nichole Quiring, in "Rush Hour," writes about the plight of the working mother: rushing, running late, not there for her child when crises take place. The subtext is also her discontent with a neoliberal world and the demands of her lifestyle, which allow her the luxuries associated with an independent income—designer handbags and silk blouses—but relegate her child to the care of another woman for too many of his waking hours.

Jean Crozier, in "You Didn't Take Any Pictures of Me," provides us some insights into mothering in poverty, both in the moment, and what the longer term ramifications of this experience can be for children and families. Furthermore, this story highlights the very important reality that poverty is not a static condition and mothering and single mothering are often at the root of many women's economic difficulties.

Sheena Wilson's piece explores the near-universal distress of rushing to the doctor with a sick preschooler, but in this case against the particular backdrop of congested traffic in an oil refinery community. "Petro-Mama: Mothering in a Crude World" links the personal with the political in a tense and evocative moment that parallels her desperation, as she struggles to help her small son suffering from an asthma attack, with our collective suffocation in a culture defined by oil production and a boom-and-bust economy. As an academic mother concerned with our environmental future, she provokes readers to question how this storied instance links the local to the global and connects past, present, and future, ending the collection with the hope that the social, political, economic, and environmental winds of tomorrow will shift, "blowing in new directions."

CONCLUSION

Telling Truths aims to creatively expose the lived realities of mothers in the late twentieth and early twenty-first century, as the authors explore how the expectations that others place on us or that we have internalized for ourselves often bump up against the realities that each woman faces as she tries to mother and discovers that her mothering is inextricably linked to the position she occupies within her specific socio-cultural context—her class and income level, marital or relationship status, age and genera- tion relative to the time period (decade) of mothering experiences, cultural background and ethnicity, gender and sexual identity, level of education, the environment and the setting—urban or rural. And of course, the child she is raising. Mothering takes place within a complex web of social, political, economic, and even environmental relations.

However, the truths revealed in this book cannot possibly en- compass all the complexities of motherhood nor speak to all the potential mothering identities. Motherhood, as the stories in this collection reveal, is not one thing to all people. And one mother is not the same parent to each of her children. To the best of our ability we have presented a diversity of voices, but the reality remains that some groups of women and mothers have more education and greater economic stability—ultimately greater ability—to speak their truths. It would have been wonderful, for example, to include the voice of a teen-mother, especially considering the ways this particular story of motherhood is currently being glamorized and repositioned by reality television. Alas, we received no submissions from any teen-mothers. For similar reasons, it might not have been possible to include a story about mothering in poverty, which is why we were so pleased to have Crozier's retrospective on being a working-poor mother. There are many other missing stories of other mothers beyond what could be included in any one book. As you read the stories we were able to publish, remain aware of the silent stories, those experiences of mothers who do not have access to power. Listen for their stories—stories yet for the telling.

Stories of motherhood are important. They allow all of us to contemplate our place in the world. As mothers, we construct ourselves every day in relationship to our children, based on ourselves and on their reaction to us, based on our circumstances, doing the best we can with the knowledge we have at the time. Likewise, our children and partners are intricately involved in co-constructing themselves, our families, and our communities. Together, as writers and readers, as mothers and parents and communities, we are rewriting and rereading and reinventing what it means to mother and parent our children at this moment in history. Baring ourselves. Bearing witness. Mothering stories, like all stories, help us create knowledge, preserve knowledge, and transfer knowledge across generations.

NOTES

[1]For more on courageous mothering see Rich's *Of Woman Born*.

[2]In *Politics of the Heart,* Baba Cooper writes about radical mothering, advocating that children be involved in the resistance against cultural matriphobia that disrupts relationships, particularly mother-daughter relationships (238).

[3]On rebellious mothering, see *The Mommy Myth* by Douglas and Michaels. For Hip mothers see Gore in *Breeder.*

[4]For more information on feminist mothering see Green in *Mother Outlaws* and more recently *Practicing Feminist Mothering*. To understand any of the aforementioned mothering terms in context, see O'Reilly's many publications, specifically *Mother Outlaws* and *Feminist Mothering* (4).

[5]In *Textual Mothers* Podneiks and O'Reilly explain the project of mapping the "shifts from the daughter-centric stories (those which privilege the daughter's voice) that have, to be sure, dominated maternal traditions, to the matrilineal and matrifocal perspectives that have emerged over the last few decades as the mother's voice—in all its rhythms and ranges" (2).

[6]According to Rebecca Jo Plant, Austrian American child psychiatrist Leo Kanner first used the term in 1942 (185). Bruno Bettelheim also critiqued mothers of autistic children, and ultimately this was

part of a cultural climate of mother-blame that "attributed child-hood autism and schizophrenia to frigid and inconsistent mothers (13). For more information on the cultural context, see Plant's *Mom: the Transformation of Motherhood in Modern America.*

WORKS CITED

Cooper, Baba. "The Radical Potential in Lesbian Mothering of Daughters." *Politics of the Heart: A Lesbian Anthology.* Eds. Sandra Pollack and Jeanne Vaughn. Ithaca: Firebrand Books, 1987. 233-240.

Douglas, Susan and Meredith Michaels. *The Mommy Myth: The Idealization of Motherhood and How It Has Undermined All Women.* New York: Free Press, 2004.

Gore, Ariel and Bee Lavender. *Breeder: Real Life Stories from the New Generation of Mothers.* Seattle: Seal Press, 2001.

Green, Fiona Joy. "Feminist Mothers: Successfully Negotiating the Tension between Motherhood as 'Institution' and 'Experience'." *Mother Outlaws: Theories and Practices of Empowered Mothering.* Ed. Andrea O'Reilly. Toronto: Women's Press, 2004. 31-42.

Green, Fiona Joy. *Practicing Feminist Mothering.* Winnipeg: Arbeiter Ring Publishing, 2011.

O'Reilly, Andrea. *Feminist Mothering.* Albany: SUNY Press, 2008.

O'Reilly, Andrea, ed. *Mother Outlaws: Theories and Practices of Empowered Mothering.* Toronto: Women's Press, 2004.

Plant, Rebecca Jo. *Mom: The Transformation of Motherhood in Modern America.* Chicago: University of Chicago Press, 2012.

Podnieks, Elizabeth and Andrea O'Reilly. *Textual Mothers, Maternal Texts: Motherhood in Contemporary Women's Literatures.* Waterloo: Wilfrid Laurier University Press, 2010.

Rich, Adrienne. *Of Woman Born: Motherhood as Experience and Institution.* New York: Norton, 1986 (1976).

Not My Children

KAT WIEBE

SUNDAY MORNING. Sun's up. Me too. I've always been an early riser, leaving warm bed and bodies behind as I investigate what has begun. Setting moon or rising sun, ocean, meadow, mountain, town—all are newly birthed and unexplored at this time of day.

Even as a girl I would rise and leave the quiet house before the others, only to return to bed and warm blankets before having to get ready for school. It's a habit that was only interrupted when I became a mother.

Sure, in the early days, I could zip him—or even them—into fleece and down. Tucked inside my parka, or snuggled into sheepskin, they greeted the day with me. The folks at the Bagel Café, which opened at 6:30 a.m., knew us. Primo and I wondered why the newspaper deliveryman wore a bicycle helmet before there were any other vehicles on the morning streets—the owls were attacking his head, he explained.

But at a certain point life became too fraught with logistics—what with school and work and homework and a nutritional breakfast *and* lunches to be made—and that early-morning exploration ritual became hit and miss, very much missed.

So today, this gorgeous Sunday in mid-June offers early dawn and alpenglow, and I am free to venture out. Just walking to the swimming pool is a sensual feast. Cottonwoods and silverberry exude wild perfume as the rising sun dispels the early morning chill and highlights the billion-year-old rock dramatically upthrust at my periphery. Closer at hand a hummingbird finds food fast at an oleaster thicket, and plain old mallards dabble for breakfast in the muck at the bottom of the stream.

Why am I free to wander this morning, inspired by daybreak and Mary Oliver and rocket-fuelled by two shots of espresso?

Where are my children, those boys whose birth so transformed my life and made a mother out of me? An attentive, stay-by-their-sides, sleep-in-the-den with them, carry-them-everywhere, rarely-be-apart-from-them type of mother?

They are at their other house, the house where they spend fifty percent of their lives, the lives they live with their bio dad and his wife, their other life—the one that doesn't include me.

Oh, but don't worry. They're safe and loved there too. We four adults are mature and appropriate co-parents. We communicate and work together in the best interests of our shared children. We've been living this way since the youngest was one, and he's seven now.

So we're all used to it.

Right now I know they are warm in their bunk, Primo on top and Secundo on the bottom. I've been in their room. It's sunny and hung with red curtains. Their bookshelf is stuffed full of Sandra Boynton and Curious George and other kid classics. There's a kite hanging from the ceiling and a growth chart and bins of LEGO and more than a few stray socks on the carpet.

When they wake up, they'll put on their bathrobes, tie the sashes around their waists and trundle downstairs for homemade waffles—while I have all the time in the world to do as I please. No clamouring voices, no requests for help with the knife, no pleas for extra syrup, no sticky fingers on my skin, no spilled milk, no recounting of dreams, telling of bad jokes, or wiping of dirty faces.

I have all the headspace I could possible need. I awoke when I wanted, lay with my warm husband, and, nose up, I headed out into an uncharted day. I know many mothers only dream of the free moments I get. They tell me this often. Family life is so busy, parenting—especially in the early years—so demanding that relationships, both with self and partner, suffer.

Just last night Andy and I made love in the living room, in front of a fire, and then we ate cake and I may have even had a scoop of ice cream. Or was it a square of dark chocolate? Did we really pass a sip of tequila from tongue to tongue?

My husband is Handy Andy. He can fix anything. "Look, if you had one shot, one opportunity," he quotes Eminem, "to seize everything you ever wanted in one moment, would you capture it or just let it slip?"

This morning I am capturing it, seizing the day with both hands, open hearted and vulnerable, present and available. I am right here.

Right here, in the pool, in water as blue as the *Mar Carribe*—in which I used to swim way back when I was not yet a mother and still roamed the world at will, one morning at a time, accumulating adventures, evolving, becoming the person that I became in order to become the woman that I am.

Sun pierces liquid and the moving medium strobes with prisms as I hang suspended, holding my breath, sobbing underwater.

* * *

It took Andy by surprise, the first time I wept after making love—and the next and the next. "Uh," he'd wonder. "Is everything all right? I mean—" Being a man, he was naturally concerned about his performance.

He didn't understand why I'd release like that, my ecstasy turned so suddenly, and thoroughly, to agony. Just part of my process, I told him. Grieving the loss of my boys—grieving the half-life my motherhood has become. He argued that the boys were fine, but my limbic brain tuned into the boys' absence despite my neo-cortex's insistence that all was well, that they were safe, and I so happy in love.

My grief when the boys aren't with me is always there. Deep, in the middle of my brain, in the place where I am a mammal, where it is imperative to touch my pups, to nuzzle and cuddle them, to herd them and teach them and always, always, have my eye on them, there is such a disconnect when they are not here.

One weekend, very early on, I let myself go: I lay on the floor and sobbed while Andy hovered in the doorway watching me.

"I'm supposed to leave you alone, right?"

"Yup, just let me fucking cry. I am sad."

He tried to understand: "You say it's so great with us—so what's wrong, are we not good?" (More checking.)

"I love you, but I miss the boys." (He showed visible relief.)

"So this is just about that?" (*Just?!*, I thought to myself.)

"It won't take away the pain," said my GP when I asked him about Prozac, "but it'll take it down a notch." He offered a prescription, if I needed it. I left his office without pharmaceuticals and gauged the pain and noticed it was always there when the boys were not.

Looking back, I am not surprised that Andy was confused. The process of separating when you have kids is complex. The divorce may or may not seem like a good thing, but separating from the children is likely universally tough. Parents—and kids—experience grief, a roller-coaster ride that takes us on an inter-twined, circular, figure-eight pathway that is dynamic, not linear. We all go from protest and denial to despair, detachment, and—hopefully—meaning. Ideally, we eventually loop into hope, exploration, and new investment. Interestingly, Andy reports that the separations from the boys get harder for him as he bonds with them more deeply over time.

Unmistakably, there is loss. Not only are the children not with me, they are with the person that I have decided I cannot live with.

You've got to see the difficulty in that—and the irony. The two adults who cannot live together must let go of their child/ren into the care of each other—to live with, to bond with, to love and adore and depend upon, and to need and miss and to look forward to being with.

This is not easy.

* * *

I went to see a spiritual teacher.

"What can I do for you?" the Latin woman in a white turban and robe asked me when I sat down in front of her. I started crying immediately.

"It's my two kids," I blubbered. "I have this 30-70 split with their dad that's becoming 60-40, and moving to 50-50 in the next few years."

"And?" She raised an eyebrow beneath that imposing turban.

"I've accepted that it's good to be uncoupled. Their dad and I are creating an awesome new way of relating after being unhappy for some years. I've got a new man in my life who loves me and loves the boys. It's all good. But I can't stand being away from my children." I cried, not even bothering to wipe away my tears. "It's just not right to be separated from them, not even for a day!"

"Oh," she raised a hand to her forehead and pretended to swoon. "All this drama. Weeping and carrying on. When there is nothing to cry about."

"They're my children," I insisted, betting she didn't have any. "It's not right for them to be away from me. They're mine!"

"Yours," she laughed. Then she became stern. "They are not yours."

That stopped me in my tracks. Not mine? I was nauseated for nine months twice. I pushed what felt like two bowling balls through my pelvis and out my vagina. I survived sleep-deprivation, post-partum depression, and left the work force. Not to mention that I gave up the life I lived for forty years to figure out how to guide two new humans through a world that had changed dramatically since I was a kid. My experience of mothering is right up there with every peak experience I have ever had, including meeting and mating. It has been powerfully joyful, satisfying, pleasurable, and transcendent. I certainly didn't intend to relinquish being the best damn caregiver they could ever have. Which meant, in my opinion, *being with them*.

I looked at her, much more pissed off than I expected to feel during a spiritual counselling session.

"Not yours," she repeated.

I knew what she meant in the theoretical sense of "They come through you but not from you/ And though they are with you yet they belong not to you." But Kahlil Gibran didn't have kids either. It's inspirational on one level. In reality my stomach dropped at the thought of my kids away from me *half of the time*.

"You are caught up in this drama," she said, more gently now. "Wasting your time with all this crying. Getting in the way of yourself and what you are meant to be doing with your life. You have an opportunity here. Everything is aligned for you. Take it. Don't mess it up."

"Oh."

"Get on with this fifty-fifty arrangement. Grow up!"

* * *

When I asked my boys—now eight and eleven—how separating families should arrange the mother-father care split, I received interesting answers. Secundo said it should be fifty-fifty. "That's fair," he said. Primo looked inwards: "A kid needs his mom more," he counselled. "Because she knows how to take better care of a young child."

Is that his experience? Or is that a universal?

I came of age reading Germaine Greer and Gloria Steinem. As a teenager I was rabidly against having children because I thought it imperative to kick the old *Kinder, Küche, Kirche* habit. Yet, when I became a mother, I wanted nothing but to mother my children, and I flouted feminism by giving up my work and devoting myself to them. I know there is chemistry involved, and biology. There's plenty of research to support mammalian attachment. But I didn't know any of it at the time. I just know what I felt.

"Does my child need me?" A woman I know is trying to do what is right for her two-year-old. "Or is it that I need her?" She and her ex are currently navigating the waters of parenting after separation.

"Is she fine with her dad fifty-fifty right off the bat? Or is it better for her to be with mom more?"

Good questions. The answers require the heart of Buddha, the wisdom of Solomon, and the genius of Einstein.

In the legal system there is no presumption in favour of equal parenting. It is something that couples must negotiate. It is the one piece I was stuck on, and the sole point for which we sought legal guidance: I did not want fifty-fifty to start. The boys were one and four when we separated. Secundo, still a baby, was breastfeeding. Primo was accustomed to my care. We settled on a seventy-thirty arrangement, working toward fifty-fifty by the time Secundo was school age.

Ironically here's where feminism's effect is evident: the trend toward participatory fathers is increasing. No longer does a father's role end at sperm donation. I applaud this change, and at the same time, admit that relinquishing the care of my children to their father—full bore—is the hardest thing I've ever done. And while I am proud of myself, and believe it's best for my boys, my dirty little secret is that I'm envious of (and a little angry with) those moms who, for whatever reason, end up with the bigger share of the care and custody of their children.

Last year my boys went with their dad and his wife to attend the memorial of their stepmom's mother. There they were with the clan that I am not part of: cousins I have not met, uncle, aunt, friends of family—all strangers to me. Their dad's parents, who used to be my in-laws, were there too, and together they participated in the ritual of mourning and celebration. A milestone in my boys' lives—for death must be accepted and understood as part of life.

Every family has their ways, their own subtle beliefs and practices. I will not be privy to that deep, often unspoken, modelling. What happens when we die, after we die? Why are we born? How is death celebrated, a life commemorated? This is for my boys alone to discover with that wing of their family.

Are they in good hands? I know they are safe, their primary needs well handled. They will have delicious family dinners and special breakfasts that I will not taste. They are probably neater, tidier, more contained than when they are with me. They will play with their cousins, two girls similar in age, whom I have never met. They may hear prayers and reference to a religious belief that is not mine.

While they were away my ex emailed me a photo of them in button down shirts with fresh haircuts. Bright eyes, ears sticking out like jug-handles and closed-mouth smiles.

I was grateful for the picture, for news of the changes in their lives, for a glimpse into the window of that world. And of course I missed them. Of course I wanted to smell their hair, and touch their cheeks, and hear their white noise—Primo's repetitive whistling and snippets of things he says to himself, Secundo's constant questions, and even the sniping and bickering that happens, inevitably, no matter the day or occasion.

The photo evoked in me a longing. It unsettled me. And momentarily I was undone. When they are away, the ache I feel is still intense, their absence palpable.

And I am able to live with this.

I am not the centre of their universe; they are unmistakably whole and my wholeness is separate from theirs, and them, though we have every intersection. We are both attached and discrete, completely sustained within and without each other. I write this for every mother—and father—who shares this loss. For us to progress, evolve, and eventually resolve, we must accept this arrangement.

"They come through us but they are not us"—I can't say it better than Gibran—yet their passage changes us. For those who are affected, it is difficult to discriminate the magic from the magician, the transformation from the agent, the reaction from the catalyst. Our Herculean task is to allow the meaning to abide, and the peace of mind to exist—even when they're not with us.

When they're not with me I want them to be happy and whole, to have joy and peace, to feel loved and connected. I don't want these qualities to be present only when I am present. I suppose, I wish the same for myself.

When they come back, I look for it. I always do. In that first moment of reconnection, I often see it: something has changed. What did I miss? A new word or concept, an epiphany or fresh development? A turn of phrase, an emerging facet of their psyche, a growth spurt? Did they not get what they need? Or did they? Did he do something better than I can? Did they like his cooking better than mine? I do. Or his Christmas presents? Or possibly, probably, the tidiness of his house?

But in a flash it is absorbed. They are seen and all is known. We pick up right where we left off. The pause button turns to play. This is how I manifest my love for these boys, and how I transform the grief that I feel each and every time they leave.

I miss you so much, Secundo said when he left, curling his fingers around the kiss I placed in his palm. I love you as big as a thousand skies, whispered Primo when we said good-bye. I love you when I'm with you and I love you when I'm not, I promised. And when they returned we slept together, Primo snuggled between my legs, his head on my thigh, Secundo beside me, his feet poking me in the middle of the night. We learned to live with the new rhythm. *All* of us adjusting and readjusting—mother, father, and the new partners who joined us and took on parenting roles. First they were with me. Then they went to their other house and I was alone with

Andy. Then the boys came barrelling back into the calm house where Andy's fourteen-year-old black Lab lay quietly on the sofa all day. Then they rocketed back over to their dad's where they made Christmas cookies. Primo practiced his letters at that house too. Secundo toddled around their family room too. We began to make our way together—in this way.

I saw the boys unexpectedly yesterday. Day four into our week without them and Andy and I were headed to the hills for an overnight backcountry campout to celebrate our fifth anniversary under a full moon. Waiting at a stoplight I glanced to my right, and there they were: two very familiar faces brightening into radiant smiles as we noticed each other. "Hey!" and "I love you!" and "I was just at a birthday party!" and "Say hi to Snowy!" rebounded between the vehicles and then Andy and I turned left and the boys went straight.

The surprise of seeing them sent pure joy cart-wheeling through my veins. Andy felt it too.

The boys may not be under my roof all the time, but they are under the loving lid of the universe. And that's how we live together, all the time.

The End of When

CHRIS BOBEL

JANUARY 7, 2011
"Shit. Shit. Shit. SHIT. SHIIIIIIIT."
As loud as I can, I hurl the expletive, each staccato repetition gaining force and volume, the sound bouncing off the interior walls of the car as I somehow, mindlessly, steer its mass through suburban traffic.

I am out of control. I know I am out of control. I am screaming so loudly at my eight-year-old that my throat is raw. She is wailing in the back seat. I hear her, and somehow, her cries make me madder. As I scream, I grip the steering wheel and lean forward.

And as I do, the internal monitor that polices my parenting makes a pitiful attempt to soften the explosion. I introduce members of the animal kingdom into my irrational tirade: "Dog Shit. Cat Shit. Turtle Shit. SHIIIIIIIIIIT!!!!"

Of course, it doesn't matter what I say, whose shit I invoke. We both know that this outburst is especially wrong, its damage irreparable. And I know that I am discharging years of pain and fear and worry and nearly fifteen months of searing grief at the expense of my little daughter. And yet, I can't seem to find the reigns.

I am angry because, after much deliberation and negotiation with a hunger-induced cranky kid, we finally settled on a place to eat out while shopping. Zoe, like many kids, is very finicky about what she eats, but her particular selectiveness is exhausting and ever-shifting. No sandwiches, but she will eat bread and cheese. Only hard cheeses, and if they are not adequately aged, they are rejected. And I won't even get into the bread criteria. Only unsweetened soy milk since milk products are banned (this is recent). No pepper, ever. The other day, she refused to eat the honey because it was not raw and wild.

I am living with a precocious eight-year-old Foodie and, on a meal-to-meal basis, it is infuriating and deeply impractical.

We finally settle on a place. I am worn down. We walk in, sit down, and she begins to pout. She won't order.

"Why not?" I ask.

"This place smells funny."

"I don't smell anything," I reply. I strain to coax her into choosing something to eat. I say, "Maybe it will distract you. You are clearly very hungry. We don't have time to drive to another place. You need to make the best of it. C'mon Zoe."

I quickly order and eat. My daughter sits and fumes. I eat and fume. I hold my tongue, but I am pissed. By the time we get in the car, I can't contain myself and I tell her off. And she fights back and the essence of her defense is that I did not try to accommodate her. *What a total brat*, I think. *This has to stop*. And I lose it.

We finally pull into the driveway at least thirty minutes late. I got lost. I can't rage and drive efficiently. I rush out of the car, slam the door, and leave my tear-stained daughter in her pink princess booster seat. I notice only a twinge of guilt, only a millisecond of hesitation. I am not done.

I stomp through the house in search of Thomas, my partner, Zoe's father. He is in the office (quietly studying mathematical formulae) and I unload my words out of my mouth, my hands jabbing the air. I tell him about Zoe in the restaurant. And then, suddenly, I tell him about the skull.

I describe a video of what happens in a crematorium, the one I found on YouTube when my curiosity got the better of me. I tell him what I learned: after the body is burned to ash, the worker smashes the skull to tiny fragments with a shovel. And I tell him that I opened the box of ashes.

But I don't tell him the whole story. I don't tell him about what it was like to open that box because I don't expect he will want to hear it. What he does know is that my pain always becomes a weapon that wounds. Besides, Zoe is still in the car and I can't really indulge a pointless bid for his sympathy when I've just damaged her. I just need to tell him enough so he understands the permanent holes I have cut out of our surviving daughter.

This is what I needed to tell him. This is the whole story.

After fifteen months of avoiding it, I studied the exterior of the cheap maroon plastic box affixed with nothing more than a file folder label typed with her name and "dates." I felt revulsion. But that's not it, really. That's my child in there. I was not repulsed. Horrified, maybe? I don't know why I was drawn to the box that Saturday morning when Zoe and Thomas were at the ice rink. I was restoring the house to its pre-snowmen and red-and-green-candle Christmas order. I looked at her photos, the green memorial candles, the little statue of Buddha my friend Judy gave me, the small earthen green pot that one of her friend's mothers made for me. And I was drawn to the box. I picked at the label. It was easy to remove. This surprised me. An invitation to go on? I accepted. I removed the label, thinking to myself: *that's all it took?* I gingerly opened the box, peering inside to find a plastic bag filled with light grey ash, closed with a white twist tie. I read it was supposed to be more white than this. The discrepancy made me uneasy. I said out loud, a bit self-consciously: "A twist tie." A twist tie, methodically grabbed from a cache by a nameless, faceless crematorium worker to close the bag of my seventeen-year-old daughter Gracie's ashes. Gracie is her name. You need to know her name. Was I expecting a gilded ribbon? An embossed seal?

Yes. I suppose I was. That's my daughter in there.

October 17, 2010

By now you want to know what happened. By now, you want to know if this could happen to your child. Gracie was travelling to Arches National Park in Utah on a field trip 2,600 miles from home. Fourteen girls, one SUV, one van, two staff drivers. While travelling at over 70 mph, the driver of Gracie's vehicle tried to get the attention of the other driver and lost control. The vehicle rolled three times. One girl died immediately of head trauma, still secured in her seatbelt. Gracie, wearing only her lap belt, was ejected through her window. She landed among the sagebrush on the stony earth, her head gushed blood.

We left for Utah in a panic, desperate to be with our girl. We tried to explain to Gracie's little sister Zoe what happened in the sparest possible terms. I remember thinking to myself, *There is no way she can grasp what I am saying; I cannot grasp what I am saying.* We called Gracie's teenage brother, my stepson Craig (who lives with his Mom in another city), and we called her aunts, her boyfriend, our closest friends. I don't remember what I said in those phone calls. I only remember standing in Terminal B of Boston's Logan Airport with the phone against my ear.

It took us an excruciating twenty-one hours to reach Gracie in the ICU. When we arrived, the neurosurgeon explained that the damage to her brain meant she would not recover. He smiled awkwardly when he told us. I hated this grimacing man, this evil messenger. As soon as he left, I excused myself and found the restroom. I closed the door and muffled my wails with my hands. Collapsing to the floor, my nose bled all over the cold white tiles.

Two days and several corroborating medical opinions later, we broadcast to everyone we knew: *Please help us say goodbye to our girl at 10:00 pm EST.* We surrounded her (and ourselves) with her art, photos, and beloved foods. We played her favourite music. Together, we bathed and dressed our precious broken daughter, preparing her (and us) for her last breath.

The nurse extricated the breathing tube. Gracie coughed, producing hideous orange phlegm. My hands fluttered around her anxiously. Her coughing clashed with my fragile understanding of her irreparable injuries. Vomiting seemed so alive. I climbed into bed with her and whispered, stroking her sweet face, "It is okay. We are here. It is okay to go."

But of course it was not okay. It will never be okay.

Forty-five minutes later, she was gone. We called Craig. He was quiet, saying little, and then posted to Gracie's Facebook wall, "I'm shattered in a thousand ways. I can't even believe that you're gone, that this is my reality. I love you now and I loved you the day I met you. There's nothin' now, there's nothin'."

Our girl's dying took forty-five minutes—the same amount of time it took me to push her into the world seventeen years and twenty-one days earlier. A devastating symmetry.

January 7, 2011

Fifteen months later, I prepared to hold Gracie again. I was terrified. I removed the twist tie and opened the bag. As I did, ribbons of dust wafted upward and I could see them, illuminated by the sunlight pouring through the dingy windows of our little study. I watched them in slow motion and they reminded me of the sketches of smoke depicted in illustrated children's books. I could see the shapes so clearly, curling upward. I actively resisted seeing the beauty. I reached into the smoky tendrils, panicked that some of Gracie was escaping. *No!* I thought. *Not yet.* I smelled the ashes and brought my hands to my face. Self-consciousness crept in: was I being melodramatic? And then a counter thought abutted: if drama was not appropriate as I encountered the charred remains of my own child, when was it, and I began to feel entitled. I smiled at this recovery, seeing myself with strangely rueful eyes as the bereaved mother.

I could taste ash in my mouth. I can't describe the sensation, or maybe I don't want to. I panicked again, this time worried that I wouldn't be able to keep this taste of my daughter in my mouth for long. Saliva and eating and drinking and breathing all would soon degrade my daughter. She was slipping away from me. She is *always* slipping away from me.

I retied the stupid twist tie and took the bag out of the stupid plastic box to study it. I had been warned about the bone fragments. There they were. So small. I wanted to reach in and touch one or two. I decided that I would keep some of them. *Later. Not now*, I thought. *This is enough for now.*

It was too much, as my explosion at my youngest daughter later that day evinced. Here is the truth baked down to its hardest, undeniable kernel: I don't know how to parent one child while grieving another.

September 10, 2013

Soon after Gracie died, caring and kind people offered hope: "That little girl will save her" and "At least she still has Zoe." Sometimes these well-meaning words were spoken *to* me, but most times they were overheard or reported back to me. This naively hopeful sentiment is offered by those who want to light my way out of my darkness. But these words are not true. There is no way out. There is no light.

Like so many other parents, I sang to my children: "You are my sunshine, my only sunshine. You make me happy when skies are gray. You'll never know, dear, how much I love you. Please don't take my sunshine away." These words haunt me today. They mock me. Someone's momentary distraction took my sunshine away. Someone extinguished the light.

My beautiful, creative, wise, vulnerable, sensitive girl is dead and now my world is dark, hostile, treacherous, hollow. Three years after Gracie's death, I sometimes sob so hard I cannot breathe, suffocated by what Gracie will never see, never do, never be.

I am triggered easily, by seemingly everything: flip flops, chocolate chip cookies, teenage girls with long brown hair, siblings teasing one another, prom dresses, college admissions brochures, pregnant women. Zoe has triggers too. In school, two months after the accident, Zoe wrote: "I have a dream that everyone stop driving cars because then there will be no more car crashes." At first, Zoe raged and exploded. She threw full throttle fits because we offered her the wrong kind of pasta or because her Papa made a stupid joke she didn't think was funny. She threw objects at her Papa, and once, at a teacher. She is still unwilling to fall asleep alone. We indulge her, because we can. And, naturally, her litany of food issues are a bid for control in her chaotic, pained life. Someone took her big sister away.

We joined a grief support group—our new tribe of the permanently marked, the interminably miserable. Ten, even twenty years later, there is no "moving on," the others tell us. There is only resigned survival. Eight months after Gracie's death, Craig graduated from high school. We flew to Cincinnati to be with him, to cheer his accomplishment, but our pride battled with our loss. Gracie's absence filled the room; her silence muted the applause. Someone took our sunshine away. And now, the sky never changes; it is gray every day.

After Gracie died in the ICU in Utah—actually, when we decided to withdraw life support—how much I wanted to get home to Zoe, to our home, to our community. I was weary from enduring this catastrophe in a strange place with strange people. I wanted to hug my Zoe and be reminded of what was left. I thought having her would "save me." Now, I know that she cannot save me. Now I know that someone needs to save *her*, from me, from her sister's legacy, from the destruction that we live in, every day, a destruction for which I take full responsibility. Please do not point out that I was not driving the car that rolled and ejected my daughter, leaving her irreparably brain damaged. Please don't tell me that what happened to her could happen to anyone. Please, oh please. I beg you. Don't. I feel responsible because I am Gracie's mother. The facts of how she died do not touch this reality. After all, a mother's job, a mother's *single most important job* is to keep her child alive.

I failed at that job, and yet, somehow, miraculously, I am still in charge of keeping another child alive. But how can I? How can anyone trust me with this sacred task? I know I don't trust myself; my credentials so lacking, so devastatingly lacking. There is no more *when* with Gracie: 'when' you grow up, 'when' you learn to drive, 'when' you graduate high school, 'when' you go to college, 'when' you have your own place, 'when' you are a parent some-day. This is, above all, my daughter's tragedy. And also, of course, mine. But it does not stop there. What multiplies this devastation is that I cannot bring myself to imagine 'the whens' with Zoe either. The end of when is total. The shadow cast by Gracie's death is so powerful, it blocks out the sun. It is grey every day.

As a bereaved mother, I found my bottom, the absolute darkest, most despairing place within me. In the early days, I allowed my-self the luxury of hope when I reached toward Zoe, my surviving daughter, the child for whom I am still responsible. But see how even the description "surviving daughter" marks Zoe, defines her by her sister's death? It is inescapable, of course, though I try to protect her. I fail and I fail. And my failures are at once grand and mundane.

I am, at my core, utterly, hopeless.

When Gracie died, so did my capacity to look ahead, to see a future, to propel myself toward tomorrow. For me, the parent of Zoe, of living, breathing, growing, changing, wonderfully vibrant Zoe, I feel utterly disabled by the end of hope. And I know that if this perfect little person I love as much as her sister cannot "save me" then I am beyond saving. And so, whither poor Zoe?

How does a parent do her job when there is no hope? Parenting is an exercise in forward motion; it is nothing if not relentlessly dynamic, churning toward WHEN. Parenting is a focus on the present with an eye, always, on the future. Our job is to grow our kids up. *To keep them alive.* We teach them manners so that they can get along with others we will never meet. We impress upon them a work ethic, a sense of self-worth, an appreciation for nature, human connection, humility, self-care—all of life's lessons are, at their root, survival skills, a tool kit for a life far beyond the one we share with our charges. A parent enlists in the job of guiding a human being through their life course until the day they, the parent, dies.

Of course, my rational brain knows that the odds are in Zoe's favour, that in all likelihood, she will grow up, she will outlive me, she will have "when." But I cannot afford to assume this for her, or, for me. Keeping my absence of hope from her is exhausting. I know that her sister's death cannot be Zoe's burden any more than it already is. I know that Zoe is entitled to *her* life, her mistakes, her life lessons, her joys, her own fears. Her own life journey must not be inescapably inflected with the horror of her sister's life cut short. She is not only Gracie's sister, after all. I know this, but I can't *feel* this. I know this, but I can't yank out what Kathryn Stockett's character Minnie, the maid who stoically mourns her dead son in *The Help* called "a bitter seed ... planted inside me."[1] Gracie's death planted that seed in me and it is as permanent as Gracie is not. Sometimes the seed expresses itself as rage, sometimes as expletive-hurling rage. Sometimes, it channels despair, or a deep abiding sadness. Or cynicism. The seed is potent and I fear it will sprout soon and take over.

Zoe deserves better, simply because she is HERE. And I, her mother, must fight that bitter seed. I know I cannot exterminate it any more than I can bring Gracie back, but can I temper it somehow? Can I contain the weed it wants to grow in my heart, crowding, and ultimately strangling joy, gratitude, comfort, tomorrow? I don't know. I don't know. Others have survived much, much worse. The brutal torture and murder of their child. The death of multiple children. But I must arrest this almost ritual listing of 'it could be worse' because that is a game for the rational and grief cannot be reasoned with. I *know* it is possible to survive and to hope again.

People do every day. And I *know* that the key to moving forward, to imagining 'when' is linked to not denying this horror, but to, somehow, surrender and tap into a place beyond knowing.

February 20, 2012

I spent a few days in my friend's rented winter home in Maine. She uses it as a base for ski weekends. I used it to escape, to be completely alone. I wanted to tear off the mask I wear—the "I am fine, I am coping," the custom-made mask that bereaved parents wear in the world. I tried to let the pain flow. I brought Gracie's journals (she filled 37 of them, from age five to seventeen) so that I could be with her, their pages serving as permission to experience the presence of her absence.

While there, I took several walks. During one, I followed an asphalt path that hugged the Androscoggin River. I heard a shuffle and voices to my left and I startled. There were two figures under the overpass. It was a man in a Carhartt jacket and knit cap and a little boy, fully equipped in snowsuit, winter hat, gloves and snow boots. Father and son, I assumed. And I heard the dad, "Put your hands here...feel that?" as the cars rumbled above, vibrating the metal girding below. A good daddy, I thought, exposing his son to something new, fostering his curiosity. But like quicksilver, I was cynical.

The bitter seed inside me gained strength: *It won't matter.* I think to myself. *You will pour your energy into rearing this boy into a man, showing him the world, answering his questions, guiding his path, and in two to three seconds, he will be gone.*

Then jealously consumed me, my feet moved me further from them. *No. He will grow up, this little boy in a navy blue snowsuit. His father will watch him transform into a man.*

I kept ahead of them, winding my way to the bridge that crosses the half-frozen river. I indulged my urge to study the moving water beneath, but not before I pictured myself climbing the wooden lattice and jumping, knowing that there were too many unknowns woven into this death strategy to render it remotely viable.

Dad and son began to cross the bridge near me. We stood near one another. Dad pointed out the little prop engine noisily cruising over our heads. Of course, it is a parent's instinct to point this out, to say "Look at this, did you notice that?" We do this because we want to teach our children about the world, equip them with facts and keen observational skills. Why? So that they survive. Well, or thrive. We assume they will survive. Don't we? Really?

I moved on, wanting to remain a mere voyeur, not the least bit interested in small talk or even the quiet collusion of parent-to-parent. I did not want to be a parent right then. More precisely, I didn't want to be the parent I have become. The parent of the dead child. The parent who failed, now hopeless.

But in that moment, I felt curious and envious and wistful for those innocent days of lazy moments with an impressionable child who wants nothing more than his parent's undivided attention. As I indulged this longing, Dad and son prepared to roll down the grassy hill. Just the right size for such a small boy (he couldn't have been more than three) and I couldn't resist smiling as I watched Dad correct his son's form. Dad demonstrated the ideal hill rolling posture, and off he went. Fun dad. No educational value here, just ecstatic abandon. And a good story for when they got home, peeling off their mittens as the hot chocolate simmered.

When I encountered a dead end, I reluctantly turned around and passed the rolling pair. I didn't want to smile at them, because the smile felt like a lie. I know too much. I know how precious this is, or at least, could be, and I didn't want to betray my own life, my own desperate reality, with a simple nod and smile implying 'aren't you cute.' I wanted to say something unkind. Something like, "He might die. He might get flung through a broken window. Someone might smash his skull, baked at 1400 degrees Fahrenheit, with the back of a shovel."

Of course, I didn't. As we passed, I whispered a hopeful prayer to myself, for the little boy in the snowsuit and his father: *Please grow up*.

The bitter seed feebly resisted.

NOTES

[1]Kathryn Stockett. *The Help*. Toronto: Penguin, 2009, p. 3.

Changing Terms

GARRETT RIGGS

M Y SONS GET INTO AN ARGUMENT on the way to school. My younger son wants to play a game on my phone to pass the time and my older son, annoyed by the sound, tells him to turn it off.

"I'll turn it down," the seven-year-old says.

"No. Turn it off," his big brother says.

"Why can't I just turn it down?" my youngest asks.

"Because Dad probably won't remember to turn it back up and what if I need to call Dad in the middle of the day or something?" my eldest says. And just for good measure, he adds, "Turn it off."

This is one of a handful of times that my older son has spontaneously called me "Dad" in the privacy of our family. Usually, he calls me "Mom" because that is what I used to be to him. Sometimes he tells me: "I can't call you anything else. That's all I've known you as for fifteen years."

He was twelve when I came out as transgender. I was in my mid-forties when I started the medical and social transition to male. My oldest son is now fifteen. We have been going through puberty together. He was my first supporter; I came out to him and his little brother before I came out to anyone else. I figured they would be the most impacted by the transition and if either of them had truly objected, I would have waited until they were both adults.

But, after I told them what I had been feeling for so long, and shared my fears that they would be upset and reject me, my oldest put my anxieties to rest with his simple, strong reassurance. "You raised me. I love you no matter what."

Of course, his humour had to slip in there, too, to absolutely let me know he was okay with it. He ended the conversation with, "Why would I care what you do? You're weird anyway."

* * *

My youngest son comes into the living room as I am watching the documentary about Chaz Bono. I think about watching Sonny and Cher on TV when I was a child and remember feeling like Chastity Bono always looked a little sad and uncomfortable in the mini versions of Cher's eveningwear. I had no idea then just how much we had in common.

"What are you watching?" my son asks and pauses in front of the television for a minute.

"*Becoming Chaz*," I tell him and explain, "He is like me—he was born in a girl body, but now he's a man."

My youngest goes back to bouncing happily through the living room in his Superman costume, practicing his fight moves and stunts. He doesn't pay much attention to the screen, but I do. I notice how Chaz's eyes seem to fill with light and life now that he is more and more comfortable in his own skin. It is a stark contrast to the images from those childhood performances. As I watch Chaz's transition unfold, I see common experience in our parents not quite knowing how to handle the news and know that my Dad, like Cher, is struggling with feelings of loss, grief, concern, and ultimately, love. They're afraid for us. They want our lives to be happy and easy. I know this because I'm a parent and that is what I want for my children: happiness, health, and love.

Some parts of the documentary raise questions for me. There are experiences of transition that I don't feel like I share with Chaz, but I am not sure; I've never been good at seeing myself in the same way that others see me. When your physical body does not line up with your interior self, it can be very hard to know how others perceive you. When Chaz's girlfriend complains about his personality changing, I ask my youngest if I have gotten grumpier or seem angrier since starting testosterone.

"No, you're more fun now," he says and picks up the cat. The cat is not an aloof, cold creature. He is a floppy fluffy companion who accepts my son's enthusiastic hugs and accepts being carried around like a baby. Nobody in our house conforms to societal expectations. Not even the cat.

* * *

I am on the margins of parenthood in many ways. I have given up my social label of "mother" and the expectations that go along with it, but have yet to attain comfort in my role of "father." I no longer share birth stories or talk about the benefits of breastfeeding with women, because I no longer look like a woman and do not know an easy way to explain how I have come by my knowledge of pregnancy, childbirth, and breastfeeding. I can share in fatherly pride and boasting about my sons' accomplishments, but I lack the history and intimate knowledge of fatherhood that goes unspoken by the men I know.

Many of the men in my life who are fathers don't fit into expected gender roles. Very few of them push their sons into organized competitive sports. They encourage healthy activities such as rock climbing, skateboarding, biking, and swimming. My male friends encourage their children (regardless of their sex) to be active; they sidestep the American tendency to force kids into constant competition. Rather than using physical prowess as the measure of their sons' maturity into manhood, these fathers worry over academic achievement and self-expression.

Around these men, I am comfortable with my parenting style. I don't feel different for encouraging my sons to develop their brains more than their brawn.

The situation is different with men who are not part of my normal social circle of academics and artists. When I am around men who are more rough-and-tumble, I know I am an odd duck and my parenting style seems too nurturing to them.

"Jeez, Garrett, you do everything for them," my neighbour complains as I carry my youngest son's backpack from the car.

My neighbour is also a single dad and we have accidentally bonded over this commonality. He doesn't know I am transgender. He assumes that I am the biological father of my children. I haven't corrected this impression—exactly when is the right time to announce to a stranger that you used to be a girl? It doesn't seem like something you blurt out on first meeting and after months go by, raising the issue seems less and less appealing. I have no plans on sleeping with this guy, so why does he need to know what is or isn't in my pants?

My neighbour has a different woman with him every time I see him. I'm never sure what the relationships are. He complains about the mother of his son, yet she turns up on the occasional weekend and spends the night. When she isn't around, there seem to be other women who spend their weekends with him.

This neighbour chides me for keeping too close an eye on my kids. His son wanders through the apartment complex, jumps in the pool, and turns up at different people's apartments throughout the day. Having grown up a girl, I'm much more wary of sexual assault and violence than my neighbour is. As a result, I go everywhere with my kids or keep them within my sight.

I also spend as much time as possible with my sons because I was a latchkey kid. There was a certain loneliness to my childhood that I don't want them to experience. All that time on my own did make me independent. But, sometimes, I think I became too self-reliant in those years. I got so used to doing everything for myself that I still find it hard to relax and let somebody else take charge.

My neighbour throws a barbecue one weekend. His strange harem of exes and currents are all in attendance. Kids run in and out. His son, with a shock of wheat-coloured hair, slips past us and opens the cooler to get a bottle of water.

"Hey, gimme some sugar!" my neighbour says to the boy.

"Come get it," his son retorts.

The boy grins and turns his freckled face up to meet his father's whiskery kiss. He takes the water and runs off to join the other kids.

This moment of vulnerability and affection reminds me of my own father.

My mother died when I was 16 and my father finished the job of raising me alone. Like my neighbour, my father was a rough-hewn builder. He sweats sawdust and single malt whiskey. He chased women and stayed out to all hours when I was little. But, he also had his sweet side he reserved for his kids. He read us the Sunday comics in bed, played Crazy 8s late into the night, and made up long, involved stories that featured our family pets.

My father also showed affection with mock violence. He would pretend to strangle one of us before pulling us in for a hug. He gave us light pinches, pokes, and pats on the rear as he passed by, letting us know in his own way that he loved us. When I was a teenager, my father was often at a loss for how to raise a girl. He asked my aunt to go with me to the doctor when any "female stuff" needed to be addressed. My father and I were both more comfortable with my boyish nature.

When my stepmother complained that I kept my hair too short or wore jeans, he ignored her. He bought me a used drum set and let me put it in the garage. He didn't mind that I wanted to start a band instead of being on the cheerleading squad. He kept the fridge stocked with food so my friends would feel welcome in the house. The most important parenting lesson I learned from my father is to let kids explore their interests and identities. He let me be me when I was a kid and that freedom eventually let me discover my true self.

"Make sure you love what you do; you'll always be able to make a living, but it helps if you love it," he told me when I was starting college and trying to figure out what to major in. He harboured a dream that I would become an architect, but accepted it when I majored in English.

"Well, you always were a bookworm," he said. His gift when I graduated was a thesaurus and a Cross pen set to get me started on my writing career.

As my older son contemplates his own career path, I think of my father's words. I, too, want my son to love his job; I don't want it to seem like a job for him; I want it to be his passion; I want what he does each day to carry him through life with excitement for what the next day will bring.

My dad taught me that love is as important as responsibility in both parenting and career choices. I try to emulate that in my own fathering.

* * *

It is always the little things that have the potential to balloon into big things. At the very least, the small stuff crops up routinely as if to remind me of my past self and the fact that she will always be a part of my present self, no matter what name we go by.

When I register my sons for school, I have to fill out forms attesting to our residence within the county and who is responsible for them. In an era of divorce, children raised by relatives other than parents, and so on, the forms ask about mother, father, guardian, and custody arrangements. Only one school has been enlightened enough to use "Parent 1" and "Parent 2" rather than traditional binary of "Mother" and "Father." Parent 1 and 2, while sounding like something from a Dr. Seuss book, makes room for the reality of families in our time: children with two moms or two dads or, in our case, a dad who used to be a mom. The "enlightened" school was a private school we can no longer afford. So, this year, it is public school for everyone. And public school means lots of forms. Forms that stick to traditional roles, thank you, very much.

To avoid weird looks in the office and possible bullying for my kids, I put myself down in the "Father" blank. Their bio-dad lives in another country, so I simply note that "the other parent lives in X" on all the places where they wanted information on the second adult.

Even though our divorce decree gives me primary residential custody, I sometimes wonder if I should ask a lawyer for advice on rewording the paperwork with my new legal name. The paper trail is there and it connects me to my children through social security numbers and court papers. But, sometimes when the debate about LGBT issues gets really heated and I see the ugly, vindictive things people do to avoid equality, I wonder if I need it spelled out more plainly. Socially, I'm their father. Do I need a piece of paper underscoring that role?

At first, it felt odd to put myself down as "father" when, in truth, I had given birth to them. But, I am father and mother to my sons. In a sense, I always have been. Their father was hit-and-miss with his parent-child engagement. Depression often sidelined him, so that even when he lived with us, he wasn't always present in their lives. I wound up being everything—the provider, the nurturer, the disciplinarian. I took on every parental role. In that light, I still feel more comfortable being a "parent" than a "father" or a "mother." When we're out in public, I say things like, "These are my sons" and let people fill in whatever descriptor they want.

Language is something many take for granted. They use it every day, but unless their livelihood depends on it, English-speakers rarely stop and think about the subtleties and nuances of the language. Most of us don't think about pronoun usage or gendering terms and phrases. Most don't spend a lot of time thinking about how language is used to enforce gender roles and shape identity. Boys are encouraged to divest themselves of emotion with things like "Big boys don't cry." Girls are admonished for not being "ladylike" in their behaviour. Women who stand up for their rights are labelled as "bitches" or "feminazis." Men who show vulnerability or sensitivity in any way are told to "man up!" Exhibiting sensitivity is perceived as a weakness in American men.

When I'm standing in line to pick up my youngest after school, I use this causal relationship to language to my advantage. I don't divulge what I feel is private medical information. When other parents call me my son's "Daddy," I accept the title. I never claim it for myself though. The stickler inside me insists on accuracy even if it is through omission.

Which brings us back to my kids and their labels for me.

Everyone around me struggled with the pronouns at first. They forgot. They mixed them. A few refused to use masculine pronouns. The kids and I had conversations about what they should call me. I told them they could call me whatever they wanted, but I asked that, for safety's sake, they use masculine pronouns when we were in public. I told them I felt weird about being called "Dad" when they call their bio-dad that. "Father" seemed too formal. We live in the Deep South so "Pop" would sound too Midwestern. "Papa" is too antiquated for our tastes.

Exasperated by the conversation one evening, my oldest said, "You know what? I'm just gonna call you 'Pronoun!'"

In reality, he avoided calling me anything when we were in public. He chose to speak directly to me rather than opening by addressing me as "Mom," "Dad," "Dude" or anything else. At home, I was still "Mom." I was often "Dude" to him, which seemed like a genial compromise.

Even though we have a loving, open relationship, there are things my eldest son keeps to himself. He is a teenager, after all. One of the things he doesn't talk much about is my transition and how it affects him. I worry that he will get bullied or teased. I worry that my change is one more thing that adds to a sense of instability in his world: he is the child of divorced parents, one of whom doesn't even live in the same country. And as the child of an academic, he has lived with semester-to-semester contracts and deadlines disrupting the family routine. He's also fifteen, an age that in the most ideal of situations can be confusing and scary.

Sometimes, I think his inability to settle on a title for me shows that my oldest son is still struggling to figure out how all of this affects him and us. I suspect there are things he doesn't voice because he doesn't want to hurt my feelings or he wants to protect me in some way.

My kids weren't the only ones who had to figure out how to address me or refer to me when speaking with a third party. My boss, co-workers, friends, and family members all had to adjust.

Despite making a few accidental slips himself, my boss made it clear to everyone at work that I was to be called "Garrett" and that they needed to use the masculine pronouns. Like my son, my boss used humour to get through the awkwardness of the early days by reminding people that I had recently earned my Ph.D. and if they were uncomfortable calling me Garrett, then they could always call me "Dr. Riggs."

Friends made the switch quickly but weren't always sure who was in on the changes I was making. Part of the trouble of transitioning as an adult is the wider and wider circles of friends, acquaintances, and colleagues one builds. I had to update my name and gender status with former schools and workplaces. Any place I could change it, I did. But my old name was still out there with publications and other accomplishments. I wasn't always sure how to handle that—noting the publications were under a different name or a pseudonym seemed like a reasonable way to handle it.

My father and siblings have the hardest time with it. They still use the old name and feminine pronouns when they talk amongst themselves. To me, they might call me "bro" or use my first initial in email salutations and the like. I understand it is hard for them, so I don't insist. As the masculinization becomes more complete, they are making the switch. Hearing my deeper voice on the phone or seeing photos of me with a scraggly goatee is helping them truly see me. Being out in public and having strangers call me "sir" helps reinforce for them that the rest of the world does, in fact, see me as a man.

Most of the time, I am genial about my family's use of the wrong name and pronouns, but I quietly assert myself by signing emails and letters from "Garrett." Except for with my father. At 81, he's been through so many hard things—the loss of my mother and stepmother, the loss of two sons, and now more recently, his sister and friends. In some ways, he has also lost his youngest daughter; sure, I have not really changed as a person, but I am not really his daughter anymore and whatever dreams of womanhood he had for me are just that—dreams. For him, I sign things with my initial. As his own compromise, he addresses letters to me as G, which is much more than I expected and one of his typical signs of unspoken love.

We're all finding that the kind of transition I am undertaking, while a private decision and process, is very public because the changes are so visible. Everyone who knows a transgender person makes a transition right along with them.

My sons and I still have the same relationship we always have had. We spend a lot of time together because we genuinely like each other as people. Sure, we bicker over who made the mess in the living room or what movie to watch, but we feel comfortable with ourselves and with each other. Marathon homework sessions and my adjuncting sometimes disrupt our insular little routine, but we still would rather be with each other than with anyone else.

This sense of comfort is what allows my eldest to come to me at the end of the day and express his fears that he might be too late in learning enough of a language to be a top-tier programmer. Or, to tell me about his existential worries about why we are here and to ask what can we do with the world to make it better. Maybe when he comes to talk about these things, he is still talking to his "Mom," but he occasionally reaches out and strokes the wiry hair on my chin and says, "Nice neck-beard, Dude."

Pivot

Fragments from Mothering Through Time

JANICE WILLIAMSON

We come into the world and there it is.
We come into the world without and we breathe it in.
We come into the world.
—Juliana Spahr, "Gentle"

2011—My friend sits on a straight-backed chair. Last time she visited, her back gave out as she lifted herself out of the sofa. Now prone on the hardwood floor, she groans about her last two weeks of pregnancy. I watch her difficult progress through these last days as though I might catch a glimpse of another time and place.

I've not been there. Pregnant. Though I have a beautiful daughter. She came into the world at a time when I didn't know her. A woman, a mother somewhere in southern China, felt her daughter between her legs. A cry as her lungs expel her first breath. I imagine tiny wet fingers folding like ribs of new leaves.

All of my mothering life, I have imaginary conversations with this anonymous stranger—my daughter's first mother—who now seems familiar to me.

2009—"A daughter searches for meaning in her mother's past," the saying goes.

"In every woman's psyche is the unconscious of her mother and her grandmother's conscious mind," says another.

And what about those cut off from their biological genealogy?

How do we separate out the biological and genetic of birthing and bloodlines from the daily caregiving and knowledge of

44

motherwork? What is shared by adoptive and birth family alike? Where do nature and nurture fuse and split apart? Where does my daughter's birth family invent her in ways that exceed our life together? If I seek to know my daughter's laughter, do I hear the voice of her first mother in its traces though the rhythm and inflections may be my own?

All a jumble, the photographs in the album slip from their sleeves and settle in the bottom of a box where time stands still until someone's hand reaches in and asks you—"Who is this?" or "When?"

5 July 2006—On my third trip to China with my daughter I correspond with a writing friend about her new book, my envy barely concealed:

Hi dear M., Good wishes to you on pulling together your manuscript. What an accomplishment. I may be hot on your heels with my manuscript if I can get it all together. I'm writing as I go along thinking that if I don't get impressions down now, I'll remember little. My brain is fuzz half the time. We're having a fine time here in China. We especially loved Shanghai and Ji'nan and Beijing and Xi'an.... Basically every place we go we're quite enthralled though having friends and making friends makes all the difference. We just arrived in Maoming and on the way here on the highway, B. wondered about the brothers and sisters she might have. A very bittersweet visit though she does like it here since the people we know offer such kind attention and insist she call them uncle and auntie giving her an extended adoptive Maoming family.

Re: relaxation. China isn't a very relaxing place for us though we still love it. We're always on display in a way and we have to explain at every turn why B. doesn't speak Chinese and how it is I am her mother, etc. But we are going to Bali to visit friends after this and Bali is apparently the most sublime place on earth. That may be why people want to blow it up.... Love, Janice

22 March 2001—First day of spring yesterday. After last week's barbecue weather, it is snowing and twenty-five below. Writing, not writing. The thick of it, the thin. Hands not typing over the keys, letters like this ... not coming. Coming. Hardly. Ever. Remember the lovers you took up as a younger woman. So much

time writhing in bed. Breath sweating pillows blankets sheets. And now. Sheets clean tonight. New: a present to myself to take the place of not yet here, threadbare and thinning spring flowers. Time's a wasting. New sheets with stripes yellow/grey and flowers rust and green and yellow, shades of autumn or late summer here where snow might fall in August.

21 March 2001

Dear K.—The best way for me to manage single motherhood is to create a community of others who share the same pleasures and conflicts. Not necessarily other writers here in Edmonton in my case, but neighbours who are biologists and musicians and psychologists for the most part. Though I still have a writing group that meets intermittently and is a real treat to visit. I always show up unprepared with no writing but they seem to like what I have to say about their work and I enjoy the contact since I'm a working-inside-and-outside-the-home-single-mother of a small child and a writer-in-waiting at the moment.

Dorothy Parker joked "Time doth flit; oh shit."

Yesterday I hosted a big meal for ten adults and five children under five. Have learned to put away the puzzles and tiny plastic primary-coloured debris and leave out toys with large bits and pieces that are easy to find. The children spend most of the gathering playing with toys in the bathtub (outside of the tub ... no clothes ... brushing their feet with toothbrushes in a little bit of water filled up with toys—some new trend in personal hygiene) or sleeping on the bed (the infant) or dressing up and pretending to cook us all dinner. Everyone brings delicious food and I provide bread, salad, olives, and "tone." Tone is what Sheila claims I excel at as I set the long table with a big white tablecloth and best dishes and your late aunt's candy dish filled with peppery olives—I'm sure she would love them and so would you. We drink mimosas and think warm spring weather while winter rages white outside. Afterwards we share hot pies from the market and ice cream. The afternoon lasts from noon to five when everyone disappears having helped to tidy up most things. These afternoons of children playing by themselves while we talk about whatever—everything but the politics in our workplace—are a wonderful time.

These friends help me in ways that matter. We arrange for our
girls to swim at the same time together so we can all go and squeeze
in an adult swim as well as their lesson. Or we take the girls to
gymnastics at the same time so we can have talks while they play
… I think if I plan one activity every day for us on the weekend—
painting or swimming or Chinese dance or Mandarin—and B. has
music and gymnastics during the week, I can master this single
parenting. The activities take some of the pressure off of me to
be the Zen attentive one always on. Though my girl is so sociable
and "in the world" that a party every night with lots of play and
loving friends would suit her fine. I would like a party every other
night as I am slowing down a wee bit. Forty-six years between us
… and now I am fifty….

1962—My mother, a fierce Red Tory, was explosive in her criticisms
of my father and his views about social issues. And she was known
to denounce the views of well-loved friends. In some households,
she was banned from talking politics.

Those were the days when many talented women with material
support from middle-class husbands were confined to full-time
"housewifery" (as Donald Barthelme would call it in his novel *Snow
White*). It's easy to dismiss the invisible anguish concealed by the
appearance of good fortune. Some suffered greatly. One of my
favourite "aunts," a family friend, was the wife of a very successful politician. Immensely creative and a statuesque storyteller, her
voice sounded like a soul singer's. She gardened madly. Her eyes,
the colour of frozen cornflowers, kept watch over her summer
table-top blooms in the midst of the well-appointed dining room.
The bright green stems drank vodka filled almost to the brim of the
heavy lead-crystal vase. This hard-drinking horticultural housewife
stashed her secret straw nearby.

"What did the children do?" you may ask. A friend of my generation reminds me that her mother during the same era tied her
to a tree in front of the house and told the older children to keep
watch over her. Not standard parenting practice today.

Everyone knew my mother would argue her way up and down.
She was a supporter of my rebellion. When I ran away from home
at sixteen and eventually left for good at seventeen, her advice to

me was, "Never do anything once for a man that you don't want to do for the rest of your life." I caught her drift. My marriage, a misery of sorts, lasted fifty weeks and I was never really keen to do it again.

10 July 2010—First sleepover of almost thirteen-year-olds. Almost identical giggles. All in the same class at school. Three study Mandarin daily. All have their passions: two classical pianists, two soccer players, and a Wushu champion. All love Bieber's hair.

12 May 2013—Thanks to my B. for a special Mother's Day outing to the Golden Rice Bowl for delicious dim sum. And I was chauffeured by the girl who is becoming an excellent driver. Then it was off to the fourth and final game of a week-end soccer tournament on a gorgeous sunny afternoon. Now it's nap time for all.

September 2013—My Uncle Bob died today, a close family friend who was my neighbour during childhood. He and his wife, my beloved aunt Peg, and their two children Robin and Barb were my extended family—unofficially adopted as fellow migrants from Brandon, Manitoba, to Ontario. Bob's wit and intellectual energy provided me with a big stash of *New Yorker* magazines piled in his basement, an archive that gave me a sense of how humour and politics mattered. And for a prairie girl growing up in rural fields outside Toronto, urbane wit and writerly insight mattered. Paris and New York beckoned. Simone de Beauvoir and Dorothy Parker became my bedside table companions—the eros of radical play and good conversation. *The New Yorker* introduced me to Jonathan Schell's 1967 long-form exploration of the Vietnam War "The Village of Ben Suc"—the landscape of a village decimated by a war machine where a Vietnamese girl longs for the cool walls of her aunt's house from within the disorderly furnace of the refugee camp where she now lives. Is this when I became a peace activist?

8 June 2013—My mother had surgery this week and every day I've felt out of sorts, not always conscious of her distress but living alongside myself looking in. My mother's surgery will be a

moderate success as she continues to walk with pain on her brand spanking new hip. But while she was recuperating, my psyche leaked memories and time shifted.

In class I teach George Elliott Clarke's new poems *Illicit Sonnets* so deliciously erotic, outrageous, and vital. And we begin to explore his play *Trudeau* where his invented character Simone Cixous sparked stories about the freeing effects of reading Simone de Beauvoir's *Second Sex* when I was my students' age or younger.

My mother encouraged me to not live out her life. And she eagerly read everything I read in my university literature and social history Women's Studies class—one of the first offered in Canada in 1973. I read Doris Lessing's *The Golden Notebooks* and my mother read it too along with everything else Doris Lessing wrote. She read Betty Friedan and Virginia Woolf and Ursula LeGuin and Germaine Greer and Margaret Atwood and later Toni Morrison, Alice Munro, Christa Wolf, and others.

Thinking about *Trudeau*—the pirouetting "just watch me" Pierre reminded me how I narrowly escaped arrest as an undergraduate student. The night Trudeau imposed the War Measures Act in 1970, I gathered with my Religion 100 class to listen to Baba Ram Dass tapes in my Ottawa suburban living room. In the midst of our discussion, a stranger appeared at my door to "check" on what we were doing. I explained that we were a study group and he left only to return a few minutes later with police who searched the house. We would have been arrested but for the welcome presence of the boarder in the basement, a gentle American deserter named Norman who owned a leather artisan store and was an avid handball player. Fortunately the detective in our kitchen was one of Norman's handball partners at the YMCA.

The many anti-Vietnam War immigrants of this era would make remarkable contributions to Canada but I have always been especially grateful that Norman's informal intervention saved us from imprisonment for extra-curricular study.

In thinking about one of the inspirations for Clarke's *Trudeau* character "Simone Cixous," the remarkable French writer Hélène Cixous, I think about my mother. "Thinking about" is too detached a mental energy to describe the embodiment of mother in this daughter; the look-alike face of mere biology does not suffice. The likeness is deep in the body memorized in time, the echo gestures and identical turn of phrase or tone of voice, the memories of her hands in my conversational gesture.

And the love.

This sense of embodiment continues in my daughter too—I see myself sometimes when she talks and our voices shift tone just so.

13 August 2013—In Ontario briefly to visit very dear long-time friends, I spend time during a hospital visiting hour encountering a mid-sixties man in utter despair and shame at his hopelessness.

This is the suffering of mental illness.

Here in an institutional building, locked doors are monitored closing one after another. Butterfly patterns on the floor mark and mock the way along corridors as though metamorphosis is inevitable. I sit in a chair, my back to the door as an invisible old woman screams from a hallway nearby. I hide my shock at my friend's shrunken frame and pallor. He tells me of his wasted life memorizing facts and I tell him of his long life teaching and writing brilliantly.

The dissonance between our two versions of his life is the gap between his insider world and my view from an almost comfortable distance. He says he once didn't want his beloved wife to become a widow. Now he is less certain of this. If I believed, I would pray for him. As it is I hold his hand and wish him a return visit to this ordinary fragile world we once shared—most days his familiar wit and irony would whittle the bitter edge from misery.

I tell him of my daughter's insight on her northern canoe trip where to think ahead beyond this natural beauty was to encounter fear of weather and river and more than a dozen portages. Focusing here and now in the rhythm of a paddle stroke kept her present to herself and safe. My friend's river is a room opening onto a garden. His weather, an electric storm of ECT. His portages, lonely nights journeying out in the cries of strangers. May this suffering place keep him safe until he can risk imagining a possible future again. I keep him close in my heart, a sharp reminder of love's comfort and the pain of life so near at hand.

1914—Grandma and her siblings were abandoned by their father after the death of their mother and all three of them grew up in abject circumstances as servants or worse. My great-uncle, a landscape painter, died in a WWI battlefield in his teens. My great-aunt, grandma's sister, died in childbirth at sixteen. The rural Manitoba home where she was fostered housed her in a room with the hired hand, a curtain separating her bed from his.

My grandmother was fostered in a different very religious family. The youngest in the household, she learned how to clean house, the only thing she knew how to do, she later told me. Stubborn and gifted, my grandmother worked her way through Normal School in Winnipeg and drove a buckboard to a rural schoolhouse before marrying in her early thirties, an advanced age then. Her husband finished elementary school and was one of fourteen in a southern Manitoba rural family.

At first my grandparents lived in a farm house with earth floors. Eventually the farm would be lost in the dirty thirties and a gravel business my grandfather started with his brother would sometimes flourish.

On a visit to my grandmother's well-tended bungalow in Shoal Lake, Manitoba, I explore the basement treasure trove only to find the faded leather-bound volumes of English Romantics—Keats, Coleridge, Wordsworth—and the Scot Robbie Burns. Tucked in a box nearby was a yellowed envelope with hair the colour of my own though longer and braided into a plait cut off soon after my grandmother's marriage.

In my house today, a row of coloured glass vases line the rail of the double-hung bay window. The shades of light mimic the refracted rainbows in my grandmother's living room.

27 November 2012—I wonder how many children of writers tell them "I don't want to be a writer like you" as your days fritter away carving words in the kitchen when you could be cooking, sleeping, shovelling the walk, or doing anything that looks more productive. Your child calls to you and you find yourself awakening from your mid-story daydream a few minutes too late—your mind state a private one that requires persistent knocking at the gate.

1974—After my parents' separation, my mother worked with

severely disabled children for many years. A friend, the wife of our dentist ran an outreach program at a local church. Eventually my mother would win the Lieutenant Governor of Ontario award for this volunteer work—that's when she told me she wished she had trained professionally but she always felt too intellectually inadequate to go to university. This is a woman whose stories contradict this tale of failure. She thinks her feelings of inadequacy might be linked to her mother's life.

1 May 2012—My mother made her annual spring visit when I was enmeshed in a political struggle. I described to her the collective outrage around the honorary degree the University of Alberta recently granted to the Nestlé chair Peter Brabeck. Our university president met the Nestlé's exec at a Davos gathering and next thing we knew, in spite of public protest, he had an honorary doctorate from the University of Alberta.

At the ceremony, students chant and some faculty stand with our backs to the stage. Why do I protest now? I think about my daughter and her generation's uncertain future.

After listening to my Nestlé story, my mother responds with her own.

In the early 1970s, she was invited to her dentist's for dinner. Introduced to the man seated beside her, my mother discovers he is the head of Nestlé's Canada.

"Oh, you must be happy to have that controversy about baby milk behind you," enthuses my mother but the executive's face turns red with fury.

"I thought he was going to jet off to the moon."

My mother had perfectly timed what I call her "intervention." For Nestlé's marketing plans were first publically documented in 1973 leading to a two-year trial judgment advising the company to "modify its publicity methods fundamentally." Critics on Wikipedia describe how Nestlé's "aggressive marketing strategy had led to the deaths of thousands of babies who did not have access to clean water with which to mix the milk powder and, who needed the enzymes in their mother's milk as an essential part of their immune system."

Oh to inherit my mother's good timing.

31 January 2014—*The Guardian* headline reads: "Nestlé chairman warns against playing God over climate change"—a good fit for my university's increasing ties with big oil and government. As if on retainer, our university Board of Governors advertises for people with oil industry experience. And the highest paid university administrators in the country rival the salaries of oil executives. Happily Brabeck's politics suit some aspects of Alberta' oil sands ethos. The article observes: "While scientists point to the near certainty that human activity is driving up temperatures, Brabeck claims 'climate change is largely down to natural cycles and society should focus on adaptation.'" Who needs pesky evidence-based science?

28 March 2014—I am multitudes: a mother who writes, a mother who teaches, a mother who cares what world we leave our children, the world we've made for those Indigenous peoples who lose their water aquifers to Nestlé bottles or their hunting grounds and health to tar sands devastation. In Alberta, the petroeconomy beckons and young men and women give up on education to secure high-paying skilled labour jobs in the oil industry. Nothing wrong with skilled labour but not when it is the favoured destination of several generations and tied to a lethal economy.

2012—According to studies, I share feelings of failure with many other women. I went to graduate school on a dare without much confidence anything would come of it. Though I passionately love/d the work.

My daughter tells me I'm too critical of her—"You want me to be perfect"—and I hear the voices telling me I'm not doing well enough if the As don't all match up in a report card arrow pointing up.

June 2013—When my daughter quits piano after a decade of lessons in lieu of school band trombone and guitar lessons, will our piano will be silent? My longing is entirely selfish as I love to hear her play Bach's gigue, a baroque dance filled with hypnotic varied repetitions. B.'s last lesson with Ruth was yesterday and they hugged and Ruth and I hugged and we remembered B.'s early days and I thought back to the first years of study as a tiny girl with her first teacher Miss Anne who moved away after a few years, a sad loss for all. But this afternoon, I'm out in the garden pulling weeds and moving plants around the way spring allows, the dark earth wet with rain—generous and fertile. Suddenly Bach stretches from the living room out the kitchen window to the garden and in my mind's eye I see the little girl now almost woman at the piano, her fingers nimble and gifted with new knowledge and practice beyond count. Then silence and the creak of stairs as my daughter makes her way to the study where chemistry beckons, her last exam tomorrow. The music an interlude to unsettle the tension that keeps her at her desk in preparation for what is to come. She'll do well and I'm glad to hear how the piano interlude calms and soothes us both.

1965—At night, all through high school, I read books by the light of a flashlight under covers. And I listen to great R&B on WU-FO in Buffalo beamed across Lake Ontario to my transistor radio. The Great Lake acts like a giant amplifier booming the hip rhythms of Aretha Franklin's "Evil Gal Blues" & "just give me a little R-E-S-P-E-C-T." I'm launched on the road to Women's Liberation that will arrive in my life a few years later. WU-FO was the only African-American radio station in Western New York State and certainly the northern-most station of its kind—nothing like it in Canada. It started in 1962 with DJ Eddie O'Jay on the air, the producer of the R&B group The O'Jays who in the mid-seventies would have fabulous hair and release "For the Love of Money."

On WU-FO, the sounds of the Civil Rights Movement played, and at fourteen, I might have heard news of the 1965 march from Selma to Montgomery. All I remember from that era is James Brown's "I Feel Good (I knew that I would)." I sewed a sequin-collared shoulderless ice blue-grey crepe dress and danced to James Brown with two other R&B fanatics in Pickering High. I can't remember their names but I recall their slicked back hair and shiny pointed shoes beneath stove-pipe pants. Shirts were turquoise or purple. They looked good and always danced together. In this era, the sexual revolution had not yet made same-sex dance partners anything other than a convenience. Sometimes they invited me to join them on the almost deserted chaperoned dance floor.

54

Across the big silent waters of Lake Ontario in the midst of rural Ontario—outside what was then an almost all-white very small town called Pickering—I had little occasion to talk about race. Though bigotry was just under the surface or right in your face at our Sunday dinners. My father was a dedicated racist, ever more committed as I eagerly rose to the bait. I was happy to learn later that my beloved high-school Latin teacher Miss Teelucksingh had a poster of Malcolm X in her Toronto apartment she commuted from every day.

Racism was the subject of my arguments with my father for as long as I can remember. I was his "artsy crafty lefty"—a kind of ideological foundling in the family. (I make no claim to ideological invention—just a stubborn resistance to nonsense.) At sixteen, I won a public speaking contest for Ontario students and was part of a high-school contingent that visited the United Nations in New York City. Between a group photograph and our speeches, I bought a present for my father in the UN bookstore: a thin cobalt-blue covered UNESCO book, *Buddhism and the Race Question,* originally published in 1958. It argued "the Case Against Racism" and caste focusing on "the worth and dignity of human existence in view of the opportunities and potentialities that man possesses for self-development."[1] Gender figured very briefly in a short commentary about Buddha and women.

In another era, I might have discovered bell hooks for my amateur jazz musician father. In her 1998 memoir of childhood, *Bone Black,* hooks writes: "Jazz, she learns from her father, is the black man's music, the working man, the poor man, the man on the street. Different from the blues because it does not simply lament, moan, express sorrow, it expresses everything."[2]

2003—This morning outside my office window a man and a woman walk down the sidewalk towards the desirable ravine-end of the street. They are pointing at something, or rather, she is pointing at something, cell phone clutched in her hand, antenna leading the way. Her black tight pants are slit up to the knees. A black sweater slung across her shoulders covers the back of a cherry pink T-shirt. Black sandals, delicate, are low-heeled. Hair is bleached blond and curling to her shoulders. Short like me, she strides to keep up with the grey-haired man at her side in blue jeans and blue t-shirt, black fleece jacket folded carefully on his arm.

Mothering a young child makes me more attentive. Adults look different. More like, well, adults. "Where's the play in them," you think, as you make your fingers move over the keyboard. And if you are a single mother you wonder whether a partner would be a good alternative. But you also recall how the partners can spiral into a surprise single-parent arrangement.

Today I feel quite relaxed in solitude. My daughter is visiting a friend and aside from another friend calling to speak with her, the house is quiet and the afternoon uninterrupted. I should be finishing up something else but this summer I've prioritized some time for my writing. What a word: "prioritized" sounds like "sanitized" when I sound it out. Does that mean it is good for me?

10 March 2013—At a university meeting today, I noticed that everyone in the room had a wedding ring but me. Some of the women had husbands, some wives. But I was suddenly stricken with the fact of my solitary status = single mother and all that ideology of the oppressed. Then my thoughts turned to longing for companionship. Though upon reflection, this mental journey was overly optimistic opportunism because the first quality that popped into my mind was the handy person missing in my life who can solve: the ice dam on the roof, the icy sidewalk out front, the wacky bathtub drip, the light fixture with impossible-to-change bulbs, the back door the dog destroyed, the back deck about to collapse, and the garage that needs to be emptied of debris. So much for romance. I need a cyborg synthesis of dump truck, shovel, hammer, screw driver, and socket wrench.

Today was also the first day my B. worked at paid labour. Last week she took a snowboard instructor course and when she excelled, they hired her at the ski hill immediately. After dropping her off, I cook up an elaborate feast for some rabble rousing friends and we plot revolution all afternoon. Who has time for this when the babies are tiny and hungry for all manner of things? But by dinner time, it is B. who is exhausted after teaching lessons to little tykes all the way to adults. Tired but delighted, she tells me how her driving lessons are progressing.

Help! I'm heading towards near redundancy.

November 2009—I am inspired by an Edmonton interfaith gathering I attend with Muslims, Christians, and human rights activists demonstrating their opposition to Omar Khadr's exile and imprisonment.

Years before I worked hard as a peace activist establishing several women's peace groups. For a few years, I take my daughter to stand with me in silence with Quaker and Arab and Jewish women to oppose the conflict in Iraq and Canada's participation in the Afghanistan conflict. Then my single mothering creates other priorities and the world of war and want melts into an uncomfortable background hum that I work to ignore.

But in the words of the coalition of speakers that November night in Edmonton, Omar Khadr seems too long neglected and I fall under the spell of his story. Keenly engaged, I feel driven to act on his behalf in response to the grotesque nature of his torturous treatment and long solitary exile.

May 2012—Between 2010 and 2012, I put together a multi-disciplinary anthology *Omar Khadr, Oh Canada.* The more public my voice, the more I hear from extremists. The Israeli Defence League, a radical group associated with violence, demonstrates outside the Toronto book launch, one of the five I organize across the country. Someone threatens to bomb the bookstore. Afterwards, personal harassment ensues.

September 2012—As part of the Petrocultures Conference, I travel to Fort McMurray and then on to Fort McKay, the neighbouring First Nations and Métis communities. At lunch we are told that not only was the land we stand on compromised by development, but through an elaborate patchwork of potential resource development their traditional lands further north are at risk. This northern pristine landscape they fly into to hunt, trap, and participate in ceremonies is surrounded by land leased through oil companies. One man describes how "when you lose your land, you lose what it means to exist."

Later, our tour of Suncor includes a visit to reclaimed land. On the surface, grasses wave, the unblemished earth stands under your feet, the waters in the pond glisten. Imagine a bison, a mirage on a distant horizon. But you notice what looks like the wooden lid of a deep well and lift it up. The deep well holds surprises as you peer into a Wizard of Oz maze of pipes constantly pumping the goop of sticky black ooze out of the landscape.

Meanwhile back in Fort McMurray jovial city representatives share Fort McMurray boosterism that on the one hand reflects a dynamic community and on the other glosses over urban challenges and the strange demography of a fly-in workplace and nearby nearly all-male work camps.

Why don't I write more about this Alberta landscape? It's what we are known for internationally. Why don't we have a widespread provincial cultural movement that documents and explores these issues in an ongoing and very public "art & activism" way?

Why don't I write for my daughter's generation? Last year, in a reading for a city book prize, I was struck how few off the locally-written books mention oil. The silence speaks to what—our fears?

Certainly not indifference.

The stakes are too high.

November 2012—Soon after Omar's arrival in Canada, I try to send my anthology to him at his Canadian prison but the officials say he can't read it because it is about his case. The university publisher finds this as outrageous as I do.

November 2013—The best part of writing books is the rapport that develops with readers. My memoir *Crybaby!* was published just before I became a mother. It developed a small but persistent and very interesting readership—over the years they still write or talk to me. And every once in a while, they send their dissertation chapters about my book or they forward a new essay. Today one of them sends the third article she's written that explores photography and autobiography—this time the focus is on my use of the empty frame.

28 March 2014—Revising a new talk about Omar Khadr, I reflect on my ongoing passion for social activism and writing. The more I

learn about the case, the more consumed I am about the injustice. Aren't there other raging social issues I could obsess about?

What is at stake? Torture in the name of national security versus justice and human security. Arbitrary citizenship rights determined by racism. The triumph of bigotry over evidence and the Rule of Law.

Omar Khadr has now been imprisoned without interruption for almost a dozen years in spite of international law that determines he should never have been imprisoned at all. He is the only minor in modern history to be convicted of a war crime and this in a disputed military court. Our governing party continues to revile Omar as a terrorist in spite of the forced nature of his plea bargain in a widely denounced U.S. military commission. They repeat the disputed judgment of a U.S. military witness whose forensic psychiatry cites a notorious racist and is more theology than science. They ignore the documented history of doctored military reports and secreted evidence. And oblivious to Canadian legal judgments in Omar's favour, they spurn international law that says he should never have been imprisoned at all.

Imagine a father dropping his son off in a war zone when most boys are given a digital war game and taught to take up battle. And imagine being captured at fifteen after a four-hour firefight. And imagine thirty interrogations in Bagram beginning when you are on a stretcher recovering from surgery. Imagine your torturer is a man who will be convicted of murdering another prisoner by using the same methods he uses on your pummelled legs. Imagine your own country betraying you, calling first for your special treatment because of your youth and then falling silent. Imagine your own country sending a Canadian interrogator to your Guantanamo prison cell knowing that you have been tortured through three-weeks of sleep deprivation and months of inhumane treatment.

Nowadays, other racialized persons are imprisoned—almost a quarter of Canadian prisoners are Indigenous though they make up only four percent of our population. And the most suspect "untrustworthy" Canadians today are constructed by our Islamophobia. Muslims continue to live in fear and silence at risk of being caught in our interminable transnational "war on terror."

I think about my daughter, now sixteen, the same age as Omar when he was tortured in Guantanamo. And I reimagine her through Canadian history. Once my Chinese-born girl would have been imprisoned for the price of a Head Tax or more likely refused entry through the Chinese Exclusion Act that kept this country free of the racist panic about the "yellow peril."

3 January 2014—Omar writes to me about my anthology: "It is too bad I couldn't read the book…. I got the same odd reason for not being allowed this book. You'd think we are living in a third world country where there are restrictions on speech and thought. But I guess I'll have to wait to read it…. Being in this hardship for so long saddens me sometimes, but seeing people's compassion towards me and others in suffering reminds me and reassures me that even if sufferings are everywhere, goodness is still there and it will overcome…."

I'm humbled by Omar's hope.

23 July 2013—My girl has been away for almost a month at camp planning and then navigating an eighteen-day canoe trip down the Churchill River. Missing her, I live very quietly in her absence. Midway through her travels, I hear news from an unexpected source. By chance our neighbours and their extended family paddle every summer down the Churchill for two weeks of wilderness holidays. In earlier days, this couple crafted artful canoes for a living, precursor to the beautiful houses they build today. While there is not much water traffic in that neck of the woods, last week they met the six canoes from my daughter's camp—ten fifteen-year-old girls including my B. and two counsellors in the wilds of North Saskatchewan. They invite me to look at their photographs of rock and forest and river—the Class III rapids more demanding than usual. They show me the map and chart their progress with the skill level of the girls in mind. The water is very high and fast, they say. The weather is unpredictable as it is elsewhere these days—colder than usual and very wet. Even in the pristine wilds of the Churchill River, there is no escaping the climate effects of a world transformed.

When I drive three hours to pick up B. from camp, her strong brown body will leap into my arms—elated and soaring with a new world of stories.

NOTES

[1]G. P. Malalasekera and K. N. Jayatilleke. *Buddhism and the Race Question*. Paris: UNESCO, 1958.
[2]bell hooks. *Bone Black: Memories of Girlhood*. New York: Henry Holt, 1996.

The Front of the Bus

FIONA TINWEI LAM

A SUMMER SATURDAY AFTERNOON. We board the number 17 bus in Kitsilano, heading to Granville Island market after a busy morning of tee-ball. I find an empty seat near the front, and haul my leggy, forty-five pound son onto my lap. One of the laughing, chatting teenaged girls sitting up front with us graciously offers to stand, but I decline. I can see the girls want to be together.

A few stops later, a well-dressed, robust blonde woman in sunglasses, probably in her early sixties, comes aboard. She's clearly not happy that all the front seats are filled and makes a remark to that effect. When the girl next to me offers up her seat, the woman turns her down, with a quick frown in my direction. I realize that she actually doesn't want to sit beside me.

"Just get all the Chinese off the bus!" the woman says just as an Asian man vacates his seat to disembark. She looks around expectantly, as if everyone in the bus (other than my son and I, and the gentleman who relinquished his seat for her) will find this remark amusing. The girls—who are white—look at her, then at me, their eyes wide in shock.

Stunned, my mind races, trying to decide how to respond. Although I've been raised to respect and defer to the elderly, I am horrified by what my young son has heard. I brace myself, and then state as clearly and firmly as I can, "That was a racist remark." Nerves taut, heart pounding, I wait for her reaction, steeling myself for the worst.

"That's right!" she smirks proudly, sitting down a few feet away in the seat vacated for her. But she isn't completely indifferent.

Obviously annoyed that I was uppity enough to actually talk back to her, she adds, with a derisive chuckle, "Better look out for your immigration papers, honey."

I look the woman in the eye. "You look out for your own immigration papers," I say. "You don't know anything about me."

The woman stops smiling. I am not exactly the kind of "immigrant" she expected. The girls shift in their seats. They don't look at either of us. Maybe they wish I'd stop talking. But I can't and I won't.

"It's appalling you would say such things in front of a child," I continue. "Appalling." I turn away, hug my son closer and stare fixedly out the window. I have no idea what will happen next. Should I say something more? Should I try to convince her that we all have an equal right to ride public transit? Cite the Charter of Rights? Start singing *Oh Canada* in French?

I can tell the woman is thinking hard. I feel sick to my stomach, imagining what she might say back. Have I unnecessarily escalated a conflict?

The girls stop talking entirely. My usually squirmy, chatty son is still and quiet too. The silence feels interminable. But nothing more happens. After a few stops, the woman gets up, walks past us to confer quietly with the bus driver about directions, then exits the bus. The girls remain subdued. My face burns, and my heart still hammers in my chest. I hate conflict. I feel no triumph.

Finally, after a few more excruciating minutes, I ring the bell for my stop. As my son and I make our way to the front door, it feels like we are walking in slow motion. I can feel the girls' eyes on my back. I have no idea what they are thinking, what the driver or any of the other passengers have heard or thought. But I do know that I feel very much alone.

If this woman had made a remark of that kind about another kind of passenger, I would have spoken up. But no one in that bus feels the need to speak up for me or my son.

After the bus is gone, I kneel down to talk to my son. I'm still trembling. "Do you know what happened there on the bus?" I ask. He shakes his head. I try and explain what the woman did. And then what I did. "Some people think that you should just ignore it when a person puts down other people. But that only makes that person think that everyone agrees with the put-down. If something is wrong, you should say so. Be proud of who you are." He seems to take it in.

But afterward I berate myself for not having said something stronger, better, to that woman on the bus. And then I worry that I've given my son a simplistic message, maybe even the wrong one. What if it had been a group of teenaged boys who'd made the same remark? Or a big man? Or a drunk? What if it had happened at night, or in a rougher part of town? My instinct to protect my son and myself would probably have overtaken everything—I would have been silent.

If only the bus driver had said something, the girls had said something, or one of the other passengers. But no one did anything. Maybe they were as conflict-averse as I am. And they weren't the object of that woman's cruel remark. They weren't Chinese. They didn't care about the history behind her words, nor feel the almost physical shock of them. A good reason to expect them to step forward? Or a better one not to put themselves out?

In the end, on that day, on a public bus in Vancouver, what hung in the air was the silence of the passengers. It came through to me just as loud and clear as the slur.

This story was first broadcast on "The Sunday Edition," CBC Radio, October 26, 2008.

Constellation

JANINE ALCOTT

I LOVE THE NIGHT SKY. Looking up at the bright points, I see all of time simultaneously. The image of the moon comes to me from 1.3 seconds ago, the planets from a few minutes or even hours ago, the bright star Sirius from eight and a half light-years ago. The light from some long-dead galactic clusters has taken so long to reach me that what I see is an image moments after the creation of the universe. This mosaic of time in the night sky harmonizes with the way I see myself: old, young, dead and yet-to-be-born child of the universe, caught in this specific lens, on planet Earth, in California, a mother of five, a writer at her laptop.

Raised by enlightened atheists, I have no religion. But my fifth child Kyle, born after a long gap in childbearing, teaches me the depth of prayer. My baffled soul converses with the cosmos in a language of instinct, myth, poetry, and scraps of scripture. Sometimes, like ancient sailors in a sea with no landmarks, I am guided by the stars. When the heroes of mythical Greece entangled their families into impossible knots, Zeus addressed the impasse by throwing the players into the stars, achieving a kind of perpetual equilibrium that acknowledged what was irreconcilable. I feel closest to Kyle when I think of us as constellations circling each other from across the sky. I don't know how else to address the impasse.

Conformity, discipline, postponed gratification—these traits elude Kyle. He cannot adjust to our market-driven, government-monitored, cubicle-strewn society. Perhaps in Ancient Greece, Kyle would have been a respected leader instead of a thirty-two-year-old homeless dropout. He is charismatic, generous, reckless, and he radiates flashes of heroism and brilliancy. But Zeus threw Kyle the wrong way—out of the stars and into Central California, where his fractured soul blasted through a condom and diaphragm to catch and quicken on the ragged edge of a hostile marriage, conceived in a moment of lovemaking that more resembled the embrace of mortal combat than tender devotion. Perhaps in protest, Kyle was born backwards: he arrived butt first, nearly dying, nearly killing me. Kyle's birth went on and on; the dying and killing still go on and on.

My relationship with Kyle may have begun, like the light from that far galactic cluster, moments after creation, but this story begins with his birth. The pain of it blasts through all my reserves of selfless love: I would welcome not only my death, but also the death of my child, if only to stop the torment. As two physicians attempt to pull him free from the birth canal, I hear my voice cry out "God help me!" and for a few blissful, pain-free moments I actually leave my body, on my way out of this world. I pause at a corner of the delivery room ceiling, and dispassionately look down on the frantically working doctors grouped around the bloody form that used to be me. But my gynecologist looks at my face, and knows that I have left. He grabs my head with both hands and yells my name, pulling me back through a dark tunnel to the scene below. Kyle is violently jerked free from my body. The pediatricians work to revive Kyle who is hidden from me by a row of doctors' backs with tied green gowns. No one answers my plaintive queries,

"How is my baby? How is my little boy?"

My ears strain for a newborn cry, but none comes. It may be that Kyle, even more than I, has willed our mutual exit from this world. He certainly resists much longer coming back into it.

Finally, the tension in the room eases, and one of the doctors lays the beat up mess that is Kyle on my stomach. My baby looks at me without a sound. I suddenly know—Kyle is a mighty warrior. I recognize Kyle as a warrior because I am a warrior. Kyle and I, we are each of us valiant, wounded, resolute, defeated, triumphant. This knowledge, born as Kyle is born, will lie in my unconscious until years later, when once again my love will be overwhelmed by pain.

* * *

Kyle was a bright but tempestuous boy trying to keep up with older siblings. As his single mom, I worked away from home while gradually pulling the family out of poverty. My son's absent dad neglected him, and his eventual stepdad disliked him. Then major disaster hit Kyle's life: the end of the cold war. The dismantling of the Berlin Wall meant celebration and thanksgiving, but it also meant closure of the defense plant where Kyle's stepfather, Brent, and I worked. We were among the few lucky ones to receive transfers from our small town in Central California to a larger company division in the San Francisco Bay Area. With four children needing college tuition the following year, Brent and I had to accept transfers. Two of Kyle's other siblings who had been living at home moved out to go to college. Kyle would become an only child, in a new neighbourhood, in a new school, with his mom and stepdad away at work all day. My son was traumatized and furious with me for ruining his life. He spent three months of allowance on lottery tickets, hoping to win big enough so that we wouldn't have to move. Finally he decided, in imitation of his siblings, that he would no longer live at home: he would go to his biological father. His dad, newly married to a woman with no children, acquiesced with apprehension.

Kyle moved, not to my carefully chosen new neighbourhood with good schools and proximity to my workplace, but to his new stepmother's house in a low-income neighbourhood. He bussed across the East Bay each day to a mediocre school. The next nine months were a disaster. Every Friday afternoon Kyle called me at work and begged me to take him to my parents' house a two-hour drive away. At his grandparents' home, Kyle shadowed his brother, sitting silently beside him while my older son worked on a computer. Kyle minimized contact with his brilliant, generous, and judgmental grandparents. My father, preoccupied with his supernova career as a physicist, hardly knew Kyle was around. My mother sporadically telephoned me to worry about Kyle. She worried, she said, because she loved him. It took me many more years to understand that my mother's love-worry was a euphemism for criticism, and that my answering panic and guilt were my little girl response to the impossible expectations of super-achieving, hard-driving parents. Meanwhile, I cringed in anxiety at the picture of Kyle as a miserable failure, and of my own failure as a mother.

Sunday afternoons, I would drive Kyle back to his father's house in the East Bay. Kyle complained about going back, but refused to move in with Brent and me. He talked to me as if I was an enemy. I watched him grow increasingly unhappy and withdrawn. His father complained that I took him away too often. My road trips decreased to every-other weekend.

Then I got a call from Kyle's father. Kyle had been picked up by the police for shoplifting and was flunking middle school. My ex-husband blamed me, and wanted to know what I'd do about it. It was pointless to argue with my ex. I'd talk to Kyle. He was going to come on a weeklong vacation with Brent and me to the Grand Canyon.

* * *

The Kyle that comes to us at the start of his thirteenth summer is a damaged being. He keeps a little beanbag cat on his shoulder day and night. He will not walk through a doorway without opening and shutting the door a certain number of times. Neither will he eat without picking up his fork and setting it down its predetermined number of times. He talks exclusively about fantasy books he reads, video games he plays, or movies he watches. He tells me nothing about himself or his life.

At the nadir of our vacation experience, I lie on a bed in a worn-out motel near Lake Powell, looking at cracked plaster walls. The heat is searing. Kyle sits on a single bed in the next room staring at the wall, withdrawn. When I try to talk with him, he looks at me with guilt and suspicion. More than anything I want to help him, and I have no idea what to do. A prayer arises from the depths of my being, like something from the Old Testament: "May the God that was with Kyle at his birth be with him now!"

An idea comes to me. When we return to the Bay Area, we plan to have a family gathering at my parents' house. I ask Kyle's brothers and sisters to talk with Kyle without any other adults present. I don't tell them what to talk about. I shepherd my parents and Brent out of the room and wait.

After an hour alone with his siblings, Kyle announces that he doesn't want to go back to his dad's house, not even to pick up his things. One of my older children later tells me that Kyle's father had told Kyle that leaving his father's house would indicate a moral failing in Kyle's character. My older child says with a laugh, "We just had to tell Kyle that Dad fucks with your mind!" Kyle later tells me that his father had said, "If you leave, you can never again return to this house." Knowing my ex, those words were probably said in a temporary passion, but like many careless words, they bring their own prophecy. Kyle never goes back to see his father again.

I drive to the East Bay one last time and pick up my son's things. My intuition says that what Kyle needs most is a parent who believes in him. For that reason, I don't take Kyle to a psychiatrist, which is perhaps one of my many mistakes. Who knows? Instead, I love him and listen to him. Every day, seconds after I walk in the door from work, Kyle follows me around talking non-stop about the plots of video games. Brent asks, "How can you stand it?" I explain that I am trying to demonstrate faith in Kyle, love for Kyle. In my mind I plead with Brent, *Why don't you help me?* But I never say this out loud. Another mistake?

Dinnertimes I am caught between Brent wanting to wind down from the workday, and Kyle, who has been home alone, wanting to talk like a radio just turned on. I listen to them one at a time, feeling the impatience and resentment of each, in turn, when my attention shifts to the other. My beloved child, the man who married me when I had five dependents: how can I fail either of them?

Gradually, Kyle walks through doorways and picks up forks without rituals. The beanbag cat is less present. Sanity returns—to an extent. Perhaps my hope blinds me to the magnitude of Kyle's depression. I wonder, what more can I do? Under it all, he is still angry with me. I dig deep trying to understand why. It occurs to me that Kyle may be angry with me for not letting him take that last-chance exit on his path into this world, but at the time of his thirteenth summer, my guilt and grief are fraught with perplexity. I have no idea what to do.

Kyle begins high school without enthusiasm, but seems to get along. He has a few tenuous friendships. He joins nothing. He does well scholastically in all the areas where undisciplined brilliance can rescue him from failure, but neglects his homework. Unbeknownst to me, Kyle spends afternoons alone in his room cutting ancient runes into the skin of his upper arms, fashioned after Nordic myths he has learned on the Internet.

Kyle graduates from high school with an unremarkable GPA but stellar SAT scores. He is conditionally accepted at MIT as a math-physics major. That same year, my father is awarded the Nobel Prize in Physics. We all go to Stockholm and celebrate. Nine months later, Kyle flunks out of MIT. He casts around for work that he can't seem to find, and begins sofa-surfing. He lives among people and in places I don't know.

The years that follow have a nightmarish sameness, composed of crisis after crisis. For a while, Kyle sleeps in the car Brent and I gave him, until the car is impounded for unpaid parking tickets. For a couple of years, Brent and I let Kyle live in our vacation home in Oregon. He turns it into a flophouse for "friends," in exchange for food and drink. They trash it. When Brent and I divorce, I go to Oregon to get the house cleaned up and sold as Brent can't bear to look at it.

My life continues like a summer pageant punctuated by sniper fire. I move to a small beach cottage in Monterrey, my older children marry, my grandchildren are born. These life events are interrupted by catastrophic phone calls from Kyle who is desperate for money, or from emergency rooms or distraught strangers describing things a mother should never have to hear (stitches for a bite on the scrotum?). At night I am frequently jerked awake by anxiety that gnaws at my innards like the stolen fox hidden under the Spartan boy's toga in Plutarch's story. I stare into the night sky so often that I buy astronomy texts and start to learn my constellations. I feel as if my love for Kyle is being sucked into a black hole like the exhausted rays of an over-exploded star.

Yet almost imperceptibly, my star-navigation through life shifts its direction. I begin to question why I give my energies to the military-industrial complex, suffering under the pressure to become ever more robotic. Part of me blames Kyle that I cannot make the life changes I'd like because I must keep my salary in order to bail him out of crises. Even while I think this, I realize it is unfair. Kyle doesn't ask me to choose financial security at whatever spiritual cost; my choices are my own. Sometimes, on the last tattered fragments of a sleepless night, feeling the implacable response of the universe that despite Kyle's meteoric fall to havoc all is as it must be, I throw back at the stars, "*you* try it down here!" No answers come from above, yet I find in myself some acceptance of irreconcilable love and pain. I also find the courage to leave my lucrative job and to seek other, less secure but more satisfying work. The perpetual rescuer will take her chances.

One chilly morning between midnight and dawn, waking with a jolt of panic, I risk looking at Kyle's Facebook page. I read such ravings of self-destruction and despair that I have to click off my computer. I try to subdue the fox under the toga by singing Leonard Cohen's "Hallelujah" while pacing my living room floor. Suddenly I catch sight of Orion hanging in the southern sky outside my bay window. I pull a blanket around my shoulders and walk out into the street, the best place to get a clear view of the stars. No cars are out yet. The wind rustles the pines, and at the bottom of the hill, an occasional wave rolls in. I know Orion is the Great Hunter, but as I gaze at that brilliant cluster, I see Kyle the Warrior. In that moment, I realize that I have known Kyle to be a warrior for a long time, since his birth, but I have forgotten. It gives me a kind of peace to acknowledge the metaphor—at last, instead of fretting over The Loser, I am lamenting The Warrior.

My star-navigation through life makes another shift.

* * *

The next shift comes early this year as I spend a month at my aging parents' home to support them in a fretful transition to assisted care. Late one evening, too emotionally and physically weary to sleep, I lie on their Persian carpet staring through full-length windows at the night sky. The light of a few brave stars struggles through the metropolitan glare, exactly depicting the condition of my struggling, burdened spirit. My cell phone buzzes. I see Kyle's name in the register and dread washes through me. With a sense of fatality I pick up. Kyle is calling from somewhere in San Francisco, drunk, desperate, maudlin, angry, impossible. After half an hour I can bear no more. I hang up. It seems that both my parents and my youngest child are falling through black space, heading for crashes where I can't catch them. I lie back on the floor spread-eagle and give myself over to non-existence. The phone buzzes, I don't pick up. Back and back through oblivion I sink, willing myself out of existence.

Just before extinction, a memory comes to me, from infancy, of drawing in my mother's milk devoid of loving-kindness. The milk is rank with ambition and dominance. To my sensitive infant's soul, the experience is excruciating. To the adult spread out on my parents' carpet, it is a revelation. I see the will to achieve, the replacement of love with judgment and admiration, passed through the womb from generation to generation, wrapping us—and those who mate with us—in a paralyzing chrysalis until the quickening flicker of love is all but extinguished. There is no one to blame: my parents can't help it any more than I can. Steely threads of ambition, sharpened by anxiety, are inextricably woven into a long rope of DNA that goes too far back to remember.

Kyle is at the very tip of the cracking whip, a comet shot from an ancestral mass, madly plunging through an erratic path. With regret too deep for tears, I feel in my body how this unloving ambition has passed through me to my children. I see Kyle as a lonely teenager, cutting Nordic runes into his arms while I attain promotion after promotion and his older siblings embark on successful careers. I recall the family conversations of mutual admiration and acclaim at holiday gatherings, the expectations accompanying gifts of money passed from older generations to younger, my father receiving the Prize in Stockholm while all his grandchildren applaud and his wife (almost) forgives his infidelity because this makes it all worthwhile—and Kyle flunking out of MIT nine months later. There seems to be nothing I can do about it, except to feel so sorry, so sorry, so sorry. I am shaken to the core.

Still, I live on. Although I feel there is nothing I can do about the truth of my family's condition, things change. I treat my parents differently. I no longer seek their approval but just love them. I feel more respect and understanding for Kyle, oddly coupled with a new firmness. My family responds to me differently. My parents seem comforted and less fearful. Kyle still asks for money but he talks with me differently. He tells me about his girlfriend, about the courses he's taking at a local community college, even makes hints at future plans.

In the midst of a busy spring, I take time out to spend ten days with a dear and ailing friend in a small desert town. Her house was once the monastery of an obscure, tiny cult. The L-shape of the old monastery forms two sides of a walled courtyard garden featuring rocks, succulents, and iconic statues. My room is at the far end of the L, an art studio complete with futon and shower. A deep verandah runs along the entire length of the house. Daytime temperatures top out at 110. Nights are full of warm breezes, brilliant stars, swaying palms, and sharp black mountains outlined against the horizon. Just over the courtyard wall is a row of orange trees, and their fragrance enhances the night air. When I go to bed, I turn off the AC, open the windows and verandah doors, and breathe in the smell of citrus and sage. As the nights tick by, I watch the waxing moon increase its band of light across the foot of my bed.

One night, between midnight and dawn, I am shocked awake in full, frozen anxiety about Kyle. So complete is my terror that I can hardly breathe, hardly move. It is as if I have been thrown backwards ten years. I have no resources left; I am overcome with panic. A prayer tears itself loose from my soul—it sounds like King David, surrounded by enemies, admonishing his God: "I am your devoted child! Help me! Help me NOW!"

And help comes. It comes in the form of a vision, as I move across the starlit floor and out the doorway to the silver rocks and dark sky in the courtyard. In that black and silver setting, I am a constellation warrior and I face Kyle the constellation warrior, the two of us wheeling across the universe of our lives. Before some unseen judge, staring Kyle in the eyes, I accuse him: "This being has burdened me beyond endurance." A question arises of its own volition—I could never have willed it—How would my life have been if Kyle had died that day on the delivery table? And I know the truth. I see myself worried and brooding, focusing on the four older children who, because of Kyle, have escaped the brunt of my suffocating insecurities. I see my alternate self consumed with guilt and a negativity that doesn't consume me now only because my love for Kyle is greater than my neurosis.

And I realize that Kyle has been a gift to the whole family, and especially a gift to me.

The constellation Kyle stares back at me, without pity or anger, acknowledging what is, was, and will be true, in time like the stars' time: all time, no time at all. The images shift, and I see a huge, dark red star shaped like a placenta, its cord attached to the Kyle constellation. I call out loud, standing in my friend's rock garden at 4:30 in the morning, "Kyle, be free of it!" I watch as the cord breaks away from him. The constellation Kyle shines blue-white and clear, slowly drifting eastwards on its own path. But the dark red blob, like a severed blood clot not yet dead, sobs with parasitic longing, hovering near. It is still attached to me! I cry out to the desert night, "Let me be free of it!"

I stand alone in the courtyard, my sleeper T-shirt fluttering around my thighs. I hear a far-off coyote howl, then another, then another. In the East, the horizon is greying and stars are fading. A cock crows. I wonder how I will live this day.

Every day since, I wonder how I will live this day. When anxiety over Kyle threatens, I shift to my constellation warrior in the stars. My image shines as I was a few seconds ago, a million years ago, a second after Creation. There is no red star. Sometimes I see the Kyle constellation there, its destiny incomprehensible to me. Other times I don't see Kyle at all. Our constellations no longer circle one another in a fixed, perpetual path. The cosmos is now a living sky. Every moment is an opportunity for destiny to change. I know that death and life come together, all at once, like Kyle's death-birth, like the night sky filled with creation and destruction all in one pattern. However I live or die this day, my response will be born in that moment.

Crazy Too

KAREN GROVE

"THERE'S NEVER BEEN anybody crazy in my family," my husband John says. The year is 1991, and I pay no heed to the political incorrectness of the word "crazy." In the moment, I also give no conscious thought to the unfairness—and inaccuracy—of this remark. Mental illness is so common there is likely at least one afflicted person in every family.

It's a Sunday evening in June, and we are tidying up the kitchen after leaving our seven-year-old middle child Roman at the University of Alberta Hospital for his fourth week in the paediatric psychiatric unit. Although we don't know it at the time, this unit, with its draconian disciplinary agenda, won't be in existence much longer. For now, however, it's the most important thing happening in our lives.

John leaves for work at 7:20 every weekday morning. I continue my half-time job at the public library. I manage to get my older son Stefan on the school bus just after 8:00 am. But we are just going through the motions. Our real focus is Roman and the paediatric psychiatric unit that has taken over our family life.

This was the first weekend we were allowed to bring Roman home since he had been admitted. Otherwise, we have been visiting him in the unit. And there, all our interactions are monitored. In the regimented world of the unit, it's made pretty clear to us that all the children's problems, including Roman's, are deemed the result of poor parenting. The belief seems to be that correcting our flawed parenting techniques will solve all—transforming our kids into the well-behaved children they were born to be.

Before our son's admission, we had had a different understanding of what awaited us.

"I recommend admitting him to the hospital so he can be seen by the greatest number of specialists in the shortest possible time," said his child psychiatrist. Dr. H. was one of twenty-five such professionals in Alberta, at the time.

"He presents with such a range of symptoms that I need some help in reaching a diagnosis."

I still believe our psychiatrist was acting in good faith and that he had little sense of the day-to-day oppressive and punitive atmosphere at the unit. When Dr. H. observed the front-line staff, they were probably exhibiting their most humane behaviour.

The disciplinary method used in the unit was "chairing": at any infraction of the rules, any questioning of the authority of an adult, a child was banished to the corner to sit on a chair until the adult decided he or she could rejoin the group. Some staff seemingly derived personal satisfaction out of administering this treatment. Others were resigned. Once in the produce department of our neighbourhood Safeway I met one of these semi-believers. When we made eye contact we both *knew* and we guiltily looked away.

Besides giving training in the technique of chairing, staff ran weekly group therapy sessions for the re-education of the parents. The diverse problems faced by the families included suicide attempts, setting fires, smashing holes in the walls, not yet being toilet trained without any discernible medical reason at age ten, and physical assaults on parents and other caregivers. Rather than demonstrating empathy and compassion, the tight-lipped social worker conducting most of the sessions bristled with negativity. Whatever trauma or difficulty parents raised, her brow remained furrowed with disapproval. She clearly thought that if only we were more capable, the problems would resolve. I found she had few useful insights for dealing with Roman's difficulties.

At one session, a nurse was speaking about organization and the importance of leaving enough time for every activity.

"Rushed children become acting-out children," she said.

"Well," I asked, "what happens if you prepare so far in advance that your oldest child has to get out of his snowsuit to go to the bathroom before your middle child can be coerced into doing what needs to be done to get out of the door. And, then, in the meantime your baby throws up on your last clean shirt?"

With iceberg eyes that could have sunk the *Titanic,* the nurse turned on me and said, "If you were organized you would never be down to your last clean shirt, and anyway, you would always have a towel on your shoulder."

I was sick with guilt over my child, and having him in this fraught and hostile setting exponentially increased my guilt and anxiety. All my memories of this time are of panic about never being able to measure up and a fears of being judged as inadequate and never having my child returned to me. I felt under constant surveillance. I knew I was being incessantly judged.

After three weeks of such interactions with the staff, John and I became panicked. We dropped Roman off for his fourth week, but not because we believed that the authorities were helping him. No. Now that we had become part of the system experts seemed to have an inordinate amount of power over us and all decisions related to our child. Our fear was that our son would be taken away from us forever.

We had naively signed his admittance papers without knowing what we were abdicating.

* * *

And yet, despite all Roman's problems, as a child he had many gifts. In the late summer of 1988, he passed all the Kindergarten entrance tests with ease. We knew he could already read in English because one Saturday morning he started reading an *Archie* comic aloud at the breakfast table. He could speak English and Ukrainian fluently. Because of his facility with language and his skill at math, we were urged not to hold him back even though he was just four years and seven months old when he started school. At first, he seemed to settle in well. As the year progressed, however, Roman became more and more agitated and inattentive. He squirmed and fidgeted outside the edge of the circle while other children sat quietly. His awkward efforts at engaging them in conversations about trains or the Catalan music we enjoyed at home were rebuffed. I'd observed that he would flap his arms and hands. This happened more in social situations outside our home and grew even more pronounced in large-group settings.

When I volunteered in his kindergarten class, I could observe for myself that my beloved son was having difficulties coping. But I too never did well as the "mother of the day," and my discomfort in the classroom setting probably did nothing to put my child at ease. I felt I was different, so it did not surprise me that my child also seemed different. Under the best of circumstances, I found being the helping parent difficult because I always do poorly in situations where expectations are not clearly articulated. As one of several helping parents each day, especially in the lead-up to important days in the Ukrainian cultural year such as Christmas or Easter, I never felt able to sustain the perky tone that was one of the unspoken demands of the job. Irony, despair, or sheer bewilderment were emotional states I could not entirely suppress for long. Sometimes they tended toward the suicidal. Often the only reaction I got to my comments or suggestions was a raised eyebrow or pursed lips. Words actually spoken would have been easier to react to.

Because of Roman's general inattentiveness and his lack of social skills, his teacher—with her twenty years of experience and her boxes of well-worn materials dragged out for all the special days in the school year—suggested Roman repeat kindergarten and start taking a small dose of Ritalin.

"Get him settled on the Ritalin over the summer," she said. "It will calm him down and help him to focus."

* * *

Our paediatrician was a slightly stout, balding older man who wore out-of-fashion wire-rimmed glasses. I took Roman to see him. I wanted a medically-informed second opinion. The doctor was furious.

"Only an idiot would suggest that a child who is already reading repeat kindergarten! What gives this woman the authority to diagnose and prescribe?"

Then the paediatrician added something I had already observed from my well-behaved, diligent older son's experiences: "Too many elementary teachers don't understand or like boys, and think there is something wrong because they aren't as well behaved as girls.

There's nothing wrong with this child and I'm not putting him on Ritalin."

These were sweet words of approval that I needed to hear. Even so, I knew that Roman's behaviour one-on-one with a caring adult—like our doctor was—had never been a problem. Issues typically arose when Roman was with other children, especially large groups of children his own age. Unfortunately for my child and for me, large groups of children are what school is about—what institutional life is about.

Since Roman was still very young for Grade One, John and I decided to simply keep Roman home the following year. He spent half days with me and half days at a daycare. He thrived. He read stories to the younger children. He enjoyed the low staff-to-child ratio.

* * *

When Roman returned to school the following year, his behaviour rapidly deteriorated. There was a great deal of pressure. Pressure that has only increased in the intervening years. He was slapped with the ADHD label. At a few meetings of a support group for parents of ADHD children, I became certain that this was not the correct diagnosis for my child. If anything, his problem was not an inability to focus but a tendency to focus so intently that he had trouble switching from one activity to another—and school is all about this kind of switching. Then, it was decided that his bad behaviour stemmed from boredom, so Roman was moved from Grade One to Grade Two.

ADHD, Tourette's syndrome, bipolar disorder, schizophrenia—these were all suggested as root causes of his aberrant behaviour by various experts who saw him during this tumultuous year in and out of the hospital setting. We had tried a small dose of Ritalin as he became increasingly agitated at school. The ADHD "lobby" insisted that if a low dose of Ritalin had make him act "crazy," then a higher dose would be just the thing to calm him down. Although I did not personally observe what happened at school after he took the higher dose, the teacher said that he ran around the classroom screaming and could not be stopped or restrained. I had no reason to disbelieve this kind teacher. She had twenty-eight or so other children in her class and yet she was considerate to me and my child. We needed a lot of kindness over the next decade of his schooling.

A breakdown at school when Roman was seven is what eventually led to his six-week stay in the paediatric psychiatric unit. In the psych ward, Roman was put on an anti-psychotic drug called Mellaril, on which he gained 35 pounds in a few weeks. His psychiatrist agreed that this amount of weight gain was an unacceptable side effect. Up to this point Roman had been a slender child with a sharply pointed chin. Even off the medication it took him a long time—the better part of a decade—to shrink back into a weight normal for his height. I think it took all of us about that long, in fact, to recover from his brief stay there. Being overweight exacerbated Roman's sense of difference. Roman would go on to take Tegretol and Seroquel and various other drugs, although the sequence of all the prescribing now escapes me, as do the reasons for the particular drugs being prescribed. I think there was a sense that if we could find a drug that improved his behaviour, the efficacy of the drug would point to a diagnosis.

During our boy's time in the psych ward, my husband and I were also wrestling with the dilemma of his placement for the next school year. The principal of our neighbourhood Catholic school told me they could not possibly handle a child with so many problems. Roman was placed in a special Grade Three class in another school. He remained there through Grade Five. The children in his very small class—all boys—had various developmental and behaviour problems. All of them were there because of their profound inability to conform to a regular classroom setting. The two young male teachers Roman had in these three years were as close to living saints as anyone I have met. They taught him to type and encouraged him to write using a computer. He also learned computer programming. They appreciated his special gifts and helped him to develop them. They enjoyed his intelligence and unique sense of humour.

These years were a relief after the terrible turbulence we had been through. However, as these classes never had more than six or seven students, and no two students were ever doing exactly the same thing, their small size and individualized approach did little to prepare Roman for his eventual return to a class of thirty students where everyone was supposed to be doing the same thing at the same time.

Grade Six was a nightmare. By this point Roman had a school-file an inch thick. At the October parent-teacher interview, we discovered his teacher was unaware of his history, had never looked at the file, and had been disciplining him by turning our son's desk to the wall. This was not unlike the chairing that had been used in the psych ward. Even after this teacher was given his file, it seemed to make little difference in her approach. A few months into the year, she was on medical leave and was replaced by a series of substitute teachers, none of whom lasted long, the stay of some no doubt shortened by the presence of my son in the class. We got through the rest of Grade Six with many calls from the school to pick up Roman. Sometimes these calls reached me at the reference desk at the library when John was out of town with our only vehicle. Although most elementary teachers are women and most have children, there was an assumption that other parents were occupied by nothing more pressing than waiting for a call from the school. It was during these years that I grew to hate the sound of the phone. I spent many of the hours I was not working at the gym, getting the thinnest and fittest I have been. Taking the long way home whenever I could, I drove around with *St. Matthew Passion* blasting away on the stereo. The suicidal feelings I had experienced during Roman's kindergarten year had abated when I was stabilized on a combination of Prozac and Desyrel but getting through the day remained a struggle.

* * *

I kept a baby calendar for Roman, where I recorded the goings on during that first year of my sweet baby's life. Reading it, I am struck by how connected I was to my friends then. Life was full of friends. They would drop in on me and me and my baby, we would go out to friends' houses for coffee and a visit. As problems multiplied, as life was more and more defined by difficulty instead of ease, I felt—and became—more and more isolated.

The year Roman was in kindergarten, the year his differences became apparent, also happened to be the year that the friends who had sustained me became literally or emotionally distant. Their absences were one factor, I believe, that led to my clinical depression. A decade later, we would again reconnect. I'd also make new friends. However, during my hardest years, I felt pretty much alone. I did not have the time, energy, or self-confidence necessary to make new friendships or sustain old ones. The other adults I encountered most often were the parents of children who shunned my son, as children naturally rebuke anyone who is different. The parents may have rejected me because deep down they were worried my son's problems could be contagious—if not physically then metaphorically or spiritually.

About a decade after his time in the psych ward, Roman would be diagnosed with Asperger's Syndrome. In the interim I struggled to get through the long weeks and months of the school years. To somehow support my child and attend to his special needs. Friday afternoons always came as a blessed relief, and summer holidays with him were mostly bliss. Away from prying eyes. Away from the judgement of others. We could just be—and sometimes be happy.

Struggling with my own mental health issues during that decade gave me a new insight and different kind of empathy for what my son has been through—especially his time in that psych ward when we struggled to support him and understand what was happening to our child. I had a glimpse of what it meant to be crazy too. And it brought us closer together as we worked to find a way through to the other side.

Push-Me-Pull-You[1]

SUSAN OLDING

A HOLIDAY WEEKEND, and I am walking with my daughter to the park. She sniffs the air like a young filly and canters into a pile of leaves. "Hello!" she whinnies to every stranger we pass. "Happy Thanksgiving!" And even, "You look beautiful today!"

I set my face in what I hope is some semblance of a smile. This smile is my shield for what I know will come next: "How adorable!" "What a sweetheart!" "How old is she?" And of course, the inevitable, the ubiquitous, "You are *so* lucky!"

When we reach the park, J. wants me to push her on the swings. Her hair streams out behind, a black banner glinting with red highlights. "Now you get on, and I'll push you," she commands. At not quite five, she is strong enough to do it too, though she forgets to get out of the swing's path on its return, and I have to stick my legs out and drag my boots in the sand so I don't slam into her. She laughs. "You stay sitting and I'll come join you," she says. She clambers up and positions herself face to face, astride my lap. Snuggling closer, she rests her head against my shoulder. "Swing, please. Rock me." This is an old ritual of ours, one begun when she was still a baby. I croon her favourite lullaby. When she looks up into my eyes, her own eyes shine with the purest trust and affection. "You're the best mum in the whole universe," she whispers. "I love you to infinity and beyond."

I am so lucky.

That night, after I've read stories to her, brushed her teeth, cuddled under the blankets and banished the monsters from the closet, I tuck her into bed and lean across for a goodnight kiss.

83

But instead of the soft pressure of her lips or the butterfly's brush of her eyelashes, I feel her small hands come up around my neck. Her thumbs are at my windpipe. She squeezes. Hard. I wonder if I am imagining this, if she's really just trying to hug me in some new and original fashion. She's creative and dramatic and physical and she likes to invent all kinds of games. Surely she's just fooling around. She doesn't really know what she is doing.

But she does know; she knows *exactly* what she is doing. She wants to choke me. To choke me.

My daughter is the human embodiment of Dr. Doolittle's Push-Me-Pull-You. Dr. Doolittle is what I privately name each of the so-called experts whom I consult in search of explanations and help. These are the labels they try on and cast aside, for none of them fits exactly or covers completely:

Difficult temperament
Regulatory disorder
Sensory processing disorder
Attention deficit hyperactivity disorder
Non-verbal learning disability
Gifted, with asynchronous development
Unresolved grief or loss
Oppositional defiant disorder
Post-traumatic stress disorder
Reactive attachment disorder.

J. joined our family through adoption at the age of ten months. Before that, she lived in a large orphanage in China. Most, if not all, of her more challenging behaviours can probably be traced in one way or another to her early experiences of abandonment and neglect, as those interact with her genetically determined sensitivities. In public, she plays two roles—the beautiful, exuberant charmer, perhaps a shade too friendly with strangers, perhaps a bit too "busy"—but precocious and delightful, just the same. Her other role is the poorly-governed wild child. Back at home, we see the complicated self beneath the masks. Living with J. is like living in a hurricane zone. You can't relax because you're always scanning the sky for signs of trouble. Winds are generally high, and it's hard work at the best of times to clean up the falling debris. And then the storm breaks, and you batten down; it roars and roars, and it's all you can do to keep yourself intact in the face of its fury. Unless, of course, you find yourself within its calm, still centre. The hurricane's eye surprises even the weariest with hope.

Her first year with us was relatively easy. She was active, yes—unusually so—but she liked to cuddle, made good eye contact, and grew and learned at a remarkable rate. Even during her second year, signs of trouble were subtle, mutable, and easily missed. All two-year-olds throw tantrums. Most four-year-olds don't, though, or not often. And if they do, their fury stops somewhere short of compelling them to fling chairs across the room.

She spins, hangs upside down, jumps down hard onto harder surfaces, and shows other evidence of early deprivation to her proprioceptive and vestibular systems. She suffers from subtle developmental delays; she did not establish "handedness" until she was nearly five. She struggles to sit still; she chatters and asks countless nonsense questions. Driven by impulse, she grabs and interrupts. She resists or defies almost every parental instruction, and she can be so peremptory with us that we have nicknamed her "Miss Bossypants." Yet at the same time she demands our constant attention. Until she reached the age of four, she could not bear to be in a separate room from me if we were in the same house. A recent move across the country has thrown her back to that emotional territory and if I happen to leave her side now without repeated warnings, she screams.

And often, in the guise of seeking closeness, she aims to harm. "I'm sorry," she will say, after landing an elbow in my stomach, after leaping headlong and unannounced into my arms, after cutting me off and tripping me up on the sidewalk. "Ouch," I shout, as she plonks herself into my lap and the top of her head hits my jaw. "Oops," she says. I can't tell if that's a smirk on her face or a smile. She doesn't, and yet she does want to hurt someone.

And why shouldn't she? The person she was closest to in all the world deserted her shortly after she was born. The fact that her birth-mother may have made that decision under enormous social or economic pressure, at great personal cost, and with only her baby's interests at heart is irrelevant to J. Deep in her cells, she knows only this—at the age of one week, she was left, helpless and alone. Then she was institutionalised, where she was neglected and unloved for ten long months. Finally, she was handed off to a pair of weird-looking, strange-smelling strangers and taken a whole world away from everything known and familiar. And all this without explanation and entirely without choice. She was powerless, and being powerless felt bad, and now that she has finally gained some small measure of security and safety in our family, she never wants to feel powerless again. Hence, her constant jockeying for control. She hones her considerable charm, sharpens her wits, and strengthens her will for violence. Far below consciousness, in her primitive brain, she knows that her survival is at stake. And her anger—the anger that should rightfully be aimed at her birth-mother or at her birth-father or at the nannies at the orphanage or at a sexist culture or at oppressive family planning laws or at longstanding customs militating against domestic adoption in China or at the vast global network that permits middle-class westerners like me to whisk children like her away from their countries of origin—all that anger, the full fierce force of it—she points directly at me. At the person who, however guilty I may be of participating in an ethically questionable system, am also the one who feeds her, bathes her, diapers her, teaches her how to walk, teaches her how to read, sings to her, plays with her, holds her, comforts her.

And loves her. Loves her. Loves her.

I live with a level of uncertainty about my mothering that is unusual even among the other adoptive parents I know. I am never entirely sure where I stand.

Around age two and a half, J. went through a phase of aggression towards other children. Or, more precisely, towards babies. At her pre-school, at our kinder-gym, at the park, even in our own house—whenever she saw a crawling infant, she would stomp over to him, loom above him menacingly, and then, with a glazed, cold, almost inhuman expression on her face, shove him to the ground. Snatching up the latest victim and rocking him, his mother might scold, "You need to set firmer limits. Give her some consequences!"

"There, there," others would sigh. "It's all because you are too strict with her. She needs you to be more nurturing."

"Never mind," counselled a third group. "All kids do that."

Or, in its nastier form, "What are you worrying about? She's normal. You're crazy!"

Any way you look at it, I'm to blame.

I've seen those baby books in which proud parents are supposed to record developmental milestones. First tooth, first step, first word.

The milestones I should have recorded, but didn't:

> First kiss not flinched from
> First time she played for more than two minutes on her own
> First adult conversation she allowed to proceed uninterrupted
> First time she did not shriek in fury when I left the room
> First time she could engage quietly in a parallel activity in my presence
> First time she co-operated immediately with a parental request
> First time she did not explode when a parent refused a demand
> First time she truly relaxed.

Then again, maybe it's better we didn't record these. The first step and the first word are assumed to lead naturally to the next and the next and the next. A simple, reassuring linear progression. But just because J. did not explode when I disciplined her last week is no reason to think that she won't explode today. Just because she has accepted a kiss in the past is no reason to believe that she won't brush it off tonight.

At the age of four, J. told me, "I had a nightmare about a mean mummy with mustard teeth. And she was always mean to me. And I sang a happy song and put her in jail and then my nice mummy came back. But the mean mummy looked just like you except she had mustard teeth."

Normal parenting does not work, or does not work reliably. Although J. understands the relationship between cause and effect, between her actions and their repercussions, she often cannot stop herself from doing what she knows she should not. My husband, Mark, and I must become a species of super-parent, the "therapeutic" parent. We're not just here to raise her, we're here to *heal* her. The Drs. Doolittle agree that what children like J. need is "high structure/ high nurture" parenting; sadly, they agree less on the precise meaning of that term. Consistent consequences, or paradoxical reactions? Time-in or time-out? *Love and Logic* or *1,2,3 Magic*? Boot camp with bottle-feeding, is what it sometimes feels like. What it doesn't feel like is natural. The learning curve is steep and I don't have my climbing equipment.

I know we are not perfect. No parent is. But I know our parenting is at least as good as that of the smug know-nothings who sneer as I drag J. kicking and screaming out of the park. Because I am Caucasian and J. is Chinese, people don't always recognise immediately that I'm her mother. In the face of what the good doctors would call her "negative persistence" and the seeming absence of a parent, people sometimes feel free to treat her rudely. "Stop that," they say, in tones I know they would never use with their own children. In tones they would never *need* to use with their own children. When they learn that I'm her mother, they can barely contain their contempt. "Do you think you could do better?" I want to scream at them. "Go ahead. Give it a try. Be my guest."

I find myself a therapist. Nobody knows what to do for J., but maybe somebody can help me. The therapist asks me to find some pictures of "mothering." For a full week, despite the fact that I look and look and look, I do not see images of mothering anywhere. Or none that strikes a chord.

How can this be? My entire existence is focused on the task of parenting this child. The only other area of my life to which I have ever brought this degree of intensity and determination and pure passion is my work. And now my work is a dim second. As for my marriage—well, the less said, the better. I never expected it to be this way. Mark and I were happy. We were friends as well as lovers. Together, we'd weathered thirteen years of highs and lows, thirteen years of boring work and fulfilling work, thirteen years of sicknesses and the return of health, thirteen years of trips, and money problems, and family problems, thirteen years that even included co-parenting his older children through their teenage agonies and angst. And still we had energy to spare; enough to want to raise a child from babyhood together. Now, when we're not fighting about how to handle our daughter, we lie conked out, exhausted, in the wake of her demands. I recall once hearing a friend say that her sons occupied a far bigger place in her life than her husband. At the time, I felt appalled and faintly self-satisfied. That will never happen to me, I thought. And maybe it wouldn't have, if J. had been different.

Early last summer, J. and I accompanied a friend and her daughter, E. to our local wading pool. While my friend and I sat talking under a shade tree, the girls splashed happily in the water, taking turns giving one another rides on a plastic float toy we'd brought along. Soon another girl, perhaps a year and a half younger, approached them. In the way of many three year olds, in the way of J. at the same age, this girl stood much too close. She tried to grab the floatie away. She tried, repeatedly, to sit on it. She wedged herself between J. and her friend and would not leave. She tugged at their bathing suits. All the while, her mother sat nearby, saying nothing.

J. "used her words." "Please. We're playing. It bothers me when you stand so close." The child ignored her. "Don't! It's my floatie!" Still, the child wouldn't go.

Finally I intervened, suggesting that maybe the other girl would co-operate better if she were given a turn. Reluctantly at first, but with increasing good grace, J. and E. agreed. "Go ahead. You can play with it for ten minutes. Then it's our turn again."

But once the toy was hers, the girl no longer wanted it. It drifted to the pool's perimeter as, with a fixed and slightly manic smile, she chased my daughter and her friend around and around.

At last J. lost her temper. "We want to play on our own! Go away!" Not that it helped. I had her serve a time-out for rudeness, and then another when she made as if to push the other child. And then another time-out and another, until she had lost a good portion of her precious play time. She accepted these consequences with relative calm, but I wondered if inside she might be feeling the way I sometimes feel in her presence, worn out by the relentlessness of her claims. What I felt now, though, was angry on her behalf. My friend and I cast hostile glances at the mother, whose only comment on the entire drama, issued with a sniff and an injured pout, was, "Those are not nice girls. Find some nice children to play with."

Suddenly, I remembered that I had seen this pair before, over a year earlier. The child, then a toddler, was playing, or rather teetering on the ledges of park equipment far too big and dangerous for her, refusing to get out of the way when older children wanted to use the slides. After asking her to move a couple of times and failing to get a response, J. simply ducked and wriggled past her. The child wailed, and the mother, until then nowhere in evidence, sprang into action, snatching her daughter away and muttering something about J.'s rudeness and my irresponsibility.

"Oh, for heaven's sake," I said. It had been a long day and this park outing was the closest I was going to get to a moment of relaxation. "Just wait until yours is three."

The woman began screaming at me then. "No wonder your daughter has such awful social skills, with you as her model! You're a terrible parent!"

It's true, I thought—though I knew, too, that the woman wasn't entirely in her right mind. No wonder her kid seemed a little "off." Who wouldn't, with a banshee like that for a mother?

Now, though, watching them again at the sun-dappled pool, it occurred to me that I might have confused the causal relationship. Because living with that child would surely drive anybody crazy.

It isn't always difficult. Whole hours, days, weeks, and even months can pass when parenting J. feels almost like parenting any other spirited and strong-willed child. And what a joy that is. During a recent car ride, she became for half an hour or so her healthiest self. On the surface, nothing had changed; she was chattering, nattering, and singing as incessantly and loudly as always. Her energy level was high, and most adults would probably consider her behaviour annoying. Yet something felt different. Something prompted Mark and me to turn to one another at the same moment, to touch one another and smile. For once, she isn't talking *at* us, I thought. For once, she isn't covertly demanding; it's enough for her to be inside her own skin. I could not believe the gift of relaxation this brought to me, the way I felt my head clear out and my heart expand in my chest.

No child could be more rewarding to parent than J. when she is thriving. She is intelligent, imaginative, active, affectionate, funny, and fun. She works hard, plays hard, and fills our lives with gusto. She is also perfectly suited to be our daughter. "She loves to eat and she loves to talk. She's come to the right family," Mark once joked. And it's true. Her passions couldn't be more similar to ours. Particularly her love of words. Her vocabulary surpasses that of some children twice her age. "I feel vulnerable," she told an adult dinner guest of ours as they walked together down a darkened hallway. "Oh, really?" said our friend. "And what does vulnerable mean?" "It means you are afraid that you aren't strong enough and that something might hurt you," J. replied. Every night she asks me to define another word; if she hears the definition once, the word is hers. And it isn't only meaning she responds to. I have seen her shiver with pleasure at a rhyme or a new phrase. I have heard her repeat it to herself again and again, just for delight in the sounds. Hers is a poet's sensibility. I did not make her this way. She just *is*.

"Family fit" is the phrase used by adoption professionals. "There must be family fit." But our problems are not due to an absence of mystical "fit." I cannot imagine feeling closer, more akin, to any child. For better or for worse, I am J.'s mother. And she is my daughter.

When I was young, my mother and I had an intense and at times combative relationship. I recall one period, in particular, when we had just moved to an arid suburb, where our house was the very first one built in a new development. In the mornings, my father drove off to work in our VW Beetle, leaving us without a car and my mother without adult companionship. All around us stretched muddy lots and vacant skies. The nearest people lived miles away; the nearest stores were further. Mum must have gone crazy, stuck alone there with a chatty three-year-old, day after endless day. She watched the soap operas and ironed my father's shirts and the family's sheets, keeping them damp and rolled in the freezer until she was ready to begin the job. I squatted in front of her on the carpet, sometimes getting tangled in the iron's cord, often begging her to play with me or whining in a high-pitched monotone that I was bored. She used to slap me across the face and call me a brat. A selfish brat. "I hate you," I shrieked back at her. "You're an awful mummy!"

These days, J. has taken to wailing, "You don't love me," whenever her father or I tell her to stop doing something, or ask her to do something that she does not want to do. Sometimes she adds, "I don't love you!" This is painful and difficult to hear—but all part of the "normal" mother-daughter relationship, and all, to me, expected.

What I didn't expect was having to learn a safe-restraint technique before my child reached the age of five. What I didn't expect was to bear bruises and bite marks on my arms for weeks once, just for issuing a time-out. What I didn't expect was to turn around one morning as I was preparing her school lunch and find her pointing a knife at my back. A child's dull-bladed knife, true. But a knife.

At last I find an image of "mothering" that resonates for me. It's a photo taken by my husband this past summer. J. and I had just finished playing dress-up—one of the "floor time" sessions that I build in as part of my therapeutic parenting role. These are one-to-one play periods when J. directs all the action. Theory holds that allowing children a strong measure of control in their fantasy play will encourage them to relax control in other areas of their lives.

In the photo, J. and I are still in costume. We sit together on the carpet. She's cuddled in my lap, with my arms around her. In her own lap she cradles her beloved blanket – the "transitional object" that some of the Drs. Doolittle see as a sign that she has internalised my love, and others think ought to be wrested away from her, as a hindrance to the purity of our attachment. J. smiles sweetly at the camera; she makes a demure and delightful Bo-Peep. I, on the other hand, sport the livid green hair and the pointed black hat of the wicked witch.

J. hates it when I am sad. Sometimes she gets angry and orders me to stop crying; if especially stressed, she might even hit me. But sometimes, instead, she tries to take care of me. "See, Mum?" she says, pulling a funny face, or quoting a silly riddle. "I can make you smile. Don't cry. Please don't cry."

"Boundary issues," my therapist says. "She doesn't know where you stop and she begins."

I'm not sure that I know where I stop and she begins either. Musing about that photo of J. and me, I wonder why I've chosen it. Because consider this: in the picture, the child is sweet and innocent and all good. But who or what is the mother? Is she the competent, playful and smiling one who holds the child and contains the child? Or is she really the mean witch with mustard teeth?

And as if that were not confusing enough – look again. Mummy is wearing a nametag, the kind that parents and tots are asked to put on whenever they participate in some semi-organised activity at the gym or the local library. Look; look closely. The name on this tag is not the mother's. It is the child's.

I do my best. I try to be the strong, all-loving parent that she needs. But a poor night's sleep, a skipped meal, or an annoying phone solicitation can cut my patience short; a death in the family, a conflict with a friend, or trouble in my work can draw me inward, away from her demands. "Mum, Mum, Mum, Mum, Mum," she shouts. Often, in her presence, my pulse begins to race, my breathing tightens and my neck cramps. Her anxiety becomes my own. Vicarious trauma, this is called. And sometimes the pressure builds too high. She'll be hanging on my pant leg, chasing me into the bathroom, issuing orders in an even bossier tone than usual, or shrieking at me—and I'll explode. "Go away! Leave me alone. Mum needs a time out!"

Of course this sends her into a tailspin. Her mother, rejecting her. It is the worst thing she can imagine. Never mind "imagine." She doesn't *need* to imagine; it is the worst thing she has ever lived, and she relives it every time I walk away. Afterwards, I curse myself. I wonder if she will ever recover. I wonder if I will ever recover from the guilt. And I wonder if at bottom, her ambivalence is nothing more and nothing less than a mirror of my own.

While we're cuddling one afternoon, J. confides, "The worst day in my life was when they cut my umbilical cord. I wanted to stay inside my birth-mother forever. I was so comfortable in there." A few days later, though, I hear her on her play phone, talking to the birth-mother. "You should *not* have left me," she says, with sizzling indignation. "I was only a baby. That was bad of you. You were wrong!"

One night J. gives me a good night kiss that sets my eardrum ringing. "I think you did that on purpose," I say to her. "What's going on? Why do you try to hurt me when I'm about to leave your room?"

"I don't want you to go," she says. It's simple, and it's obvious, but articulating the idea seems to help her. The next night, instead of hurting me, she bars the door to my exit.

Her rages are less frequent and less violent. She is one of only two in her kindergarten class to have earned three stars for "home reading." She can focus on her drawing for half an hour. Frequently, she asks before she grabs. At daycare, she is making friends. So many signs of progress.

But on our worst days, I still fear that I am raising a sociopath. At minimum, a "borderline."

She will be pregnant, drugged, and on the streets by the age of sixteen.

She will be in jail by the age of twenty.

At thirty, she will ruin some psychiatrist's life with false accusations of sexual improprieties.

At forty, she will wake up alone, with no partner and no child.

She will never really learn how to love.

She will never really love me.

Every night she wakes. Sometimes shrieking with fear; sometimes bellowing in rage. But tonight, she comes on quiet feet and stands silent next to our bed. I wake up and follow her back to her room. If she crawled in with us, Mark's sleep would be disturbed, too; this way, at least two of us will get some rest. Three years ago, that would not have been true. Back then, she was so anxious at the intimate presence of another that she would stay awake and keep us awake all night, jumping, hitting, rolling, pulling hair. I count it as one of my incontrovertible victories over her past that now, when sharing a bed with one of us, she returns to sleep within minutes.

Under the canopy of her double bunk bed I feel a double layer of darkness. We settle in. When she was younger and still struggling with pronoun usage, she would have barked, "Put your arm around you. Put my arm around me!" Meaning that she wanted me to hold her. Those pesky boundary issues, again. Now, instead, she gently but firmly grasps my arm and wraps it around herself, tucking it in just so. I brush her fine hair away from my chin, adjust my hand so it won't get pins and needles, inhale the scent of her apricot shampoo.

An hour or so later she cries out, thrashing and kicking and whining. She grinds her teeth with a sound like a rake on cement. A bad dream.

"Shhh, It's all right," I whisper, my promise to her a kind of prayer. "Everything will be all right. Mummy loves you. Mummy loves you."

Rolling closer, she fishes for my leg with her foot and snuggles against me. She finds my arm and drapes it across herself once more. I don't know what tomorrow will bring—whether she'll bend flexibly with the day's demands and look at me with love in her eyes, or whether she will harden herself to shield her wounds, and blindly, helplessly hurt me. But for now, her breathing calms and slows, slows and calms. She pulls me close. She does not push me away.

NOTES

[1]Excerpt from *Pathologies: A Life in Essays* by Susan Olding. Copyright © 2008 by Susan Olding. Used by permission of FreehandBooks/Broadview Press.

You Don't Know What It's Like

MARTHA MARINARA

IT WAS ALMOST A YEAR before I stopped ducking or flinching whenever my daughter wanted to kiss the top of my head, touch my arm, or hug me. Multiple disabilities—autism, ADHD, a low cognitive capacity, fine and gross motor control deficiencies, a seizure disorder—caused my beautiful, dainty daughter's adolescent angst and misery to manifest as violent behaviour. For close to five years, a kiss would become a bite, a touch would turn into a pinch. Head butts, slaps, and kicks were my reward for helping her brush her teeth, tie her sneakers, or hand her something to eat. All of my mothering, all my instinctive nurturing, could not stop her violence. I thought that I had everything under control and could keep her aggressive behaviours in check. But it escalated beyond my abilities to manage and spilled out from the borders of our home. I did not seek help. Through all of the physical pain, broken furniture and windows, ripped books and toppled shelves, I loved my daughter. My mother's heart continued its contract; its pink muscle sent love without the knowledge of its own sacrifice.

Annie came into my life just before her second birthday, and she felt so sweet in my arms that my heart broke and remoulded itself around her small frame. (I've changed her name for this essay partially to protect her identity, but also because my daughter cannot tell her own story.) Annie weighed less than seventeen pounds, she could not sit up by herself, she could not say any words when she became my daughter. Annie was diagnosed with moderate spastic cerebral palsy. She was months behind other children her age. I was told by a team of doctors at Newington Children's Hospital that she would never walk without braces, ride a bicycle, or take dance lessons. Convinced all the doctors were wrong, I thought with love and good food, she would "catch up" with her age group. And she did, at first.

Annie had arrived at LaGuardia Airport in April, and by July she was walking and then running around our house and yard.

And then, just after she turned three, Annie began having seizures. Our life became a routine of neurologists, medications, physical and occupational therapies, a specialized school, and hours at home attempting the same simple tasks over and over and over, piling one alphabet block on top of another. We had to learn a new language of neurology. We had to accept that the MRI scan photo-sliced her brain like deli meat, showing layers of optic nerve, cerebrum, cerebellum, sinus walls, coils of mind flesh flat on the monitor screen. It became a kind of torture, slicing her brain open like this, looking for secrets. We fought and we hung onto messages in hidden folds. I accepted round heel bruises on my chest and scratches on my neck through the cotton fog of anesthesia. I thought, *this is only fair—after all, I brought her here.*

When I look through photographs from those early years, I can pinpoint and then follow Annie as she slipped away from us. There is a picture of her wearing blue and white striped overalls and a red shirt. She is trying to put a plastic laundry basket on her head and laughing while looking right at the camera. In later photos, Annie stopped making eye contact. She became engrossed in playing with small toys, keeping other toys clutched in her hands, and the camera could only capture the side of her face or the back of her head. Later family photos show her almost outside the frame as she turns to pull or walk away; physical closeness, even with family members, began to make Annie anxious.

Other behaviours soon manifested. Annie began to pinch me in frustration when she couldn't make herself understood. Surprising sounds—a siren, a car backfiring, a balloon popping, or a vacuum cleaner in another room—caused her to scream for hours even after the sounds dissipated. If she scratched or bit me when I tried to comfort her, I immediately forgave her. Annie became scared, unhappy, and tired. I constantly excused behaviours that should have alarmed me.

Within a year, she became almost impossible to touch. Parenting a toddler who could not hug presented emotional difficulties for me that I wasn't expecting. The bonding has been a slow draw. We tried to build something by ripping pieces from each other. Our bits of spine, thigh bone, eye and heart muscle were held together with cell jelly, toothpicks and glue.

I knew something was very wrong with my daughter, and it was something besides the seizure disorder, the ADHD, and intellectual delays. Annie was ten years old before a doctor in Savannah diagnosed her with Pervasive Development Disorder, and before I learned that her behaviours earned her a position on the Autism Spectrum. This doctor patiently explained sound defensiveness, tactile defensiveness, the confusion of sensory input that all made it painful for my daughter to look at me when I spoke to her and made a shower hurt like needles on her skin. At this point, I was a single parent. I was alone and devastated by the news. I took her home where I thought we would be safe.

The first time my daughter hit me for no reason, she balled up her fist and pounded the top of my head while I was bent over tying the white laces of her red Converse high tops. Her older sister had bought them for her with money from a job at the Greek deli down on Habersham Street. Annie started hitting me in the head every day as I tied her shoes. People who have heard this story have asked me why I didn't tie her shoes by holding her foot up, by keeping my head away from her fist. I wish I could answer this question without sounding psychotic or delusional. I thought she would stop if I just kept everything together. And, a small part of me felt as if I had failed her somehow and deserved the abuse.

Everything Annie broke, I picked up and glued back together like she hadn't just thrown a plate at me or knocked over the book shelves. I had to push the thought away that *Everything, every thing in my life is broken*. I swept up glass, mopped floors and wiped down counters as if somehow the outside could reflect the inside. At that time, I taught at a small college. I went to work every day wearing long sleeves and pants no matter how hot and humid the weather. Annie pinched so hard she left bruises on my arms and legs. If no one asked me how I was doing, I found it fairly easy to get through the day, performing being a professor. My serene intellectual life continued until I left campus.

Annie and I did have some good days and she could be so sweet. She always remembered people's names, the parts of musical instruments—fret, sound hole, strings—she could recite the Catholic Mass, sing "My Girl" like an angel. No matter what page I opened in a book, she could tell me what was written there. To this day, Annie still collects pieces of bark, rocks, piles of paper in every colour, and bottle caps. One day I opened the refrigerator to find every container—milk, salad dressing, Dijon mustard, dill pickles—missing a cap or a lid. I don't know what she sees in her collections or how they call to her. I wonder: are they like harp strings or strobe lights, soft and colourful as butterflies or lined up in slivers like shiny silver coins in her mind? I also wonder what caused this cognitive difference, this simple, elegant twist in her DNA? Would she change herself if she could? Would I change her if I could?

One night, nursing the bite on my shoulder with ice wrapped in a kitchen towel, I leaned against her bedroom door, watching her chest rise and fall, the movement under eyelids the colour of bruised pears. I knew without getting closer that her hair and scalp would smell like geraniums, the spicy smell from the stems, like earth grazing on sunlight. My daughter looked beautiful in that moment, her cheeks still flushed from the evening's exertions. I know all parents make jokes about how their children look like angels when asleep. Asleep is the only time I can see my daughter as more than flashes and hurt: I can see her whole.

Less than an hour before, her room had been a battlefield. I crawled on my knees, flashlight in one hand, picking up shards of mirror with the other. In a rage at me over picking up her room, she had torn the mirror off her bureau and flung it across the room where it hit the wall and shattered. There was a cut on my leg that needed stiches; I had wrapped my leg in a towel. I closed it with Steri-strips and surgical gauze (I owned an EMT-sized first-aid kit). But, as I crawled on the floor, trying to contain the debris in a small pile, the flashlight beam reflected off the pieces of mirror, blinding slivers of light making it impossible for me to see myself.

Annie had begun hitting her classmates and teacher so she was moved to a behaviour disorders classroom. At least twice a week, I had to drive to her school to pick her up because she had purposefully wet herself.

There are no societies for this, no ribbons for awareness, no annual fundraiser, no caring compassionate crowd walking five kilometers. Everyone looked away from my obvious bruises and scrapes because there is no cause for altruism when a mother "allows" her child to abuse her. Close friends lectured me about domestic violence and told me to walk away. But how could I walk away from my child who cannot care for herself?

A colleague who asked about the bruises on my arms, who listened as I poured out my life, suggested that I call a resource called Quest Kids and make an appointment. When we arrived at the site, which was housed in a church, a bald, tall, and lanky man named Eb, looked at Annie with kind, intelligent eyes, and shook her hand. Annie's handshakes are fast as touching hands is not easy for her. Eb told me that children could seldom manipulate him. After an informal intake process that took place in a playroom, Eb walked us to my car. Annie began to cry because she had "lost" her doll, but couldn't remember where she'd left it. After twenty minutes, Eb found the doll inside the wooden play oven and Annie laughed. She knew where it was all along. Eb laughed. Annie said, "Eb, I was talking to your truck and your truck didn't say anything." He answered, "Annie's World. I wish I could live there."

From the behaviour therapists at Quest Kids, Annie and I learned what to do when she pinched or hit me. We learned about "good hands" and counting slowly to ten; each time she stopped counting or yelled, she had to start the counting over again. I learned more effective "time out" techniques and how to physically control her without hurting either of us. We learned to shop for groceries without Annie grabbing food off the shelves. I awarded "good behaviour" with tokens she could cash in for treats and privileges. Annie learned better manners—please, thank you, you're welcome—to stop talking over people so I could have conversations with her sister and other parents, to take turns when playing games. The behaviour therapists worked with her teachers and other school support staff so the same behaviour modifications took place at home and school. Eb Blakely saved my life and Annie's life as well.

Life improved. I learned to enjoy our differences. Did it really matter that Annie hugged hot water heaters in Home Depot? Or talked to lizards and ignored people? Time passed and Annie, now thirty years old, has a job and lives in a supervised group home a few miles from me. She seldom exhibits aggressive behaviours. Sure, she argues with her housemates about clothes and what to watch on TV. She complains about her job which is mainly folding towels or stuffing envelopes, something she finds hard to do. But she has friends and is recognized everywhere we go—church, Target, Publix, banks. Once when I worried about what would happen to her after I died, Eb told me to stop worrying. "Annie has the most important talent there is: people like her."

My daughter and I can now hug, and I know that we will be okay.

Ethiopian Incense

P. R. NEWTON

IT WAS A HOT, dry Edmonton summer day. One of those days when the temperatures swell above thirty degrees Celsius and the heat sinks into your bones. Feeling thankful for the shade from our old tree and my blissfully cool sundress, I laid out a large blanket on the lush green grass of our sun-soaked yard. I stretched out my legs with a sigh of contentment. My two boys, three and five years old, splashed in a blue baby pool filled with icy water from the hose. Their silliness and screams of laughter filled my heart with peace and happiness. I cherished these moments with my boys. Letting my body relax under the warm sun, my thoughts wandered as I watched the wet, joyful chaos in front of me.

My mind went to an article I had read that morning. I contemplated how the water that my children were so carelessly tossing about is more precious than gold to millions of families without safe water. In Ethiopia one of the greatest needs is fresh water. Simple, clean, safe water that I can get from any tap with a simple twist of the wrist is not available to over forty-six million Ethiopians[1]. Articles like the one I had read earlier always touch my heart because of my history and connections. I saw so much suffering when we travelled to Ethiopia to adopt our youngest son. My beautiful doe-eyed boy is seemingly happy and healthy but he has suffered immense pain and trauma. His heart has been shattered into sharp, jagged pieces that scatter into the winds slicing into my Momma heart as I try to shield him, protect him, heal him, and love him.

Born in a country where safe water is a rarity for many communities, my son suffered immensely in his first year as an orphan stuck in a system of overcrowded and under-resourced institutions and orphanages. In Canada, a country filled with so much bounty, it is hard for me to fathom how much suffering there is in other corners of the world. That is, until I came face to face with it.

As I weighed the burden of being in a first-world country, with first-world issues, a postal van pulled into my driveway.

The door flew open as it was still rolling to a stop, and out popped an energetic lady with a halo of frizzy red curls. In her hands she clutched a large brown box. "This would be for you!" she exclaimed, all smiles as she thrust the box into my hands.

Noticing the return label, I smiled. It was from a fundraising initiative started by a dear friend to bring safe water to families in Ethiopia. Talk about timing. Just as my thoughts started to overwhelm me with the burden of knowledge about the needs in Ethiopia, I was reminded that good things are being done, improvements are happening.

Two weeks earlier the charity had hosted an online auction selling merchandise purchased from local artisans during a recent trip to Ethiopia. All proceeds went to build wells in Ethiopia. Between my love of Ethiopia, my desire to give back to the amazing country that gave us our son, and an addiction to online shopping, it was easy to get excited and part with hard-earned cash.

My hands moved quickly as I tore open the box and called over my shoulder for my boys to come and see.

The first thing to hit me was the smell. The distinctive incense of my experience of Ethiopia—roasted coffee beans, spices, earth, smoke, and heat—washed over me. My mind flooded with memories of the crowded, hectic outdoor markets of Addis Ababa and the amazing trip that marked the completion of our family with the addition of a gorgeous little boy.

I ran my fingers over the smooth silk of a hand-woven purple scarf that lay across the top of the contents. The colour was vibrant and beautiful. I thought in awe about the amazingly talented women who had spent hours labouring to create this purple perfection. They spun the silk directly from the silkworm cocoons, hand-dyed the fabric, and then tediously wove all the threads to create this stunning, unique scarf. No machines were used in the making of this beauty.

Next in the box I discovered two sets of coarsely-woven traditional shirts and shorts I had bought for my boys. The bulk of the fabric was slightly off white, with soft blues and greens embroidered in stunningly complicated patterns around the collar and cuffs.

"Boys come here, I want you to try these on!" I beckoned excitedly as I fondly remembered our exciting and thrilling time in Ethiopia. The smell and contents of the package took me back to the bustling markets, visits to the pottery co-ops, driving the insane Addis Ababa streets, and the most memorable moment, visiting the orphanage and holding our son for the first time. My smile broadened, energized by the memories.

My older son, a biological child, stepped up and obligingly held up his new clothes, even giving me a little spin to show off. He laughed hysterically as he attempted his version of a traditional Ethiopian dance.

My younger son, my beautiful Ethiopian son with large soulful eyes, waited until his older brother moved away before he stepped up slowly, ever my cautious and curious boy. As he bent over the box he stopped the moment the smell hit his nose. He became frozen, in time and space, as if someone had hit the pause button on a television show.

I gently laid a hand on his shoulder, "Isn't it beautiful? Doesn't it smell wonderfully like Ethiopia?" I spoke with exuberance, still caught up in my own thoughts.

My son did not move. Pulling my attention from memories to the present, I looked at him closely. Something was wrong.

"Are you ok?" I asked, giving his shoulder a gentle squeeze.

Slowly he looked up at me. His pupils were dilated, his eyes unfocused and filled with emotion. Emotion I could not adequately quantify—sadness, fear, longing, anger, sickness, sorrow, aching, apprehension, worry, and anxiety all seemed to engulf him.

Tears welled up in my eyes as he backed up, repeatedly saying "No, no, no." His voice pitched higher and higher and pierced the air with each exclamation. His fight-or-flight response kicked in. His arms flailed at an invisible enemy and he took off running across the yard.

In that moment I glimpsed my son's vulnerable wounded spirit and gained a deeper understanding of his fears. For my son, his memories of Ethiopia were not of excitement, happiness, and the thrill of a new family. His memories were of hunger, suffering, loss, pain, anger, trauma, hurt, and fear.

Pulling the scarf from my neck, I put the clothing back in the box, closing the lid tightly. Standing up slowly, I absently wiped my hands on the soft cotton of my dress as I walked tentatively towards my son. He sat tucked in behind some bushes, back against the fence so no one could come up behind him, his brown eyes wide and unblinking as he gently rocked.

Sitting beside him, close but not touching, I remained quiet. I waited for him to make the first move, fearful I could startle him more. I had learned from earlier PTSD attacks that to enter his space now would result in violent retaliation. During this moment, my son's actions and reactions were not his own: they were borne from trauma and such a deep-seated fear that it consumes his mind and body.

Thankfully, this time, we were in the safety of our yard; I could let the attack run its course. Let the fear naturally dissipate. His body could have all the time it needed to come back to me.

It's not always possible. When we are in public his safety is often in jeopardy. All natural instincts for self-preservation become clouded by the instinct of fight-or-flight, a much stronger visceral reaction. In those instances I am forced to take the brunt of the violence. Screaming, biting, kicking, punching. I let him pummel my body as I struggle to hold him close. My body is expendable. His needs and safety are always and forever first in my mind.

This blistering hot prairie day we could both ride out the storm, side by side, together but separate. Progressing in his own time. It was a welcomed change for both of us. He never, ever wanted to hurt his Mommy, and I knew it was not him hitting me. It was the fear. That day I was able to give the fear its space.

After what seemed like an eternity, my son turned, climbed into my lap and buried his face into my chest as he started to sob. Our bodies melted into each other as we both cried. His heart wrenching tears releasing his fears, sadness, anger and pain. My tears fell from all the injustice, needless suffering and trauma in the world—but especially for my beloved son.

That night I carefully washed all the clothes taking one final deep breath of the complicated Ethiopian musk on the fabric before submersing them in soapy water.

The next day I hesitantly brought out the clothes again, now smelling of lemony soap, and this time my Ethiopian son proudly wore his heritage clothing. The scents and pain of yesterday were forgotten. As he danced and played with his brother to a rhythmic beat, my heart filled with joy knowing that these memories, memories of love, laughter, joy and hope, were filling up my son's heart, healing his wounded spirit, helping him move forward from the trauma, and into a better future.

We danced together. The prince of my heart and I, hand in hand, dressed in our Ethiopian finery. Finery lovingly created by immensely talented hands who live in a land scented by the powerful incense of roasted coffee beans, spices, earth, smoke, sun and who may or may not have access to safe water.

NOTES

[1]World Health Organization/United Nations Children's Fund Joint Monitoring Programme for Water Supply and Sanitation. "Progress on Sanitation and Drinking-Water: 2013 Update." Web.

Ephemera

Searchings on Adoption, Identity and Mothering

KATE GREENWAY

A PHOTOGRAPH

It is an unremarkable photograph of people I don't know. You've seen ones like it hanging in hallways of institutions, tucked away in attics, thrown out in estate sales or languishing in bins at the back of musty collectibles stores. This is not even the original: a copy of a print, sepia toned, some etched creases and foxing but the image clear. A fawn water-marked border frames a scene that has been repeated year after year. Three rows of girls, arranged formally, no doubt tallest to shortest, on a wooden stage. The class photo.

"Quiet please girls."

In this version all the girls—young adults actually, maybe just over twenty years old, though it's difficult to judge—look into the camera, smiles fixed on their faces. Those in the front row sit with hands clasped demurely in their laps. Sensible sturdy shoes lead to legs crossed at the ankles not at the knees, as is proper for young ladies. They wear white blouses, mostly collared, long-sleeved and buttoned to the neck. The more daring among them flash bare arms, or sport a mark of individualism: a strand of pearls, a jaunty neck tie, a flicker of lace. The skirts are mid-thigh, likely navy or grey but it's hard to tell. Black would have been unsuitable. No short hair: the style is shoulder length but pinned at the temple or neck to secure curler-set waves and swept bangs.

"Chins up, shoulders back."

A photo of privilege, of belonging. Lives suspended for a moment, giggles suppressed. "Kappa Kappa Gamma Fraternity 1948-49" reads the caption above the names. These women are identified only by first initial and patrilineal surname—names that will soon be discarded, no longer traceable.

"Look at the camera now."

My attention is captured by one young woman, front row, third from the left. Her hair is clearly blond, lighter than most of the others. It catches the light, side-parted and neatly pinned. Her head is cocked at a slight angle. On her left wrist, a slim watch. She is one of the bare-armed and her blouse appears collarless, with faint vertical patterning, perhaps pleats or flocking—it's not easy to make out. Her jaw is rounded, cheeks full and forehead high.

I am forty-three years old. I have never seen this woman before.

This is a photograph of my mother.

EPHEMERA

Imagine you have been left at birth with gifts from someone whose identity you will likely never know, someone who is intimately connected with you and your life, your very reason for existence. What tales do these objects hold? Are these treasures? Historical artefacts? Holy relics? Mysterious clues?

Imagine that pieces of your self are hidden from you, that what others take for granted is, to you, actively denied. Stories told or not told, memories that shift and dissolve under light.

My life, my identity, is formed of ephemera.

Ephemera: transitory matter not intended to be retained or preserved. The word derives from the Greek, meaning "things lasting no more than a day." Some examples of ephemera are catalogues, greeting cards, pamphlets, posters, tickets.

Adoption records.

I have always known. There was no traumatic discovery or reveal, an uncovered hidden document or overheard remark. Yet the uncertainty, conjecture, partialness I feel is real. It is private, personal, and yet also socially constructed and reinforced. Mine is a closed, non-agency adoption, enacted in secret. The frustration and indignity of not having access to my own origins. Mystery leading to fantasy. Freud believed most children daydream of other parents, a phenomenon he called the "family romance." But for me, the romance is real: there really are two sets of parents to whom I truly belong. Search attempts are variously dismissed or encouraged as curiosity, obsession, neurosis, therapy, or a diverting pastime. I inevitably face the wary questions of family, friends, and colleagues: "...but why?" And to me, the answer seems both self-evident and elusive.

What does it mean to live as an adopted person or birthmother whose personal history is ineradicably interwoven into an outdated system—one that valued secrecy above all? How do we now negotiate a world where the stigma of illegitimacy has waned, yet the resulting shame permeates our very existence? In an age of open records, how do we confront absence—the fact that there is nothing to find? How do the few stories left and unleft to me through the ephemera of objects, words, and images, embody my own lived reality or that of my mother's, and how do I respond, as educator, artist, woman, adoptee?

NOTE

My adoptive mother kept the layette my birthmother had dressed and swaddled me in: a rough woollen grey and yellow fringed blanket, and a cream knit beribboned dress edged in delicate lace, handmade in Italy, with matching bonnet and booties. My mom preserved it in pristine condition, stored carefully in a cedar chest crafted by her own grandfather.

And tucked into the lid of the chest is a small folded note: *These were on Kate when we brought her home from the hospital. They were supplied by her natural mother. God bless her wherever she is and our thanks for allowing us to share her baby.*

From time to time now I sit on the floor, pull these out of my own linen closet, and remember the mother I knew and the mother I didn't.

M(OTHER)

Even the nomenclature of multiple mothering is problematic: the term "birthmother" equates the act of mothering with gestation and delivery, a bio-essentialism suggesting that "other" mothering is somehow secondary. "Adoptive" mother feels like an unwieldy apologia, a second-best status that cannot shake itself free to be simply "mother," denoting an artificially constructed relationship. I think about what it means to be a mother, have a mother, have mothers. What language do I use? Natural Mother. Biological mother. Birthmother. Real Mother. Is it possible to find language that complicates and celebrates rather than reduces the strata of relationships and statuses involved in family building? I read books with titles like *Voices from the Adoption Triangle* and *Who Is My Mother?*—the adult version, it seems, of that childhood primer. As the story goes, the baby bird hatches. He doesn't understand where his mother is so he goes to look for her. In his search, he asks a kitten, a hen, a dog, and a cow if they are his mother.

They each say, "No."

AN ENVELOPE

In my teens, mom would present me with cheery newspaper clippings showing reunited birthmothers and children, and brightly suggest that if I wanted to search, she would be fine with it. But I did not. Rebellious adolescence or latent fear of rejection held me back until well into my twenties—a decision I would come to regret. My father never really spoke of adoption to me, a tacit agreement.

Eventually, I register with the Adoption Disclosure Agency, a backlogged, underfunded government body (who suggest, it turns out correctly, that if and when they begin my search there will be little to find). I try my hand at detective work, lying to librarians, utilizing city directories and newspaper CD-ROMS, pre-Internet. Sometime after mom dies, my father agrees to the release of information contained in the private adoption files held by Jeffrey and Jeffrey, Barristers and Solicitors, a step I need to gain access to documents. I am not allowed to search my own identity without permissions: parental, paternal, legal.

One spring day a large brown envelope arrives. In it are all the papers in existence about my heritage. Most reveal very little other than official logistical arrangements. Until I lay eyes on the contents of my original Adoption Order. Strange and wonderful, with the affixed gold seal of the County Court of Middlesex, a single paper that altered many life courses. My racing pulse quelled by gulped sauvignon. I discover, my original name—Martha Anne. The person I never became, or perhaps slivers of a hybrid, multiple self. And then I see my birthmother's signature, likely scribed under the surveillance of what I assume were the disapproving eyes of male authority, affirming she signed away all rights to this child. A handwritten document appended to the official writ confirms that she was an *unmarried* mother—a fact not to be forgotten or forgiven. It was then that she became real.

M(OTHERING)

Adoption is created fundamentally through loss: the loss of the child, loss of the mother, of agency, biological connection, familial identity, ritual, and story. The veils of secrecy and layers of shame and guilt imposed on the process by non-disclosure law, family reputation, and public morality exacerbate these losses. Birthdays—a yearly embodiment and reminder of conflicted origin and surrender—acquire a double-edged significance.

Perceptions of adoption perpetuate definitions of what constitutes "normative" motherhood, family, and identity. Biological connection versus "otherness" appears to be central, present even from earliest Oedipal myths of missing parents and suspicious lineage, to the "chosen child" tales more recently presented to young children's brokered understanding of their new familial context. Notions of good and bad mothering, the sacrificial mother, the stern morality tale against the transgressions of female sexuality, or "bad seed" child flatten the story further. Have these concepts shaped my relationships, and my desire not to parent, the figures of "absent" and "present" mother resonating through the "unmother" that I have become? Am I rejecting a cultural imperative to be defined as a woman only if I desire to procreate and nurture? Am I judged solely on the ability to have or keep a child? Like my mothers, I, too, become suspect.

CLUE

The game of *Clue* takes strategy and imagination, or at least it

did in my childhood mind. The thrill of finding tidbits of information. Sifting and eliminating data with cards revealed only to
you. Putting pieces together to form hypotheses. Withholding
your thoughts gleefully until the final triumphant reveal: Colonel
Mustard in the Billiard Room with the candlestick! (It must have
been *some* candlestick—nothing I possess would render more than
a headache.) Miss Scarlet in the Library with the lead pipe! So I
guess *Clue* is what I have been playing with my past.

A game of *Clue* is what led me to the William McReady Archives.
I Googled her name. Tell me you haven't done it. You wonder just
what's out there in the ether about you. You sit alone, maybe at
night in your room so no one can see this somewhat self-indulgent,
narcissistic side. And if you find something unpleasant, it's just as
well that no one else knows. In her case, a cryptic listing of file
box numbers, secreted away in a university library basement, as
I discover her job as an editor in a major publishing house whose
entire oeuvre has been donated to academia.

Imagine someone saved the contents of your file drawers at
work for posterity: budgets, memos, correspondence, to do lists,
management directives, some with annotations or scrawls, doodles
or comments. Ephemera. What would this say about you? What
story would it tell? My own files are crammed into cabinets that
don't close, so full that the tops of them are chewed off. My birth-
mother's files are neat, though many have mysterious handwritten
amendments in the marginalia of figures and columns. Letters are
mimeographed in purple ink. Carbon paper and onion skin mix
with a few messages on scrap.

What I'm looking for is small, I think. Her handwriting. Some
indication of her expression, her turn of phrase. Any personal
notes. A timeline—she left "secretly" to have me. But when?
Surely the sudden disappearance and return forged a complicit
understanding from colleagues. When was she back and what
might that say about her? Career-driven? Guilt racked? Maybe
there will be a hint about my father, since his name has never
been revealed. "He played tennis and had a bad arm." That's the
sum total of my paternity. Would there be love notes in the file?
Maybe one particular man mentioned frequently? "Hey—, meet
me at the water cooler at 3:00?"

But in this game, the clues have been omitted.

CONTACT

Phone call, back office, no warning. Five minutes prior to full teacher staff meeting, ten years after registering my search.
"Contact has been made with your birthmother."

I take hastily scribbled point form notes about my own life from the dispassionate voice on the other end of the phone-line, as if I am in a college lecture. This is absurd.

I write: *She was overwhelmed with emotion. Not sure what to do. She asked for time to think. She had no information on my adoptive circumstances and agreed to receive info. She is 73 years old. Medical history: Lumpectomy. Heart arrhythmia. Spot on lung (Smoker). She told birthfather regarding pregnancy. She didn't want to discuss it further. No further direct contact. Indirect contact was maintained. Therefore he was likely a member of her social circle.*

She had no choices at the time. She was comforted to hear that I had brothers and sisters. Two beagles—"Oh my."

She cried. She needed time to think about contact.

Not outright denial. Nor acceptance.

I am allowed to send a letter through intermediaries. I sit at my polished dining room table with sunlight streaming in the window and I write to my mother. I write all day, page after page. To summarize my life? To delineate how I wish to interact with her? What is the appropriate tone? What are the moments that define me, make me real to this stranger-mother?

It is no matter. The letter will be returned, after her death, scant months later. Unopened.

SCRAPS

Early. I am in the parking lot of the funeral home where the meeting is to take place. It is an oddly gothic place to hold an adoption search support group. I walk into the air-conditioned cool, a welcome reprieve after the heat of the humid evening. The meeting room is up a flight of stairs, made more daunting by the after-effects of my fifth and sixth chemo treatments. A strange lethargy and ache in the calves make walking, even in the smallest increments, feel impossible. My swollen legs and ankles burn at the extra effort the stairs demand.

Distant voices drift, and coalesce into seven or eight people sitting on couches and chairs at the furthest edge of a room that appears to be some kind of kitchen. These people seem to be the regulars, who make the trek every two months to discuss what they have done, who they have seen, what new morsels of information have been revealed. Advice is being solicited and sometimes given without being requested.

All the stories relayed are convoluted. They encompass whole lifetimes—the plots unfold around multiple characters, in multiple acts. Mine included. My birthmother was confident, capable, a career woman in a man's world. She was thirty-five when she had me, returning to a promotion months later, not the stereotypical reckless or ignorant teen. She married a colleague and had one child. I have a half-sister barely a year younger than I. My birthmother is now dead. These things I know. But mostly, there is a collage of imaginings, gaps, and silences.

I came because I was curious. I'm not a real believer in self-help. And I don't play well in groups. But here I find at least some commonality, a place to listen and to share. What is it I want? Release? Remembrance? Redemption? Perhaps a story I can make for myself. I occupy intermediate places, multiple worlds, see ghosts in the mirror reflecting no others I know. Foucault might admonish that we are without pure origins, but I think it is the hope of some concept of personhood, some type of life narrative, however fragmentary and illusive, that fuels my ongoing quest for self and (m)other.

ONE DAY

November: Remembrance Day. A day to pay tribute, to pause, to consider losses, to mourn those absent. This is fitting. Sunlight does not dispel the chill of approaching winter, and I am dressed for a city lunch, not a walk outdoors. On a whim, I park my car. The tiny cemetery office is open, and the attendant provides me a detailed, hand-drawn map of numbered rows. In yellow highlighter she indicates the path I need to take to find the plot I'm seeking.

"And there may be a poppy wreath. Oh no, that was a while ago," she says. The computer does not indicate whether there is an upright marker or not.

"You're welcome."

I narrow the search to a quadrant under an almost bare tree heaved from the earth by descending roots, framed on one side by the cemetery's edge where the gravestones peter out to a low rumble of traffic. The map shows I have gone too far. I try again. Not far enough. Wrong row. This row? Back again. Leaves obscure the flat, mottled white stones and darker veined granite.

"In 2009, special care was last purchased," the attendant had said.

"By the family?" I ask.

She offers a woman's name that means nothing to me. A friend perhaps.

"Extra weeding and watering."

Thus strengthens the grass that relentlessly, greedily, creeps, obscuring names and dates. My hands begin to numb in the chill. I sweep aside stacks of golden leaves with the toe of my boot. The name I am searching for is not revealed. I brush a wet pile off a marker that reveals only a fraction of the chiselled message once left, a single word.

Mother.

But not mine. Even in death I cannot find her.

LATE ONE EVENING, A GHOST

You'll think I'm lying. Or crazy.

I have just arrived home after the second night of parent-teacher interviews. It is a dreary evening. Rain has teemed down all day. Almost December. I would have gotten home even later but the sick dog is getting worse. His regime of pills is causing nausea. Yesterday he threw up water. He shakes. Involuntarily. He doesn't like to be away from me now. Or maybe it's the other way around. I am hand feeding the sodden, shivering creature bits of buttered white toast from a china bowl like an invalid of yore, trying to trick him into thinking he is stealing food from a dinner plate. He is not convinced. The TV has been on all day to keep him company. Judge Judy is delivering her verdict.

The phone rings. When I have to say hello twice I am about to hang up on what I think is a telemarketer. A female voice asks, "Is this Kate?" Her voice is soft, distant, but not aged. I can't quite hear. I am not really paying attention. Snatches of words come through while the TV continues to blare. The remote is on the table and I don't want to disturb the dog nestled beside me. He is finally still. I'm distracted but trying to figure out to whom I am listening.

The female voice continues. I think she mentions giving Bandit, my sick dog, a bath. Something about a picture. Is this my mother-in-law? A long-distance friend with a pre-Christmas catch up? No one identifies themselves on the phone nowadays: niceties of a bygone age, I think to myself irritably.

"He melted cheese all over.... We had to do it again."

I surrender, disturb the dog, and reach to press mute on the remote.

"I'm sorry," I interrupt firmly, flatly. "Who is this again?"

"This is Kate Greenway's mother."

Silence.

The impossibility makes me feel physically ill. The voice returns.

"Maybe I've dialled incorrectly. I'll try again."

"Okay," is the sum total of all I can think of to say before the click.

I am listed only as K. Greenway in telephone records, not Kate. Both mothers are dead.

There is no explanation for this.

"This is Kate Greenway's mother."

Words I wish to hear again from one. Words I wished I heard for the first time from another. The wet, muddy dog shivers and sighs against me. I press *69. "We're sorry. The last number that called your line is not known."

Now I am the one shaking. I feel suddenly very alone. Yet, I hang up the phone and wait, ridiculously, for a ghost to ring again.

WHAT SHE CARRIED

She carried it with her from the age of thirty-five until her death. Sometimes it was in the forefront, immediate and unignored, tugging at her composure. At other times, it was like a murmur, not quite articulated, but ready to be glimpsed if she would allow it. Like a reflection caught in a puddle of water or refracted from a window, there and not there, distorted and coloured, but not shapeless, not unrecognizable, waiting for acknowledgement. It might have called to her in quiet times, in the moments before sleep came, a dream that was not. It was part of her and yet separate, like a cancer she cut out but could not quite eradicate, nor would she want to, since it *was* her in elemental and ancient ways. It would have begun as either a slow dawning awareness or a sudden enveloping realization, either way in the apprehension that nothing afterward could ever be the same.

And she would carry this deep inside her, where it would remain cradled long after the rest played out. It began in an act and ended in an act, but had not ended, not for her, not ever. It was pleasure and panic, grief and emptiness, inevitability and control. She carried it in different ways, according to the time and context: with shame, or fierce independence, or with a relinquishing of will to other more capable hands; with guilt, or defiance, or regret, but always, always.

And she never shared it with others: her future husband, her siblings, her child, none, save for the stern matriarch who whisked her away, and in a deliberate parting from the other. For it was ultimately hers alone to bear. That is, until just before the end. She had cocooned it, blessed it, made peace with it, unwrapping it carefully when it pleased her to do so, and then just as gently swaddling it in the layers of remembering and forgetfulness she faithfully chose as her attendants.

She might have carried it with love, but I have no answer for that. She carried it—that's all I can tell.

Reflections on Becoming
a "Real" Mother

LYNN GIDLUCK

ONCE UPON A TIME I dreamt of being pregnant. All the time. Morning, noon, and night. It was all I could think about. The sight of a baby or a pregnant woman could bring me to instant tears. The thought of attending a baby shower or visiting families with children filled me with dread. I wanted to do everything I could to avoid situations where people might say: "I know your career is important, but don't put off having a baby too much longer or you may not be able to have one." Or, "Tick, tick, you're not getting any younger."

I was over thirty when I got married. Like a lot of women, I spent many years before that worried I *would* get pregnant. I think back to all the movies I watched or books I read where the woman seemed to get pregnant the first time she ever had sex—whether it was teenage love or sexual assault. Yep. It seemed so easy. I had no reason to believe I would have any problems getting pregnant (when the time was right). I was reasonably healthy and not *that* old. You get married. You have kids. You live a happy, contented life. Simple. Not asking too much, is it?

But no. Month after month after month. Soon a year went by. Then another. Endless tests—poking, prodding, legs in stirrups. Waiting. Waiting. No reason why I shouldn't be able to conceive— everything looked to be in working order. Five rounds of artificial insemination. Back and forth to the hospital with my husband's sperm in a little plastic jar in a brown paper bag—all to no avail. Like a time bomb, I was ready to explode at any moment. People at work knew something was wrong. Their former happy-go-lucky,

Suzie Sunshine colleague was not joining them for coffee and only talking to them when they talked first. I was morose and catatonic. My marriage was suffering because I had become so obsessed with becoming pregnant that it was all I could think about. Sex became a mechanical chore, a means to an end, something only partaken of on the right days. I kept my feelings close to my chest. I suffered in silence. No one knew the full extent of my grief. I wanted to be a mother more than anything else in the world.

My husband and I briefly considered in vitro fertilization but the odds seemed stacked against us. What if we spent a whole pile of money that we didn't have and we were unsuccessful? If we had to go into debt to have a family, we wanted some kind of guarantee that we'd have a child at the end of the process. We made an appointment with the Social Services branch of our provincial government instead and quickly came to the conclusion that our best option was international adoption. This was the late 1990s and China was the country most child welfare agencies in North America were pointing couples like us toward. The adoption process was perceived to be relatively smooth. Most children available for adoption were healthy and there was a growing community of families with children from China living nearby who could act as a support network.

The decision was made and there was no looking back. I didn't look at adoption as my second choice. I didn't see adoption as a disappointing last resort to becoming a mother. Grief for how my body had betrayed me was replaced with excitement. Was it really possible? Would I finally become a mother? We met with a social worker who grilled us about whether we were prepared to be parents. We filled out what seemed like hundreds of forms and then we waited, and waited and waited. One day we got the call: "Congratulations! You have a daughter waiting for you in China. Start packing your bags." Six weeks later we boarded a plane to China and our lives changed.

We went through this process not once but twice. We were over the moon with happiness. I was a mother after all these years of waiting and I was in love. Soon I had two perfect daughters. Sure—I hadn't given birth to my girls but I felt like a real mother. I was reminded that they were adopted every time I looked into their beautiful Chinese eyes but I didn't see them as someone else's children. I was their mother—plain and simple. They were my daughters. I had all the same responsibilities as any mother. I loved them unconditionally. I cared for them when they were sick. I was doing everything other mothers did—driving them to art classes and soccer and putting *Dora the Explorer* Band-Aids on scraped knees. Reading *The Cat and the Hat* and *Green Eggs and Ham* so many times that I had the books memorized. I had the same insecurities as other mothers: Was I spoiling them? Was I too strict? Not strict enough? Should I force them to practice the piano—to learn Mandarin? Was I letting them watch too much television? Should I be trying harder to make sure they ate healthier foods? Why was I so exhausted all the time? What school should we enrol them in?

I also learned pretty quickly that when children are of a different racial heritage than their parents, the family stands out. I got used to the grocery store questions: "Are they adopted?" "How much did they cost?" "Are they real sisters?" "Do they speak Chinese?" "Are you worried that their real family will want them back?" "Do you have any children of your own?" I started to worry not only about the typical everyday stresses of childrearing, but also whether I was equipped to help my girls navigate the murky waters of racial identity and racism. I read everything I could get my hands on in my attempt to help my children grow up to be healthy and well adjusted. I collaborated with a friend—who also has children from China—to do research on race, racism, and racial identity. This gave me the rare opportunity to combine my personal life with the kind of research-related work I hoped to one day have the chance to do on a full-time basis. I was fortunate to be able to learn from other parents, like us, who had transracial families.

Fast-forward five years. The impossible happens. I find that I'm pregnant after all these years. Yet I was not immediately ecstatic. *What's wrong with me?* I wondered. *Isn't this what I had always wanted?* I felt selfish. I was happy before I discovered I was pregnant. I thought my family was complete. And I was just about to begin a post-graduate degree. I was starting a new chapter of my life. My first thoughts were actually—*I can't be pregnant. I'm too old for this.*

Less than a week before this big news I had been chatting with my sister, a nurse. By the end of the phone call she had convinced me that both of us were going through peri-menopause. The hormones seem to flood through you more than they used to. You pack on a few extra pounds and get tired more easily. Your once regular visits from Mother Nature are more sporadic. Check, check, check, check. I could tick all of the boxes. Oops. Wrong. Who was I to know that all of the same signs are also an indication of pregnancy? By the time I found out, I was four months along.

I had actually been angry with a person who dared to point out the obvious to me. One afternoon, as I was picking up my girls up from daycare, I was greeted with a question from one of their caregivers:

"I probably shouldn't ask this because it's none of my business but—are you pregnant?"

I thought to myself: *Good lord, people think I'm pregnant. I'm a mess. I have to do something to address this.* I choked back tears before replying, "No, I'm just getting old and fat. I guess I should get a membership at the gym," something I proceeded to do that same evening on the way home from my oldest daughter's Mandarin class.

I'm not even sure why I decided to buy a home pregnancy test. After so many years of infertility and, well, truth be told, an almost celibate life, being pregnant was about as likely as winning the lottery. My girls, as much as I loved them, exhausted me. Sex was the last thing I was interested in and most nights I fell into bed dog-tired. But I bought a test and peed into a cup and a pink plus sign appeared. I didn't really believe it so I bought another test and sure enough, it came back positive too. I was in shock. I couldn't believe it.

Instead of being happy, I was ambivalent. I was scared to voice my real thoughts for fear of looking cold and callous. My life had just started to get a little easier. The kids could amuse themselves without constant supervision. I no longer feared that if I turned my head for even a moment they'd fall down the stairs or otherwise place themselves in grave danger. One of the first thoughts that ran through my head as I accepted I was pregnant was that I'd have to wait even longer to do my Ph.D. Would this baby mean the loss of my dream of becoming a researcher and one day teaching at a university?

I showed my husband the pregnancy test. He said, "I think you should go to the doctor. There must be some kind of explanation for this. How can this be? I sleep with our youngest more than you."

My doctor told me what I had already accepted to be true. I was pregnant and not just a little pregnant. No wonder the woman at the daycare thought I was expecting. It's as plain as day that this was more than just a few pounds of extra weight. In photos taken around this time at a staff retreat I look like I swallowed a watermelon. I was also throwing up. How was I to know that morning sickness doesn't always occur in the morning but anytime of the day or night? I thought I was just starting to be more sensitive to greasy foods and needed to take better care of myself. I probably didn't even need to dip the stick fully into the jar. The fumes alone would have produced the pink plus sign.

Our oldest daughter, who was in kindergarten, told everyone on her school bus and all her teachers. I started getting phone calls before she even got off the bus that afternoon: "You must be so excited to be having a child of your own." "How about that! A real mother after all these years." "After the pressure was off, you just relaxed and let nature do its thing."

The underlying message that came through people's excitement was that the tiny baby growing in my tummy somehow "trumped" my other children. My adopted children were not as special as the child I would be giving birth to in a matter of months.

One of my husband's relatives even said to me, "Now that you're having one of your own, are you going to give the other two back?" Granted, this woman was elderly and not bright. Most of the reactions we got to our news were not as extreme as this one was but still, the message I got was clear. My girls from China, who I love so much my heart aches to think about anything bad ever happening to them, were somehow not as special or precious as their new baby sister or brother growing inside me. They were not seen as my *real* children and I was not seen as their *real* mother.

I started becoming guarded in my responses. I was excited about having this child. Sure, it took me awhile to get over the shock and re-think my life goals, but I got there. I became secretly happy to have a chance to see what it would be like to physically give birth to a child, to be able to nourish a baby with my own breastmilk, and to see what it was like to mother a newborn. I was also scared. I had passed through the first trimester of my pregnancy without prenatal vitamins and having had a few glasses of wine. I was over 40 and automatically high risk. My family physician tried to make light of my fears: "Well, you're not a crack user, are you? I'm sure there's very little to worry about."

What really kept me up at night, however, was the thought that other people's reactions to this baby, or worse yet, my own response to their comments, might be interpreted by my other children to mean that I loved this child more than them. On the one hand, if I gave the impression I wasn't absolutely overjoyed to be pregnant I might leave the impression that the baby growing inside me was unwanted. I didn't want my future child to ever think that. On the other hand, if I said something to indicate my real happiness with becoming a mother again (and this time in a different manner) then I might hurt my daughters' feelings. I didn't want them to ever feel second-best, like a consolation prize relative to this newer addition.

I responded to any comments about having a "child of my own" by patting my tummy and saying, "This child is our 'bonus' baby. Adoption from China has become a much more difficult process, with longer and longer timelines, so we had pretty much ruled out the idea of having a third baby." I gave the impression that I had always wanted a third child. I felt like a fraud.

Some days I'd respond by joking: "This poor child doesn't have nearly as good a chance of being attractive as the other girls do with parents that look like me and Pat. This poor kid will be wearing coke-bottle glasses by the time it walks."

On other occasions, and usually with people I wasn't as fond of, I'd actually be honest. I said, more than once, "Of course, I'm sure you don't think for a second that I could possibly love a child I give birth to any more than I love my two girls?"

I even lied on occasion: "I prefer adoption to this whole being pregnant thing. Look how huge I am. I look terrible. And, sleeping is almost impossible. Oh, the indigestion."

Secretly though, I loved my pregnant body. I thought I looked beautiful. My skin was never smoother; my hair was never so shiny.

Sure, I waddled like a duck and could barely fit in the tiny desks at the university where I was taking the final qualifying class for my Ph.D. program—an introduction to statistics—but I was happy. The thought of having another little person join our family filled me with joy. And I reconciled my plans. I had waited this long to go back to university: what was another year or two?

But with the joys of pregnancy also came a whole slew of difficult questions and comments from my girls: "Did I grow in your tummy?" "So, where is my real mummy? "Can we go to China to visit my real mommy?"

I explained to my daughters that being a mom is about more than just giving birth. I poured through a million books and lurked on adoption listservs to find the right answers to explain the complicated realities of why my daughters' birth families were unable to raise them. These were all questions that any adoptive parent eventually has to answer but usually you have more time. When my children asked me questions about their *real* mother I'd joke that I didn't consider myself a *fake* mother to them.

It dawned on me that, until I got pregnant, my girls thought babies came from airports. We had been to the airport so many times in their young lives to welcome home families just returning from adopting in China. Of course, my children knew that they were adopted. There's no way of hiding that when you look completely different than your parents and get the kinds of intrusive questions from strangers that transracial families regularly receive. But, my pregnancy opened the door to a lot of important, albeit difficult questions about what adoption is really about. It was no longer an abstract concept for my girls. It was a reality. And the questions and comments didn't stop after my third daughter was born: "Do you think I drank milk from my real mommy?" "How could someone ever give up a baby?" "My real mom must not have loved me very much to give me away."

And there were two milestones in my youngest daughter's life that meant more than I ever expected they would: 11 months and 17 months. These were the ages my two older daughters came to be a part of our family. Many people had asked me the question (in the presence of my older daughters): "How old were they when they were adopted?" These occasions highlighted to my girls that they had a life they knew very little about—back in China—before they became part of our family. They had seen their little sister go through so many changes. They saw how dependent she was on me. How much I doted on her. I had very few answers for them about their lives before we met them. There was very little, if any, chance that we'd know anything beyond which orphanage they had lived in before joining our family.

Prior to going through the physical acts of pregnancy, childbirth and breastfeeding I had obviously given a lot of thought to the life my daughters had in China. But it was all very academic, very abstract. With the arrival of my third child, I had moments of sadness when I realized that I had missed those first months of my older daughters' little lives. No matter how strong my bond with my older daughters, there is no escaping the fact that I had missed out.

I am happy that I had the opportunity to experience what it was like to give birth to a child but I refuse to believe that I am somehow a better mother than I was before my third child came into my life. I remain thankful I was granted the opportunity to have not one but three children—each unique in her own way. I will continue to be hyper-vigilant to any suggestion that I could possibly love a biological child more than an adopted one. Families come in all shapes and sizes. Love is love.

Nine Months to a New Me

MELISSA MORELLI LACROIX

*Let us make pregnancy an occasion
when we appreciate our female bodies.*
—Merete Leonhardt-Lupa

M Y BREASTS ARE SUDDENLY BIGGER, fuller, more round, more obvious than I'm used to. They peek out the top of my tank top, make more than a handful for my husband. It's not my usual place for weight gain, but we are on holidays and I'm eating too much and not doing aerobics. We'll be home soon, and I'll get back into my routine. I'll start eating well again, and my weight and my body will return to normal.

I hurry to the bathroom much more frequently than usual and arrive just in time. I've been drinking more water. It's been so hot.

My period doesn't come, but it will. Surely. When it finally does come, it's not normal. It's pink and brown and spotty. It must be because we are travelling.

I have some abdominal pain, which is normal since I have my period. I wait for my heavy flow to begin. It doesn't.

I count the days backwards to my last period. Could I be pregnant? If I'm pregnant, I shouldn't be bleeding. If I'm not, I should be bleeding more. What's going on? It's possible that I'm pregnant, but it's also possible that the thousands of kilometers I've travelled this month are playing tricks on my body.

I want to buy a pregnancy test, but my husband thinks it's a waste of money. "Besides," he says, "the store-bought test could always be wrong. If you're pregnant," he reasons, "you'll have to go to the doctor anyhow. If you're not, you'll know soon enough."

We get back home. I rest for a few days. Nothing changes. I go to the doctor.

"I'll order some tests," she says "but in the meantime, act as if you're pregnant. Take folic acid. Wear your seatbelt below your abdomen. Don't drink."

The phone call comes early in the morning as I'm drying off from my shower. I run for the phone. As I lift the receiver to my ear, I notice that my body is shaking.

"Your test came back positive. You're pregnant."

"I am? Great." I hope I sound happy, but I'm really not sure what I think or feel now that someone has told me what my body has been trying to tell me for weeks. Somehow an appointment with the obstetrician is made for later that day.

Because of my spotting, I'm sent for an ultrasound. There on the screen, I see the little tadpole-looking human being with a functioning liver and brain attached to the inside of my uterus. I see my baby's heart beating.

* * *

The student who sits next to me during my "Humans and Their Environment" class eats Rice-Krispies squares, Cookies by George, bagels with fruit-flavoured cream cheese. I want to eat these things too, but I can't. As part of my recovery from compulsive eating, I don't eat between meals. *This too shall pass*, I tell myself. *I will not die if I do not eat until mealtime.*

I listen to lectures about land use and human consumption. *I may not die*, I think, *but I might vomit.* As the days pass I become more and more nauseous when I go too long without food. One day I eat a few crackers in the middle of the afternoon. Another day I eat an apple and some cheese. I feel better when I keep my body fuelled. I know it's okay. It's good to honour my body in this way. I've started wearing my husband's jeans. They're too big, but at least they don't press against my stomach. I still wear some of my own clothes: flowing dresses and skirts that hide my increasing girth. My recovering self tells me that I'm not fat—I'm pregnant.

"Look where and how your body is growing," a friend says. "It's not fat."

I know she's right. Still, it's difficult to see the distension, the refilling of my stretched abdominal skin.

* * *

I'm hungry. Some days I need to eat every two hours. I eat fruit bars, cereal, cheese, oranges. Even though I eat often, I'm not obsessed with food. I'm hungry and I eat. Still, I must consciously remind myself that it's okay, that I must eat for my health and that of my baby's. The doctor tells me not to worry about my weight, but I don't know how to gain weight without worrying.

My stomach is getting firm. The baby is growing. The elastic-waistband sweatpants and loose tops I wear make me feel bulky and fat. I know I should buy maternity clothes, but I'm tired and busy with school and work. There doesn't seem to be time to go shopping.

I notice a pregnant woman at church. Even with her round belly, she looks thin. I'm jealous. I want to look like that. I want to have a baby bump protrude from a thin body as an obvious sign of my own pregnancy. I want people to *know* that I'm pregnant, not wonder and be afraid to ask in case I've just gained weight.

* * *

Friends and aunts start asking me if I feel the baby moving. I don't. I go from one day to the next with the knowledge that I'm pregnant, but with no inward or outward sensations to confirm this. I look at my naked body in the mirror in order to see my pregnant self. My mom tells me she never felt her babies move until her last month of pregnancy. I think that's probably when I'll feel my baby too. But one Sunday evening, with still almost five months to go, a little bubble rises from somewhere inside me and then disappears. I assume this is what everyone has been so eager for me to feel.

On the ultrasound monitor I can see the baby growing inside me. It's folded up like a contortionist. The technician points out black blotches, and I'm comforted to see that a brain and other essential human organs have developed in the darkness of my inner cavity. I don't feel a connection between my body and the baby on the screen. Still, I ask my friends if they want to see the picture of *my* baby.

I feel fat in my increasingly tight wardrobe. I finally go shopping one Friday night. The saleswoman at the maternity store is extremely helpful. She pulls at least twenty tops and six styles of pants off the racks for me to try. I curtain myself into a cubicle, strip down to my underwear and bra, and buckle a little pillow belly around my waist. I try every item of clothing and sort them into piles: yes, no, maybe. The saleswoman brings more outfits. After an hour and a half I'm hungry and tired, but I still haven't decided what to buy. I choose my favourites by looking at the price tags in the yes pile. I try them on again without the pillow and decide on two pairs of pants. Then I select five tops including a lycra shirt with big blue flowers that I think makes me look undeniably pregnant. I leave the store wearing a new outfit. I feel attractive and happy, and I make no attempts to hide my maternity-store shopping bags like I so often did with the ones from Penningtons.

I'm pleased with my new clothes. They fit and display my pregnancy. I'm comfortable and my body feels like it's mine. For the first time in my life, I'm proud of my convex stomach.

* * *

I convince myself that eating a Rice-Krispies square in the middle of the afternoon is just like eating a bowl of cereal. But shortly afterwards, its sweetness makes me feel nauseous and guilty. I worry that I'm on the verge of losing control of myself and my food intake. I breathe and the worry passes.

A friend tells me that one of her formerly overweight friends slathered baby oil all over herself to keep her skin hydrated during pregnancy. Afterwards, she found that some of her pre-pregnancy weight-related stretch marks had disappeared. Since my body is also scarred from years of obesity, I decide it's worth a try. I buy some oil at Safeway later that night.

While I lie on the couch studying, my stomach moves by itself. I put my book down and watch the spasms. That evening, when it happens again, I show my husband. Surprised and amazed, we laugh at the uncontrollable motion of my belly.

* * *

I notice that the pouch of stretched-out skin that has been hanging below my bellybutton for the last five years is no longer flabby. It's full. I stand naked in front of the mirror and see a pregnant, not fat, me reflected back.

One day I realize I can no longer bend at the waist. My stomach gets squashed when I try to tie my boots. The baby presses on my lungs and I feel winded. I move the plastic kitchen stool to the front door so I can put my shoes on without suffocating.

I also now struggle to get vertical from horizontal. I experiment with different ways of getting out of bed. Swinging my feet over the edge and rolling out is the easiest. When he's around, I ask my husband to pull me up from the recliner in the living room. In class and at the computer, I lean backwards so my stomach doesn't squish out above and below my waistband like a balloon squeezed at the middle.

Most of my family hasn't seen me since summer. On the phone my mom repeats that she can't wait to see me at Christmas. As soon as I walk through the door, she wants me to take off my coat so she can see the baby and touch it through my sweater and skin. My aunts comment.

"There's hardly anything there," one says.

"Are you eating enough?" the other asks.

When my dad sees me, he hugs me from behind wrapping his arms around my belly. It shatters my unfounded belief from years ago that my large body was an embarrassment to him.

* * *

The doctor tells me I've put on some weight. "You've gained five kilos."

I mentally convert five kilos to eleven pounds. I'm horrified. It's been years since I've gained weight that quickly. The doctor is unconcerned. He chalks it up to Christmas and assures me I'll be at the right weight when the baby comes. I try to believe him, but hours later I'm still wondering how long it'll take to lose those eleven pounds after the baby is born. Other women tell me I'll lose the weight quickly if I nurse, but it's hard to believe them.

At our prenatal class, I notice that almost all the other women have nice round bellies that extend like advertisements for pregnancy while they remain slim. I think I look rolly and fat compared to them. Even though rationally I know that my lycra shirt—the one I bought because it made me look pregnant—is partly to blame, I'm still near tears. I feel like every roll from my breasts to my pubic bone is being accentuated by those big blue flowers undulating over my curves. I can't distinguish where I end and my baby begins. I'm envious of the other women and their protruding bellies. I want to look pregnant too—not fat. I decide never to wear that shirt ever again.

* * *

The prenatal classes and the pregnancy books scare me and don't answer my questions. What will my vagina be like after passing a baby through it? Will I lose urinary control? Will I leak and smell? Will I still experience sexual pleasure? How much blood will I lose after the birth? For how long will I continue to bleed? Will I lose the weight I've gained? When? How long will it take? Will I still want to eat so often? Will I be able to keep some perspective about the roll of skin that will once again hang deflated around my waist? Will I be able to remember that it isn't fat?

"Is the baby still moving around?" the doctor asks.

"Yes, but less." He makes me go to the hospital for a non-stress test. I lie flat on my back with a thick band strapped around my waist for two hours. Every time I feel the baby move, I push a button and it is recorded on a data output sheet. According to the heartbeat monitor, the baby is active. The nurse is amazed that I don't feel anything at some of the surges. I joke that it must be because I have a lining of fat that absorbs the impact.

"I don't think so," says the nurse. "You don't have any fat."

I'm surprised by her comment. Even after five years of maintaining a healthy weight, it still surprises me when others don't think I'm fat. I joke with her that my fat is compressed, like Thinsulate.

"Any day now," the doctor says. I dress in my favourite maternity clothes, fix my hair and pose for a late-pregnancy photo-shoot. My pregnant belly is round and beautiful—until I sit. Then it rolls over the band of my pants. It doesn't do that when I'm naked. For the first time in my life, I prefer my naked body to my clothed body.

Later that night, I stand in front of the mirror and look at the body reflected back to me. I run my hands over my belly, saddened

The Lucky Ones

ANNE CAMERON SADAVA

"NORAH YOU LOOK FABULOUS!" says our male dinner guest looking admiringly at my seventeen-year-old.

His wife glances at me and inquires softly, "Is everything okay?" I know what she means but I haven't faced the question myself yet.

Recently I have only seen Norah fully clothed and swathed in artsy scarves, or bundled in her bulky blue housecoat, but a few days after that dinner I come upon her in front of a mirror lifting her shirt for some reason. Hip bones protrude from her concave abdomen like sand dunes from a sunken desert. The truth that I've been trying so hard to avoid hits me square in the eyes: anorexia.

"No way," says my husband Mike, in whose eyes she is always perfect. "I was really skinny too at that age. She's fine. You're just a worrier."

"No way," say both her older brothers who adore her. "Don't worry Mum. She's way more together than either of us. If she says she's okay, then she is."

"Oh yes," says my friend who has known her all her life. "Thank goodness you've brought it up. I've been wanting to, but I wasn't sure how."

"I'm perfectly fine," Norah says angrily. "I'm just eating healthy food." Less and less foods seem to be "healthy" as time goes on.

She tells me: "I can't eat when I first get up." "I'm going for a run. I don't eat before exercising." "I'm not hungry right now." "I ate at school." "I ate at work." "I'll eat later." "I can take care of myself."

My daughter radiates tension and defensiveness like an invisible force field.

Surreptitiously I start haunting the kitchen after everyone's in bed, counting the slices of bread in the bag, the apples in the bowl, the eggs in the fridge, and checking the garbage for evidence. It feels horrible not to trust my own daughter. However, while her words say one thing her body shouts another.

We find ourselves sitting in a familiar office waiting for Doctor B., the GP who delivered Norah seventeen years ago. As my daughter leafs through magazines, I catch a sideways glimpse of what she's reading: it is an article about the rise in obesity. It stresses that omnipresent advice she does not need: eat less and exercise more. I look away and see a fading Kodak poster of chubby-cheeked babies sitting propped up in a row. I used to like looking at those well-fed babies, but not today. It doesn't seem long since Norah's little body was round and healthy too, progressing rapidly up the weight chart on a tidal wave of breast milk and mother love, reassuring me that I was doing my job well.

Doctor B. arrives and weighs Norah, who seems surprised to learn she is well below the minimum body mass index considered healthy. The doctor quietly asks about her eating habits and feelings about food. Norah gives all the right answers. Charming and convincing, she assures the doctor that she will eat a bit more and gain back some pounds while in France for an upcoming student exchange. They laugh about how French food will make this easy and I try to believe it. The doctor tells us to come back if this doesn't happen. No need to cancel the trip.

As the month-long exchange trip slowly wears on, with occasional brief cheery emails from France, my pendulum brain swings back and forth: *I believe she will come back healthy.* No I don't, I only want to believe that, but I know she won't. *Nonsense! I can't know that. Why be so pessimistic?* I'm just being realistic. I'm the only one who recognizes the truth. *Or maybe I'm jumping to the worst conclusion too fast. I must try to relax and have faith in her.* No, I must be ready to insist that she gets help whether she wants it or not.

In friends' homes, on the streets, in parks, in stores, my eyes seek the reassurance of other bodies as thin as my daughter's but

I find none. I see only young women glowing with health in the summer sunshine. I covet the beautiful flesh curving over the bones of other mothers' daughters.

While Norah's away, I read everything I can find about anorexia. I read about all the preventive things parents should do to counteract the pressures of modern media and the fashion industry on young girls. Surely we've done those things? At least most of them? At least as well as most parents manage to? I read about the attitudes and examples related to food that should be shown within families. A healthy diet but not health-obsessed. Lots of veggies and fruit every day. Pop and chips rare but not forbidden. Regular family mealtimes. Check, check, check. I notice some of the criteria do fit. We are middle-class. Norah is high-achieving, a perfectionist, a dancer. She had a plump phase in late childhood. And yes, she has increasingly restricted her eating habits and taken up strenuous exercise. I seize upon anything that does not fit. The literature says anorexics are usually socially isolated, but Norah is quite the reverse. Depressed? No sign of that. Lacking confidence? She used to be very shy, but not anymore—a drama teacher recently said, "Norah owns the stage." Poor relationships with critical fathers? Again, just the opposite. A history of abuse? Unthinkable. Mothers who are controlling and overprotective? Am I? I never thought of myself that way, but it might fit.

Can such a thing be in one's genes? I become haunted by memories of my own struggle with the same demon thirty-five years ago, before eating disorders were ever talked about as they are today. I remember the way monstrous threatening calories dominated my thoughts for a year or two back then, and how hard I fought to keep them from entering my body. I remember hearing the word "anorexia" for the first time, and being surprised that there was actually a word for this private prison I had thought my own unique invention. It's a battle I've been sure for all these years that I'd won for good. I haven't spared a conscious thought for it in decades. Now it rises up vividly in my memory as it is relived in front of me—as does the face of my own mother worrying over me.

But why Norah? My daughter's childhood has been so different from mine. I grew up in a Scottish household ruled firmly by an old-school ex-military father, and in an isolated all-girls boarding school. By late adolescence I was desperate for the independence and freedoms of life in the rapidly changing student world of the Sixties, but it was an extremely difficult transition to make. Surely Norah has none of the reasons I had for struggling on the brink of adulthood? While her reasons may be different, my daughter's struggles apparently take the same form as her mother's.

Perhaps Norah has always been too perfect. Both our sons, in their mid-teens, treated us with adolescent disdain, slacked off in school and tested limits in typical teenage fashion. Between them they crashed a van, had a couple of minor run-ins with the law, abused a number of substances and caused us many sleepless nights. Norah has never put a foot wrong. I can't even remember a single tantrum when she was a toddler. Never a rude or defiant word right to this day. Never a poor mark in school or a foul mood. She's been singing, dancing and acting her way through adolescence while acing all her academic courses at the same time. Too good to be true it now seems.

After a very long month, Norah returns home from France and looks "just about the same," says my husband. She's even thinner. Hugging her I feel only bones. I try to welcome her back and listen to her tales of adventure and impressions of France before broaching the dreaded topic. I finally do so during a car ride. There is a long pause as she looks out the window, "It wasn't quite as easy as I thought. I guess my brain has been playing tricks on me a little. But I know I can do it Mum. Please let me do it my own way. I don't want help. Please trust me. Give me another month."

Eyes on the road. I wonder if I am ruining my relationship with her for a long time to come but I say, "No my dearest. We must get you some help. I've made an appointment with Doctor B. tomorrow."

Just as I feared, when Dr. B. weighs Norah she is seven pounds lighter.

We sit in a psychiatrist's office at the eating disorder clinic. Norah is tense and resentful and Mike is sceptical and bewildered. The psychiatrist, jovial and relaxed, talks about anorexia being "forty percent genetic." What does that even mean? I am forty percent responsible, but in a way I could not help? What about the other sixty percent? I must be responsible for that too, in a way that I of all people should have been able to prevent. He also lists statistics regarding recovery rates, relapse rates, and the chances of anorexia leading to permanent damage and death. Norah will have some tests, and then attend the clinic's nutritionist weekly, and the psychiatrist monthly, but there's a waiting list for individual counsellors. "We'll let you know when one is available. Her case is not quite severe enough to require hospital admission."

A few days later, I make roast chicken, which Norah used to love, with stuffing, potatoes, gravy and green beans. The familiar delicious smell fills the house. Sunday dinner has always been one of our best family times, but there are only three of us left at the table now since both boys have left home. Norah cuts a small portion of chicken into tiny morsels and chews them at length or pushes them around the plate. She picks up one piece of bean at a time on her fork. Each bite I witness going into her gives me an irrational amount of hope, and each one left on the plate an equal amount of despair.

"How was your rehearsal today?"

"Fine. How was your day?"

"Fine. Have a little gravy?"

"No thanks."

I pass my daughter a box of chocolates. She cuts a single chocolate in half, nibbles on one half, and puts the other half back in the box.

And so we go on. I try not to watch how much she eats but I cannot help myself. I try to pretend I'm not watching, but I know she's not fooled. She tries to make it look like she's eating more than she is, but she knows I'm not fooled. I find myself eating more than I want, as if it would encourage her. She avoids mealtimes altogether whenever she can, and I am both relieved and devastated when she does not show up. How can I nurture her? It is the question consuming my mind day and night.

I continue to read. I read about sites on the Internet where anorexics encourage each other in self-destruction. I watch how much she is online—not much to my relief. I read all the pamphlets from the clinic several times through. Be encouraging without putting on pressure, they say. Provide frequent small nutritious high-calorie snacks. She declines them. Have her eat at least five times a day. They don't explain how.

Nobody from the clinic has communicated with me since that first day. I feel shut out. Is that deliberate? I'd like an appointment but I read that mothers of anorexics are pushy and controlling and need to back off. I hesitate to phone and be that exact thing. But isn't there any more advice for mothers? To my relief I find a colleague who has a daughter going through the same thing. We start stealing the occasional fifteen minutes at work, in quiet corners, to share information, feelings and tears.

Time crawls, and a treacherous minefield stretches between me and my precious daughter. I see her suffering but I cannot reach her. I find myself hesitating over every word that comes to my lips for fear of a misstep pushing us farther apart. I rack my brain for memories of anything that helped me long ago when my mind was trapped in that dark, fearful place. Certainly nothing my mother said to me helped. I only remember resenting her endless fussing. Day follows painful day.

Still no word of counselling and the clock is ticking. When Norah turns eighteen I will no longer have the right to insist on treatment. Mike and I arrange private counselling for Norah once we realize we cannot wait any longer for the clinic. Norah is disparaging about the counsellor, who she says is more interested in our cheque than in her, but she goes.

Soon Norah will leave school and she is saving money and wants to travel. Will it be controlling, if I oppose this plan? Letting go of a healthy child at eighteen is one thing, but letting go of one who does not eat enough to survive? What is right? I have no idea anymore. I am lost in a maze of questions with no answers.

Then, one day just after her eighteenth birthday, Norah and I walk arm-in-arm on Whyte Avenue in the weak spring sunshine. We go to buy a yoga outfit and she chooses size small rather than the better fitting extra-small. "I want it to fit for a while so I'll probably need this one," she says and I am quietly elated.

We stop for coffee at a little café. She drinks hers black and turns down a muffin, but we cup our hands around the steaming mugs, and talk about things other than food. My daughter tells me some of her hopes and dreams for the future. She says: "Mum, I'm so glad we can still do this. We haven't let the eating business ruin our relationship altogether." Tears prick my eyes. I hold onto those words through many a long night.

And slowly the darkness starts to lift for Norah, as it once did for me. She eats a little bit more, puts on a few pounds and looks less skeletal. Meanwhile, her busy life continues and when summer comes again she graduates from high school with many accolades and plans her travels. Things are still very tense around the topic of food, and she is still very thin, but she has definitely made progress, and now my husband and I are in agreement. It is important to let her go and to have faith in her. I understand my daughter's desire for adventure and for the freedom to redefine herself, but I am still afraid that she'll try to make her money last by skimping on food.

I accompany Norah on the first leg of her trip, a flight to London, as I'm on my way to spend two weeks visiting my frail mother in her English nursing home. Calm and composed Norah marches ahead of me to check in for our flight. Her slight frame in its loose-fitting jacket is dwarfed by a huge backpack. On our long flight, as if to reassure me, she eats every scrap of the meal—salad, bun, lasagna, dessert—and I feel a surge of gratitude as I deliberately file that memory. An airplane meal has never looked so nourishing. At Heathrow we disembark, unsure if it's day or night, and walk side-by-side within the stream of travellers along dingy yellow fluorescent-lit hallways. Pictures of Beefeaters and British Bobbies welcome us to England. I brace myself for our goodbye when suddenly the arrow to Baggage Claim diverges from the one to Connecting Flights. With a quick peck and "Bye Mum, love you," my daughter heads off amid the throng without looking back. She's gone.

As my daughter starts exploring Europe, I sit by the bedside of my mother who is now well past being able to talk about her own experiences as an adolescent or as a mother. I wonder about her body image, coming of age in the 1930s. Polio trapped her in bed, then a wheelchair and later an iron leg brace, right at the age when other girls were out dancing. Wartime rationing restricted the diet of the whole nation. My mother had a very different adolescence than her daughter. What sense could she have made of my self-imposed starvation? Perhaps even less than I can make of Norah's.

In the nursing home, I spoon-feed this frail shadow of the woman who once tried so hard to feed me. She is now so shrunken she probably weighs less than Norah, but she obediently opens her mouth for every bite. I wheel her around the gardens, trying to keep her comfortable and reassured, letting her know I am beside her. I wish we'd had a conversation sometime in the intervening years about my anorexia. I wish I had shared my thoughts, and acknowledged what she must have gone through. Walking in her shoes now, I silently apologize to her for never initiating such a conversation. I marvel at her restraint in leaving that choice to me.

In emails and rare phone calls during the long months that my daughter travels on her own around Europe and then Morocco, the burning question I cannot ask is: "Are you eating enough?" It is the first question in my head when I wake up in the morning and the last at night before I sleep. I ask Norah to send photos, not to see scenery so much as the flesh on her bones. They rarely come and when they do my daughter is behind the camera.

* * *

Norah is fine now. She survived that trip and many others in the six years since that nerve-wracking time. She survived anorexia. Now she sits at our table, age twenty-four, during one of her flying visits to Edmonton. Sunlight pours in the window, reflecting my intense gratitude as I drink in the sight of her, glowing with health and happiness, her sweet round face full of enthusiasm for life, an independent young woman in every way.

I show Norah what I've written about her and ask how she would feel about me sharing it. I'm a little nervous, wondering if it is presumptuous egotism, this urge to tell what is really my daughter's story. Wondering if it's an unfair intrusion even to ask.

"Well it was not fun to read," she says, "and I remember some of it differently of course, because it's just your perspective. Some of it I hardly even remember at all. Maybe I don't want to, but I think also my brain wasn't working that well. Recently someone posted a photo on Facebook from Grade Twelve. I looked like an alien, but I didn't see that then."

My daughter is fine with my writing being shared. "There are such taboos about it," she says, and "I want to help break them."

Norah talks to people about her experience quite often because so many people go through something similar, many more than are recognized. Many have much worse stories. She and I are the lucky ones.

Daring more now, I ask her how to end the story. What was it that freed her mind from that obsession and helped her eat normally again? She hesitates. It was not one thing. She is not sure, but she mentions two specific moments. One was seeing other girls in the waiting room at the clinic. She didn't want to belong there with them and remembers committing herself to recovery as she waited. Another was in the *hammam* (public baths) in Morocco. Looking at the wide range of shapes and sizes of naked women unselfconsciously washing and visiting together, and feeling the sisterhood amongst them all, Norah says she felt a new comfort with her body. I find humbling irony in the fact that my western daughter, raised amongst supposedly liberated feminists, found comfort with her body in the openness of Islamic women's tradition.

Casting back for my own answer, I remember one turning point when I unexpectedly caught sight of a stick figure in what I then realized was a mirror, and another when a doctor said my fertility was at risk. But mostly for me recovery was also as Norah describes: a slow process. She credits a combination of supportive friends, time and new experiences, of learning how to relate as a sexual being, and of gradually finding the life she wanted, and the confidence to live it on her own terms. She can't talk long as she has to rush off and get on with living it—meet up with friends, go to yoga, prepare a drama class she'll be teaching.

And eat? I no longer even wonder. My daughter will eat when she's hungry.

Goodbye, Girl

LESLIE VRYENHOEK

"WILL YOU DRIVE ME BACK THERE?" With those words, Raquel pulls me in to the full circle of her idea. I can't seem to say no to that backwards epic of our years-ago journey. Maybe it's the rewind I want, time moving in reverse until we're both younger, our lives bursting with potential.

Anyway, it's impossible—too far, too long, I'm too busy. I can't be expected to drive back six days alone. But then our moving-away neighbours mention they need someone to drive their car to the mainland and my schedule clears. Next thing I know, we're fitting Raquel's must-haves tightly into the neighbour's Subaru. The rest of it—the detritus of her steady march through university, the what-not from forays in apartment living, the shifting accessories of a girl becoming woman—"All that," she says, "you can throw away." All that is scattered all over the floor. I want to tell her just one more time to clean her room but I don't want to start anything. Instead, I silently accept that, weeks from now, I'll be cursing the mess she's left behind.

Raquel has other turmoil on her hands and his name is Luke. Beside the car, they cling together in grief. Kisses last a lifetime—and they have to. They've agreed this is goodbye, absolutely the end, none of that long distance crap. No agony of hours on Skype to drag out their grand finale. Raquel's stepfather and I stand on the sidewalk and pretend it's the bitter Newfoundland wind making the tears stream down our cheeks. Luke isn't the first boy we've watched Raquel kiss goodbye, but he might just be the best.

Finally, I call it. We have to traverse this whole island before dusk, before the moose are on the move. When I hug my husband, he mutters, "Don't kill each other," and he doesn't mean in a highway accident, though he's mentioned that, too.

After we're fastened in, Luke leans through the window to whisper one last "I love you." Raquel whimpers. I sink my teeth into my lower lip, the car into drive, and I think *Christ, five thousand kilometres of this.* Heading for the Trans-Canada Highway, I expect her to say, "Stop. Turn around, I'm staying." I'm hoping for it, really, but she doesn't say a word, not until she asks to drive when we stop for gas. She's dry-eyed, cried out for now, and she'll stay that way until the next harsh reminder of what she's left behind.

But this isn't really a story about young lovers torn asunder: it's a much more arduous farewell tour. It's the story of our last mother-daughter road trip together.

* * *

I was a too-young mother, a single parent barely formed up myself as I raised two daughters in Winnipeg, the three of us hammering away at fixer-uppers and bouncing fickle dreams around on long car trips. We'd put on plenty of miles together before the longest haul of all: the drive from Winnipeg to St. John's nearly seven years ago. Only by then, there were just two of us. For me, it was a destiny-calling kind of adventure. I was in love and chasing what felt like a last-chance for happiness. Raquel, just out of high school, was looking for a fresh start far from the turbulent adolescence that had exhausted us both. But at 19, my older daughter Caitlin claimed to be too rooted in Manitoba so I left her living in my house, safe under my roof, tethered to me by so much stuff.

Providence did not smile on our journey east. We said goodbye to Caitlin in a steady downpour. I'd barely got the hang of steering with an overstuffed U-Haul dragging behind when Raquel's fever and closing throat made Kenora Hospital a necessary stop. Two days later, the antibiotics were working but the rain kept coming and the chains that lashed us to our belongings began to drag. We lightened our load, abandoning books and pots roadside, leaving behind the heirloom cut-glass punchbowl my mother had passed on to me.

* * *

Today, sunshine has lifted Raquel's spirits. I'm back at the wheel as she slides in Disc One of our audio Spanish lessons. She thinks another language might be helpful in finding a career. We're talking a lot about her career lately—or her lack of one, her uncertain path now that she's finished that BA and has a résumé full of restaurant jobs.

By the time we reach our hotel, we've learned to say hello, then goodbye. We can ask for *la direcciones* and we've introduced ourselves, over and over again, to each other in Spanish.

The next morning, hours to kill before the night ferry, we head to Gros Morne National Park so Raquel can see the glory of the west coast before sailing from this island. We hike the windy Tablelands, where millions of years ago a continental collision pushed the earth's underside up over its thin skin. We show off, naming rocks and plants, knowing what's what because we stopped in at the Interpretive Centre first. We wander off-trail, clamber up the rocky edge of a stream to a waterfall. Later, we drop to our knees and peer in wonder at the frail beginnings of new rock forming in shallow pools. Every few minutes I make Raquel pose for another picture like I can hold her in these moments forever.

Back on the highway and heading to the Port aux Basques ferry, Newfoundland really starts turning it on. The low sun sparkles on ocean waves while a full moon rises white against a denim blue sky. Entering the terminal, we pass under a sign that reads "Thank you for visiting our province." Raquel slams her hand over her heart as if to hold it in her chest.

We endure a night of smooth if mostly sleepless sailing, earplugs no match for the loud talkers, for all that prattle that passes for Newfoundland friendliness. I think this, and then I think, *This is just the kind of thing I won't be able to say aloud once Raquel is out of earshot.*

Trouble begins when we exit the ferry, a loud rattle rising from underneath the car. But this backwards journey west is not cursed: there's a full service garage down the first road we try in North Sydney. A man whose shirt says *Rick* tells me to come right in. Rick recognizes the rattle. "It's the heat shield on the exhaust. They rust, come loose and can't be reattached. But they're easy to remove," he says, "You'll never miss it." He lets us stay in the car and hoists us high. A torch is lit before I think to yell down, "Wait! It's our neighbours' car!" Rick yells back, "They'll never miss it either!"

Thirty minutes and forty dollars later we're back on the road, looking for breakfast. We don't see a proper diner in this town so we try the Zellers. We're thinking about the in-store restaurant where we ate every week in Winnipeg with my grandmother, little Raquel slipping under the table, disappearing down aisles and inside circular racks of clothing. But the restaurant in this Zellers is gone and so is just about everything else. What's left forms a tight knot under a banner proclaiming 70% off. We waste a lot of time gathering up the best bargains—pants and canned drinks and tissues—forgetting how little room there is in the car.

The cashier tells me she's worked here for thirty-odd years, ever since she was a teenager, but her job will vanish with the store. Both of her barely grown children have moved away for work. I ask what she'll do now and she shrugs: "Stay home and wait for grandchildren, I guess."

After our Spanish lesson, Raquel announces she's going to nap and pulls a pillow from the backseat. "Oh, God," she moans. I know instantly what's happened. The pillow smells like Luke. She buries her face in it and weeps for at least twenty kilometres.

In Grand Falls, New Brunswick, we drive the length of town to see the falls. Peering into the tumult, I tell Raquel it reminds me of whitewater rafting in Tennessee. I've been doing that all day, letting things along the road serve as reminders of something else. "Remember the night we pitched the tent in the Grasslands on a bed of cactus?" "Remember when a football game broke out on the sidelines of a massive roadwork tie-up on Vancouver Island?" "Remember the food poisoning in Indiana, how hard we laughed about the bald guy on the I-90 billboard, the nasty fight we had on a sidewalk in Fredericton?" Recalling until it seems our quarter-century together has been just one long road trip. And maybe it has.

Zip lines stretch across the Grand Falls gorge from one side to the other. It's late and they're gated and I'm grateful. Raquel would want to try it. A decade earlier, on a hike in Alberta, she'd insisted on climbing a more difficult path by herself. When she called out for help—matter-of-factly, like she was calling out for someone to bring her a roll of toilet paper—I spotted her on a small ledge, a steep wall to one side and a sheer drop on the other. A big leap to safe ground. I froze, paralyzed by seeing my baby so precipitously balanced, unable to trust that my shaking hand could catch her. I had to send Caitlin, always so steady, down the steep pitch to bring her sister across.

* * *

It took me two years to understand that my very grounded older child needed the absolute opposite of tethering. She'd taken the brunt of my bossiness all her life, been my reliable assistant for so long it likely felt I'd nailed her feet to the floor.

When I went back to Winnipeg from Newfoundland to get Caitlin out from under my suffocating roof, I drove straight from the airport to the bakery where she worked, not anticipating the hairnet or the way she shooed me from the counter when her regulars showed up. Waiting for her to finish work, I sipped the lemon tea she'd made and quelled the urge to rush over and wipe up cake crumbs. Instead, I busied myself with a list full of verbs—repair, scour, fix, and paint. It ran the length of notebook page. At the bottom I wrote, *Get rid of crap!*

We had eight days to get it all done, to ready the house for market. I wanted to reap a good return, to make a little nest egg for a girl whose growing up was complicated by way too many nests. I hoped, too, for the chance to reno our mother-daughter relationship, to shed the cumbersome baggage that weighed us down.

In the house, I walked from room to room, trying to see beyond the scattered debris and the thick grime that obscured everything. When we'd moved in, I'd tacked the letters J-O-Y over the kitchen doorway but the J was now missing, leaving just O-Y.

I found a working vacuum in the basement. Caitlin looked genuinely surprised. I asked what she and her roommate used on the floors. "Oxygen," she deadpanned. "It's quite plentiful." I had to remind myself that after two years, there wasn't a single hole in the plaster, that they'd put down new flooring in the back porch. That there were bills marked *PAID* on the counter and good food in the fridge.

Each day, I rolled out of bed and into my painting clothes, resisted the urge to assign tasks. Caitlin was, after all, an adult now, not some teenager I could send on errands. I tried to keep the mother superior out of my voice, to be more of a gentle persuader than a drill sergeant. Finally, she said, "Mom, it would be easier if you just told me what to do." So I gave in and I gave orders, made her a list of her own. She looked relieved.

Late at night, I started in on all I'd left behind—photos and memorabilia: report cards, concert ticket stubs, scrawled notes, newspaper clippings, and old diaries. So much to sort through.

As we worked, Caitlin said she might like to go back to school, study something as unexpected as linguistics. She told me she'd really liked being in charge of the house but it was fun having me home for a while. I looked over to where her steady brush had made a clean line between wall and ceiling and I realized, in my absence, she'd already sorted it all out.

* * *

At the top edge of the windshield as Raquel and I bisect Quebec, I see the first rainbow cloud, a cirrus-shaped smudge of colour. I think it must be a tint on the windshield but when I slide down in the passenger seat and look from all angles, it doesn't change. Finally I ask, "Do you see that cloud?"

Raquel says, "Yeah, but I wasn't gonna say anything. I thought it must be the windshield."

I lean out the window to snap a picture. It's hard to make out in the photo but it's undeniably there—a rainbow, in the shape of a small cloud. An hour later, we've edged into Ontario and there's another one, unmistakable. This one's smaller, less distinct but definitely wearing its rainbow pride.

In a hotel room in Ottawa, having sorted out the neighbours'-car-for-rental-car swap, we Google "rainbow clouds," laughing nervously because we know it's crazy, because we're road crazed. In a fraction of a second we're looking at dozens of images that look just like what we saw.

"Circumhorizontal arc" is a refraction of sunlight through ice crystals—possible only at the right time of day at the right time of year, when there's just the right type of clouds. Plus you have to look up to spot it. Yet we saw this remarkable thing twice—two separate rainbow clouds in two different provinces on the same day. Giddy with our good fortune, we go to a real restaurant, eat salad and steaks and talk about Luke, and then about his predecessor, about how shattering heartbreak can be and what love might look like when it comes to stay.

Raquel tells me that she's scared of making a mistake she can't unmake, that she's afraid this next part will be even harder than she imagines—regrowing roots, finding a career, building a grown-up life. She's worried she'll be homesick for St. John's, just as she's been homesick for Winnipeg all these years.

Always missing someplace else: it's the cut-glass punchbowl I never meant for her to inherit.

Ontario goes on forever as we crawl along the low-speed southern branch of the Trans-Canada. Raquel wants to find somewhere interesting to stop—someplace like Tommy Bartlett's science centre in Wisconsin or that amazing maze in South Dakota. She didn't plan to just *drive*. She wants to *do* things. We've been getting along great but we've only passed the halfway point and there's an edge to her voice that experience tells me to heed. I consult the CAA Ontario Guidebook, circa 2003, pouring over attractions. Nothing on this route sounds interesting so I just read aloud the part about Thessalon: "Twenty-five per cent of the world's turkey production. Can you believe it?" We laugh and laugh and later, when we see two domesticated turkeys on the shoulder, proud as peacocks for the escape they've made, we feel like we've really seen something.

We see more things: a brown bear ambling into the woods, a dead moose being loaded into a pickup, an Amish man with his horse. Three dogs of different sizes complete a near-suicidal crossing in front of our car and Raquel yells, "Holy homeward bound!"

We've made good headway so we linger over dinner and take a slow swing through Sault Ste. Marie to find an open liquor store. It's that kind of soft-balm evening that suggests a drink on a patio under the stars. But once we're back on the highway, I realize we've pushed it and that twilight is winking into darkness.

There's just enough time to get nervous before a sweeping curve delivers us to the Voyageur's Lodge & Cookhouse. The proprietor, locking up when we arrive, unlocks and says she's got just one suite left and she'll give us a sweet deal because it's only got one bed.

When I awake, my daughter and I are pressed up against each other. I watch the familiar outline of Raquel, shoulders rising with each breath; I breathe her in. Beneath the tang of hair conditioner and last night's wine, she smells the same as she has since she was born, a smell like new rain on tall grass and all her own. I wonder if this is the last time we'll share a bed, if we'll ever be close like this again. She doesn't stir until I've got the coffee dripping, until I'm washing out the wine glasses from the night before.

Voyageur's Lodge is a full-service establishment, with a restaurant and a general store. Just across the highway, a sandy beach hugs the lake, sandbars fingering into the water. If enchanting had a cousin living on the side of Highway 17 in Batchewana Bay, this would be her. I tell Raquel, "I'm going for a walk" and she tells me not to take long, she's hungry. We agree to meet in the restaurant in half an hour.

I take the beach out and come back along the highway. It feels so good to move without wheels underneath but I rein it in at thirty-five minutes. When I stop back at the room for my purse, Raquel sits at her computer, half-dressed and sipping coffee.

"You're not ready?"

"Can't I just enjoy a cup of coffee?" That tone.

I say something about a schedule to keep. Or maybe I yell it and then we're both shouting, pointing out each other's unreasonable flaws—my despotic urgency, her nonchalant tardiness. She storms away, slams her suitcase while I loudly wash the coffee pot, amazed that we can travel so far yet steadfastly remain who we always have been.

With breakfast and a hundred kilometres behind us, we've calmed down, brightened up. In Wawa, we go looking for the big goose, the best we can do for a goofy attraction. Raquel camps it up, lets me take her picture beside it, one leg extended back, arms out, goose and girl taking flight.

Later, while she's in a gas station bathroom, I call to check in with my own faraway mother. Mom tells me she's just sold the dining room set, the big table that staged family dinners dating back before I was born. I run my memory over the curved back of each chair, each occupant, and I realize I've been thinking about this trip all wrong. It's not the distance in miles that will separate us. It's the inexorable thrashing of time.

* * *

In Winnipeg, Caitlin and I had filled a borrowed van with decades of accumulated crap—boxes of corroded plumbing parts, dust-covered canning lids, yarn from when I thought I might learn to knit. So many broken electronics. So much Styrofoam packaging. At the landfill, a stiff wind at our backs, we emptied the van, tossing our crap onto other people's broken pieces. A Styrofoam slab caught an updraft and we watched it lift, white as a cloud against the prairie sky as it sailed over heaps of cast-off aspirations before settling out of sight.

In the end, I kept very little from that house: a folder of my daughters' best school projects, a few decorations. And at the last moment, just before I relinquished to Value Village the wedding dress in which I'd married their father, I reached into the gold box and snagged the veil. Featherlight, easy to pack, one size fits all. "Hey Caitlin," I told her, "you could wear this to work today instead of your hairnet!" She declined, though three years later it formed part of her trousseau.

The rapid renovation complete, the real estate agent suggested an asking price beyond our hopes and we agreed to split the profit. I dropped her at the bakery on my way to the airport, knowing we were turning a blind corner, the terms of engagement between us forever altered. I hugged her again, begged her again to keep the house perfect until it sold. For the millionth time in her life, she nodded agreeably. And then I watched Caitlin sail away, unencumbered, into her own sky.

* * *

Raquel and I learn to tell time in Spanish, to talk about family and shop for a green blouse. Or at least she does. She's running far ahead of me, able to catch and hold phrases while I get a little more lost with each lesson.

When she takes the wheel, I study roadside signs. The moose on the warnings are different in every province. In Newfoundland, they're dumb behemoths standing over crumpled cars. In northwest

Ontario, they're charging bulls, beasts with intent. I think about collecting a set of these signs, about where I could display them and I almost ask Raquel her opinion on that. And then I realize who this is, this young woman sitting next to me for just one more day in a rental car. She's the only person who knows all the rooms of my life. She's lived in them too, these past twenty-five years. She knows why something matters, what parts are funny and why. She knows who was there and she knows who suddenly wasn't. She doesn't need a backgrounder on any of the players just as I don't need context for whatever event she's retelling. We both know if there were wounds to be dressed on some particular day.

Now our lives will diverge; we'll drift from understanding each other's narratives. Raquel will have her sister Caitlin and other family around, for which I'm glad. But I'll be alone on an island at the edge of her known universe, blood to no one. My memories will become dead weight the way a language does when its second-to-last speaker dies.

I stop myself there. I know better, know you can't claim your own child as a best friend or make her your archivist, not without doing damage. Besides, there are other things to worry about as dusk settles—like that beast moving slyly toward the highway in front of us. Raquel brakes expertly, crawls past, flashes her lights at oncoming cars and barely gets back up to speed before the next moose steps out from between the trees. Those signs aren't kidding, these big bulls mean business of the funeral home kind. We white knuckle it to the next motel.

It's raining when we fill the tank for the last time in Kenora, where years earlier we made our first stop. Just a few more hours, the home stretch, the miles in which I'll have to ditch my spot in the centre of this family and become, instead, adjunct to the lives my daughters are making. I avert my eyes so Raquel won't see the deluge I'm holding back. I hand her the keys.

Up ahead, the clouds part but I can't look yet at that looming horizon. As we cross into her home province, I focus only on the two words I'll hold in reserve should this girl ever need me again. "Rainbow clouds"—a private language, a delicate bridge across the expanse.

Let's Make Glitter Cards

A Mother's Journey Through Parental Alienation

SANDRA MCENHILL

T HE CHILDREN DON'T GO to Grandma's anymore. She lives two blocks away, but they have to go to Cathy's house after school now. Cathy is a stout, sanctimonious babysitter who thinks I'm a dreadful mother. Later in court she will say my daughter is sad because I never baked cookies with her. I pass Cathy's street on my way home from work each day. As I do, my mind fixates on that one crisp autumn afternoon.

My children race towards me, blonde ponytails flying behind, blue eyes bright. I imagine them saying, "Mom! Can we go to the park? Can we ride bikes? Can we get popsicles?" But that is not what they are saying. They frantically pass me, fly across the street and disappear down the alley behind Cathy's house. Baffled, I swiftly follow and glimpse only the sleeves of their pink jackets intertwined and hanging onto the edge of the fence. They are hiding from me. *Hiding from me?*

I want to call out, "Let's go to Grandma's! Let's bake cookies like we used to. Let's make glitter cards."

But I am silent. I am breathless and drowning. I turn away, hauling behind me the unspeakable weight of my unholy, disrupted maternal bond.

I didn't know about Parental Alienation then. I knew only a primal sorrow. Raw and relentless.

* * *

I look back on my indescribably gratifying initiation into parenthood when our first golden baby girl was born on autumn's vivid sunlit rays. As devoted first-time parents we gently swathed her in love. It was a delight to watch her toddle around in her red and white jumpsuit with her beloved book about Patrick and his grandpa. She and I would read it over and over, snuggled on the couch, lying on the floor, in the bathtub, or on the front step in the late summer sun. She laughed when our cocker spaniel followed her around sniffing out the arrowroot cookies she carried in a little bag. She would tell me in her cherub language that "It's waiming, no pakk today."

"Yes darling," I say, "it is raining. We won't be able to go to the park today."

She lit up my world in unexpectedly joyful ways and I was so in love with her, I was blind to everything else for an entire year. I had no inkling of the chilling destiny we had yet to live.

We added two more beautiful baby girls to our family. There were many years of happiness and contentment, a new house, mortgage, and little trips to Jasper House Bungalows. Alongside these joys and new beginnings however, there existed a vague disconnection whose genesis I cannot pinpoint. We found ourselves perplexed as misunderstanding, impatience, and resentment crept more habitually into our sacred family space.

* * *

In the midst of our breakdown, we wallpaper the hallway, walk the dog, enjoy family bike rides, scream and withdraw and wound each other. When the kids go to bed, I go out with my friends. I ignore all his needs and he seethes and churns. I am selfish. He is irrational. He feels wretched. I feel trapped. We don't know how to pause the suffering and recover the love that is swiftly becoming twilight bound.

I stumble through these days with the kids. I take them to the park and bake cookies.

"Can I put the chocolate chitts in mommy?"

I make them play dough and we do simple arts and crafts. Glitter cards are their favourite. We sit at the kitchen table and spread out the coloured paper, markers and glue and they excitedly line up the tiny bottles of glitter. We draw flowers and houses, children and bikes, and they carefully apply the glue and sprinkle the glitter.

"Look Mommy, this bike has silver wheels and the girl has sparkly gold hair."

My beloved babes are bursting with joy as they work on their precious glitter cards. When they climb onto my lap to proudly show off their creations, I kiss their soft round cheeks and feel their angel breath on my neck.

When the marriage finally disintegrates, the children live with me. Sometimes, they do not want to go on visits with their father because he is irate and after picking them up, he drives away in a rage, doors slamming and tires squealing. In response, I inexplicably follow the rules of parenting after separation and tell them that it's important for them to spend time together. They come home upset and confused.

"Daddy says Jesus is not in your house."

Within a year I begin to date and although it is distressing for my oldest child, I mistakenly imagine that in time she will come to accept this new reality just like thousands of other kids. I didn't listen closely enough or hear her pain. I allowed myself to be distracted and I let her down. I was unaware that her father was already busy stirring the soul of her sadness and playing on her anxieties for his own benefit. I was blind to the bleak image that was being painted, stroke by stroke, grey and black.

* * *

One day, he refused to bring my oldest daughter back to me after her visit at his home. Hysterical, I eventually discover that she is hiding at Cathy's house. My frantic attempts at retrieval are futile. Her father doesn't seem to care about her bond with me; he doesn't want to talk or mediate. She never returns to my care. Soon after, on a stifling hot day in August, I allow my middle child to go for a visit but I tell her that I am conflicted about sending her. She happily reassures me she will be back on Sunday. We both believe this. She never returns to my care. I imagine that she eventually cries as she is pulled into a motherless underworld. I ache for her pain and her loss, her innocence and vulnerability, and the unjust arrangement that has been imposed on her.

She is isolated. Our mother-daughter bond is disrupted. She follows her sister's lead at her father's prompting and is torn between the two halves of herself. Eventually she will believe that that this is what she wants.

In the beginning, she sends cards to her little sister and me. "I miss you. I want to see you guys so much."

She doesn't understand why she can't. I don't understand why she can't. The separation is unbearable. I feel weak, ineffectual and responsible. I cannot comprehend what I have done that could warrant such horrifying retribution.

"Grandma is so sad," I want to tell them. "Everyone misses you and loves you. It's not true what your father says about our family."

But I say nothing. I can't put any more pressure on them. They are sad and angry enough as it is.

Their father hastily transfers them to another school without informing me. They are now out of the old neighbourhood, far away from my house and cut off from grandma. I come to know less and less about their day-to-day lives, their soccer schedules, brownie outings, homework, or friends.

My lawyer finally gets me a court order for an eight-hour visit. When I get home from work that day they are frantically wailing in my living room.

"We don't want to be here," they cry. "We want to go back to Dad's house."

For the entire eight hours I am out of my body.

God please help us.

They have idealized him and demonized me. Later my lawyer tells me that their behaviour is abnormal and irrational. She says even children who are severely abused want to see their mother. I stare at her. I can't make sense of that.

There is nothing fertile or alive left in me. I rely on my mother, family, and friends to take care of me. They are the goddess Baubo, bringing me food, making me laugh, helping me to forget my sorrow. My mourning is deep and confused and I am in a state of complete powerlessness and guilt. *Is this my life? Should I have tried harder to keep the family together? Is this what I deserve?*

The children ignore me at soccer games and school concerts. The eldest one is dismissive and her sparse words sting for hours afterwards.

"You shouldn't allow her to talk to you that way," my friends say. I allow her to talk to me that way. I say nothing when she tells me that she won't ride in the same car with me to my sister's wedding. I breathe when she won't dance with me at the reception. I breathe when she doesn't return my phone calls. I know that she is hurting and angry. I know that she feels responsible for fixing her father's pain. When she glares at me, I still see round blue eyes and chubby cheeks. *It's waiming, no pakk today.* I now refuse to send the youngest child for visits as I am afraid that she won't return.

* * *

One day the school principal calls to inform me that her father has just removed my youngest from her kindergarten class. My subsequent phone calls to him are met with hostility. I am shaking, sweating, terrified. My family gathers and we decide we must retrieve her or she will become lost like the others. Six of us show up at his home and a screaming match ensues on the doorstep. I swiftly move through the house and gently lift the sleeping little one out of her bed. I later learn that the older two were huddled in their room, afraid that I would *steal them.*

"I am so sorry," I say, "that you had to experience that."

I bargain with God to let me raise the youngest one until she's eighteen. I'll give up anything. I'll go anywhere. Just give me this. I can't lose them all. I still go to work each day and walk around and breathe and eat sandwiches. But I don't know where the food goes because I am hollow inside. I dutifully attend the parenting assessment sessions and on the day that the document is finally complete, I pick it up from the psychologist's office and race back to the car, my heart hammering and a psychotic break fermenting. I'm too scared to look so I drive to a quieter spot several blocks away and flip to the last page—the recommendations.

* * *

The court trial lasts four days. It is horrifying. I am fighting for my life. My sister and trusted friends accompany me. They surround me with love and support. Lies are told, re-told, and recanted. In the babysitter's testimony, she theorizes that my eldest child is jealous of her child because her child has a mother to bake cookies with.

According to her, I never did that with my child. *Can I put the chocolate chitts in mommy?* She tells elaborate tales about how I did not sit with my child on the grade-four field trip. I recall that I had taken a day off work to go on that trip. My poor alienated child ignored me the whole time. I could only feel sad for her and the burden she carried. She pretended to take no notice of me, but I liked to think that some small part of her was happy I was there. That in some small way my presence reminded her she is dearly loved.

The trial is deeply humiliating. I am forced to listen to judgments about my family and my mothering. Absurd reasons are made for why I should not have custody of my children. One witness says my child told her she didn't want to see me. The judge asks this woman if she has any familiarity with children of divorce. She has none. Coming from a cozy intact family life, she has no inkling of the bewilderment and pressure experienced by a child in a custody dispute. The judge dismisses her testimony on account of her lack of credibility. This doesn't erase the hurt. After another independent witness speaks, it is discovered that she is actually a friend of the children's father. Therefore her testimony quickly loses credibility as well. I stare at these people in in the witness stand. I want to lunge at them and scream that they know nothing about my profound attachment to the beautiful children that I birthed into this world. I breathe. I hold back unfathomable fear and sorrow during these gruelling days. I cry myself to sleep each of the four long nights of the trial.

In his capacity as expert witness, the appointed child psychologist strongly recommended that the two younger children reside with me due to their father's alienating behaviours. He explains that children in this situation need their parents to respect bonds and build bridges so that the children can easily travel back and forth between mom and dad. He concludes that it is too late for the eldest child to be returned to me—too detrimental to remove her from her father's care. At the conclusion of the third day of trial, I am quivering and overwhelmed. A friend drives me directly to my therapist's office even though I don't have an appointment. I cannot speak for fifteen minutes. He helps me to sort out my conflict about bringing my middle child back to live with me. I want to be with her more than anything, but she and her older sister will be devastated to lose each other. I envision the middle one running away from me in order to get back to her sister.

The judge has seen the truth of this situation since the beginning. She speaks for a long time about parental responsibility to put the children first. To allow the children to love the other parent. To respect the child-parent bond. To make it easy for the children to access the other parent. This is essential for healthy psychological functioning and identity formation. She states that interference with this process is emotional abuse. She says she wants to make it clear to all parties that the mother has chosen to forfeit custody of the middle child for the child's benefit, not her own. She says the mother believes the child is already settled with her sister and father and moving her now could be troubling. She gives me joint custody of my older two daughters and sole custody of my youngest. This gives me the legal backing I need to be involved in their lives and it protects the youngest one from alienation. The visitation arrangement from that point forward is for the girls to spend every weekend together, alternating between my home and their father's home. The youngest child can spend two weeks in the summer with her father but they cannot be consecutive weeks. This will help to protect her from the forced maternal estrangement which is likely to occur.

When the last day of trial is over, I am somewhat calmed. I return home with my imperfect arrangement, eager to put this despicable chapter behind us. After supper I attend a soccer game for the middle child but she shrugs off my embrace. I don't know what she has been told about where her father had been for the past four days or how her child brain has processed the adult proceedings that she should have been shielded from.

We begin the period of twice-monthly court-ordered weekend visits with varied levels of success. In time, my feelings of depression begin to lift. I start to feel able to take control of the situation. One day I am close to their school and I stop by IGA. I buy turkey and tomato sandwiches with harvest cheddar Sun Chips and orange juice boxes and take them to the school office pretending to myself that my daughters forgot their lunches on the kitchen counter that morning. I like the feeling of being a normal mother

in a junior-high school hallway with other mothers dropping off
books and food and checking in on their kids.

* * *

Later when they are fourteen and twelve, I have an opportunity
to drive them to school in the mornings. I'm excited to have this
parental task and to be able to bring lunches for them. I make the
food as interesting as I can because I imagine that these lunches
can break down walls and move mountains. I bake chocolate chip
banana bread. I buy the best juice. I gently tuck the lettuce leaves
in between the slices of meat so that the bread won't get soggy. I
carefully wash their apples. Each night when the supper dishes are
done, I slip into a trance and complete this ritualistic intentional
act of love and hope. The next day we will drive to school and
talk a little. I will hand them their brown bags with their names
printed on.

"Bye guys. Have a good day." They slam the car door and rush
to class. *I love you.* The tears that fall as I drive away are softer
and more hopeful.

In time, I realize that a gentle thaw has finally found me. It quietly
creeps on its empty belly and slides under my door at night. It rises
up from the basement and slips through cracks in my windows.
I live in cautious gratitude that they might be returning from the
underworld.

In the years that follow, they are at my house often. At first
they come with a hesitant vulnerability and muffled warmth.
The reconnection is fragile but I am uplifted and make them
perogies, help with their English papers, and prepare them for
their social tests.

They wrestle with each other on my couch. Laugh. Shout. Bring
their girl dramas. Eat my spanakopitas and ice cream floats. They
come sobbing in the night with their boyfriend troubles and I
make tea in the pink flower teapot then we sit by candlelight and
gently walk through the minefield of adolescent love affairs. Their
resentments splinter and crack and we take small jubilant steps
forward. It becomes tougher for them to resist my imperfect and
persistent mothering. Their father has begun a new life and his
anger gradually fades to indifference. It is increasingly challenging

for them to believe the negative accounts that have been foisted on them. The weeds of alienation struggle to maintain their roots.

I phone their teachers. I get on the parent council. I take them on little trips. I drive them to sewing, swimming, and art. I help them create their first resumes. I file their first tax returns and knock forcefully on all doors that lead to their worlds. The universe gives me hundreds of ways to love them, help them, and be their mother. I am always the feminine force behind the scenes of their lives, holding them close to my heart and creating a sacred space for their emotional return. Gradually they openly love me back. The glaciers melt and warm waters gently trickle in. One Sunday afternoon in May they give me a Mother's Day card that intimates affection and tenderness. The spell is breaking.

* * *

We eventually take trips to far away places and share wonderful experiences in the here and now. They have become strong, lively, and passionate young women. They do not speak about the alienation, about those distant, aching days of desolation and neglect. Their feelings and memories from that time are hidden from me. Perhaps it is not for me to know their secret hurts. They have also felt profound motherly devotion and their earliest formative years were filled with love and wonder. Later on, they were exposed to a deeply rewarding and important experience they would not otherwise have had with new siblings and a stepmother. I ponder the destiny factor that seems to have threaded its way through our shared encounter.

I feel humbled to have been given the holy task of guiding these souls on their paths, through the sunny meadows, the glitter card days, the muddy waters and the jagged ground. I am finally making sense of the lost years, forgiving myself and releasing the pain. I am a good enough mother.

Behind the Gate

ANN SUTHERLAND

O UR 1950S-ERA DETACHED GARAGE is narrow and musty. It was built sixty years ago, long before the advent of the family van. The garage wall on the passenger's side is lined with shelves that hold flowerpots and baskets, camping equipment, and scraps of two-by-fours and plywood. The cramped space makes it impossible for me to get my two-and-a-half year old son buckled into his second row car seat. He must wait in the yard behind the back gate while I ease our 1993 Dodge Caravan out onto the driveway.

We've been held hostage for a week by a cold snap. Yesterday, a February Chinook swooped in like a caped superhero, bringing with it warm winds and the seeds of spring. Yesterday's melt also created a thin film of ice overnight that makes the sidewalk slick. The snow always looks tired this time of year. The wind has deposited bits of gray ash-like debris on top of the snow, and the warmer air has crystalized it, turning each flake into jagged pieces of glass.

My son, stuffed in his older brother's hand-me-down snowsuit, stands behind the gate. He squats and concentrates on patting the sharp snow with his mittened hand.

I tell him to wait. I yank the gate closed so he can't waddle onto the driveway and back alley. There's no need to latch it. The fence has shifted and the gate sticks so badly when it's closed that I have to kick it open.

I hoist the garage door, my left foot sliding on the slickened driveway. The springs groan as I push the door up along the track. I get into the van. It roars to life with the flick of my wrist, and I begin backing it out of its dank cave. It's a delicate manoeuvre.

Too close on either side and the mirrors will hit.

I inch my way out. I am sitting even with the garage door opening. I back out a few more inches. I look to my right to make sure the mirror clears and from the corner of my eye, I notice the back gate.

It's open.

* * *

The moment I discovered I was pregnant with my first son, I crossed the threshold from being motherless to being a mother even though he wasn't yet born. It's appropriate that materni-ty—the state of being a mother—sounds so like eternity. Once you become a mother, you become one forever. Your obituary will say, "loving, devoted mother" because above everything else you did in life, that is who you were and that's how you will be remembered. You also become a type of mother for eternity. The sacrificial mother, the patient mother, the alcoholic mother, the careless mother. Sitting in the van, and seeing the back gate open, I do not want to become that mother, the one who did and didn't do that, a label that would haunt me.

My husband and I are careful parents. We childproofed our home with locks on cabinets, gates at the stairs, electrical outlets covered, car seats properly installed, a crib and toys that met safety standards. Mothering was not to be left to chance. I chose to stay home and raise the kids. I wasn't leaving the upbringing to chance either. If I was a mother, that meant being a mother one-hundred percent. This was my new identity—"mom," under the subcategory of "stay-at-home."

In some ways, my world with babies became bigger—there were two more humans in our midst. In other ways, my world became smaller, a place populated by bowls of soggy Cheerios, a swamp of boggy diapers, and Dr. Seuss rhyming couplets. My vocabulary was reduced to monosyllabic mumblings. Those early years of motherhood are not mentally stimulating. I was too tired to read books that would excite my brain. Instead, I flopped on the couch, happy enough to watch a mindless reality show, which wasn't my reality. It was also my locking-myself-out phase. While my husband was at work, I'd lock the boys and myself out of the house. I'd lock my keys in the van, sometimes with the kids in it. Luckily that never happened on days that were too hot. Yet somehow, through sleep-deprived, muddled days, clarity came when I least expected it.

* * *

I grip the steering wheel and slam my foot on the brake. I turn my head. The gate is open, but that's as far as I can see—a wide gaping space between the garage and the side fence. I can't see if my son is behind the gate, safe in the snow.

I tell myself to put the van back into the garage. I tell myself that no, he's still in the yard. I tell myself to take ten seconds to get out and look. The one thing I don't tell myself is the thing I can't bear to face—that I've done the unthinkable. I drive those thoughts a thousand miles away. Things like that don't happen to a family like ours because we are responsible, loving and so careful. We will not be one of those stories splashed across newspaper headlines and shouted on newscasts: "Parent accidentally backs vehicle over child." Our story will not end in tragedy.

I take a breath. I put the van in park. I open the door. It's only four steps to the back of the van. My breath catches in my throat.

I see him. He's crying and helpless, his eyes pleading with me not to hurt him, begging me to not back our four-thousand pound van over him. At the age of two-and-a-half, my son understands that the difference between life and death is a space of three feet from the back right wheel. Somehow he has opened the gate and fallen on the icy driveway. Trapped in his slippery snowsuit, he can't get up. His screams were not loud enough for me to hear him over the engine and radio.

I rush to scoop him up. "No, no. It's okay. You're fine." I whisper long shhhhhh's into his cheek. "You're safe."

When I tell my husband, I make it all sound less terrifying. "Thank goodness for mother's intuition," I say lightly, patting myself on the back. I don't want to dwell. I don't want my husband to see me as reckless.

Later that night, my mind won't let go of what could have happened. I keep asking "what if?" What if I hadn't looked to the right? What if I hadn't seen the gate was open? What if it hadn't occurred to me that my son had opened the gate and gotten out?

163

My imagination plays out what could have happened. The only thing I can't imagine is how I would have lived with the consequences had the unthinkable happened. The grief and guilt would have been so overwhelming that it would have crushed me. I don't sleep that night.

A few days later I mention the incident to a friend.

"What stopped you?" she asks.

"Mother's intuition."

She nods. She understands. All mothers understand intuition, whatever that is. It is unexplainable and the only words I have to try and explain it is a catchall phrase to describe what can't be described. I can replace that phrase with sixth sense, hunch, inkling, instinct, gut feeling—that nudge that tells us something is wrong before we know we know it.

* * *

The truth is that mothering is a precarious thing. Too little of it and your child becomes feral, running willy-nilly through streets at midnight. Too much of it and you crush the life out of her or him. Mothering is one letter short of smothering. I want to protect my kids, but not stunt their growth. The gate is there to protect them, but at some point it needs to be opened for them to go through. The trick is keeping them safe on either side.

Now, after all these years of being a mother, I have a word to replace "intuition": fear. The fear we face in being mothers is not the kind of fear found in a horror flick, the kind that makes you panic and scream, a terror that can paralyze you. The fear I'm talking about is the kind of fear that is quiet. The kind that lies just behind the gate, always there, a thin layer between the snow and grass.

We want to keep our kids safe and it's the fear of them coming to harm that keeps us vigilant and hyper-aware in moments when we need it most. As mothers we don't want to admit fear as part of our vocabulary. I have been reading about intuition and even the experts have a hard time articulating what it is other than "gut feeling." What it is not, the experts say, is fear-based. But it is.

* * *

I never talked with my son about the incident until I started writing this piece. I ask him if he remembers the time I almost ran over him when he was a toddler.

A puzzled look crosses his face.

"No. You almost killed me?"

I cringe. "Not on purpose." I tell him the story. "You don't remember any of it, of how scared you were?"

He shakes his head.

* * *

The van is again parked in the back driveway. We've removed the rear seat so we can cram in all of our son's worldly belongings. In a few minutes we'll be driving him two hours to where he'll be attending his second year of college.

"That's it?" my husband asks.

"Yep," my son says. He slides into the middle seat as my husband slams the back hatch down before the boxes of books, pots, plates, clothes, blankets and sheets, pillows, sports bags, a beanbag chair and backpack can tumble out. I pull the back gate shut and hop into the front passenger seat. My husband starts the ignition.

"Wait." My son shuffles through the box beside him. "Have you seen my Adidas bag?"

I twist around to face him and point to the floor. "It's right there. At your feet."

"Oh, right."

"You're good, then?"

He nods. His mouth spreads into a smile. We drive off, east on the Yellowhead Trail, into a blindingly glorious morning sun.

Tell Me About Today

BOBBI JUNIOR

VINYL CAN BE CLEANED, disinfected. I stand to the side and watch as traces of vomit, feces, and other bacteria surrender their power to the hospital cleaning lady. She completes her task and moves on.

Now I can sit. I like the chair. I like the tall back. I can rest my head, but still look alert. Somehow, in this context, looking alert feels like a requirement. My eyes are cast on the book open in my lap. The goal of this activity is to appear engrossed, so no one can tell what I'm really doing—closing my eyes. If I appear engaged with my book, nurses and therapists may leave me alone as they deal with their life-and-death tasks. Some parents need to talk at this stage, but for the life of me, I can't find any words. What is there to say? I'm lost in a twilight zone. My hidden agenda is to rest. Nap. Doze. For some reason it feels irresponsible, like sleeping in church. Sleep. When did I last do that? Two days? Three? Four days ago? Will I ever sleep again? I used to be so good at it. Before. With a capital B.

But this is After. With a capital A.

Somehow, what was my life no longer is. What used to matter doesn't. It's as though I've stepped off the planet and into a netherworld. Nothing that was relevant a few days ago bears any weight now. My oh-so-important to-do list, my calendar of events, tasks to complete, places to go.

What matters now? God help me, only sleep is on my mind. Sleep and this chair.

I've never been in PICU before. Never even heard the term, come to think of it. P.I.C.U.—Pediatric Intensive Care Unit.

Pediatric. Draya would be mortified if she weren't so drugged on morphine. She's fifteen, practically grown up in her eyes. My child, my eldest. An undisciplined bundle of natural talent—singer, dancer, writer, overflowing with passion and compassion. Rough edges too. Never afraid to confront, rarely with any tact; a strong sense of right and wrong; fiercely independent, private, always in control ... and now?

Oh, no. Visitors.

They drift in silently, searching the twelve exposed beds, looking for a familiar face. Nine of the beds hold little ones—infants and toddlers are most common here. One bed is occupied by a twelve-year-old, hit by a car while riding her bike. The last bed is empty. That boy, Draya's age, died yesterday.

I watched as his body seized, then stopped. In a choreographed ballet, nurses swept through the unit, whisking parents out the door. I grabbed my purse. Another mother didn't. In the hallway she patted her pockets. "Oh, no. A chance for a smoke and I left my cigarettes inside."

I took a bill out of my wallet, "Buy a pack. Pay me later." She hurried off. A child had lost his life. A family had lost a son. But this is survival. She needed a smoke. His death had gifted her a window of opportunity. Why waste it?

Nowhere to go, I sat on a hard cushioned bench in the waiting room. A voice came from the alcove where a pay phone lurked.

"Yeah, he's gone ... I don't know ... I guess we can come home now ... I'll ask ... Okay ... Bye."

It costs 25 cents to notify people your kid is dead? You'd think it would be free.

A boy who was alive is no longer.

Forgive me if I say there was little distress as I listened and observed. My reactions were primal: watch the event, grasp the outcome, and move as directed.

Stop. Sit. Wait. Go back when the body has been removed.

In PICU each family is an island. Interaction is minimal.

Besides, that was yesterday. Today, a new event requires attention—visitors. They come in pairs, perhaps for moral support. I peer at the women as they scan the beds. Their morbid curiosity borders on voyeurism. Yes, I know these people. Ours are the faces they seek. This will demand much more from me than observing a child's demise.

Etiquette dictates I must be gracious, appreciative. They've made the effort to come all the way here. Paid for parking. Located the unit. I dress my face in what I hope is a socially acceptable expression and wonder if my inner aversion matters. It's a moot point. Politeness prevails.

I default to timeworn social graces, scrape strength from a bone-dry well, and smile.

Dear Lord, this place, this circumstance is so foreign.

"How are you doing?"

Obligatory hugs. My book falls. One woman picks it up.

"Such a shock," she says. "We came as soon as we heard."

"What a tragedy," the other whispers, staring at my child lying on the bed.

A breathing tube juts from Draya's mouth, attached to a machine elevated just behind her head. A feeding tube runs down her nose. Monitors flash and beep, recording any vital function she's still able to produce.

"How badly was the driver injured?"

"Were they good friends?"

"Do the doctors think she'll recover any movement?"

"Is she really paralyzed? For life?"

"But she's moving her hands…"

"She'll lose that as the swelling increases? How can they be so sure?"

"Oh. Bone shards in her spinal column. Severed at the neck. I see."

Facts ascertained, next, the piece I dread.

"I don't know how you're managing."

"You're such an inspiration."

"Such strong faith."

"I could never handle it so well."

"How do you do it? I can barely look at her!"

Their questions prick my brain like sleet stinging unprotected flesh. In my head I'm begging, *Leave me alone. I don't have the energy to make you feel better about our trial. Go away. Just go away.*

Instead, I clamber up to the occasion as we volley Christian clichés.

"She's in God's hands…"

"Jesus is your strength…"

"The Lord will undertake…"

We bounce platitudes back and forth, like a deflated beach ball. Thunk. Thunk. Thunk. Finally their parking time runs out.

And all I want is sleep.

Days pass. Others come. "How can we help?" they ask.

Their intentions are good, but their efforts fall flat because I can't tell them. I've always been the helper, never the helpee.

"Be sure to call if there's anything we can do."

They don't grasp that such an action entails comprehensive thought: the ability to identify a need, formulate a plan, find their phone number, make a call, explain the need, arrange the details. All those steps.

I don't even know how to sleep anymore. Even a baby can do that.

But once in a while, visitors come with a heart to help and the ability as well.

These ask questions I can answer. "What's happened today? Is Rick coming up after work? How is your son getting to school?"

Simple. These are facts. I can make a sentence about this. Blundering from my mouth are clues for those who listen closely, clues to what I might need.

One friend stays, just stays for the first few days and nights. Sitting off to the side, quietly attentive, she runs errands, makes calls, listens or talks, taking her cue from me.

My step-mother brings a Chef's Salad every time she visits, with a plastic fork and a napkin—fresh food I can eat by the bed. Draya is afraid to have me gone too long.

Another buys us a monthly hospital-parking pass. He understands that we'll be here that long and longer; something I haven't been able to consider yet.

Someone else hears how my feet are aching from the old flat shoes I stumbled into that pivotal day when the phone rang. This friend brings me a pair of Air Nikes. So light, so comfortable. Years later I can still feel the relief of those runners on my feet.

Two weeks into our nightmare, a friend and I sit in the empty Mother's Room, a space with cots and a shower stall, my temporary home.

She offers comfort.

I respond with fury.

She leans forward, gentle, yet fervent. "God understands how much Draya's hurting, how hard this is for you. He watched His own son suffer and die on the cross."

Risking lightning from heaven, I retaliate. "God knew Jesus's suffering would end in a few hours. Draya is paralyzed for life. There's nothing the same here."

Silence. Have I hurt her? I don't care.

But then she looks up, confident. "Jesus knows," she declares. "Think about it. John 1:3 says that before Jesus came to earth as a little baby, he had all the power of heaven. It says, through him all things were made; without him nothing was made that has been made. And in Colossians 1:17; He is before all things, and in him all things hold together. Imagine how disabled, how paralyzed it must have felt for Jesus to come to earth as a mere man and live his whole life like that."

Now I am silent.

Maybe the Lord does understand. Maybe enough to help us through. Grudgingly I accept this token of encouragement. During the months that follow, white-knuckled, I hang onto His hope as events play out, praying He will see us through.

Days blur one into another. Then weeks. Dr. W. does a quick assessment before Draya's move to rehab. In the hallway he casually splinters my brittle veneer. "I find that teens who become paralyzed are usually dead in five to ten years. They don't pay enough attention to bowel and bladder care."

Four days later I stop sobbing.

I meet another mother with a son who is quadriplegic. She offers context, "The first two years are the hardest."

"Two years?"

Seven months pass before we bring our daughter home. Then the years begin.

YEAR ONE

Supplies. Equipment. What does a quadriplegic need?

A friend scrounges a discarded hospital bed. Someone else covers the cost of the foam mattress we are told will prevent pressure sores. A man from church sells medical equipment and donates a used patient-lift. This is an unexpected blessing. Draya is 5' 7" of dead weight. Much as I want to, I cannot gather my child in my arms.

Fitting the equipment in our little house is an exercise in futility. Supplies spill out of her bedroom and into the dining room. Furniture is shoved against walls so Draya can manoeuvre her wheelchair through the small space. The table is raised on blocks so she can get under it to eat a meal. A friend with a chain saw widens the doorway to the living room so Draya can join us to watch TV.

Ongoing trials and multiple errors are relentless, effective teachers. How do we balance meds to keep her body functioning? Which symptoms are related to her condition, and which are signals that something is wrong? How do we use catheters, soakers, blue pads, sterile water, gels? Where do we buy everything? Where do we put everything? Who provides the care I can't provide? How much support are we entitled to and who pays the bill? How much can I do myself before I have to allow strangers more access to our home, our child?

We are grateful for the agency that sends caregivers, but we never know who will arrive for any given shift. Most are trained to give meds, and to bathe, dress and undress elderly or post-surgical clients. Draya's needs are beyond what all but a few have encountered. I spend hours training each new person.

Foolishly, Draya believes she should have some say in her care: "Can you not use the lift that way? I'll fall out of the sling."

One caregiver retaliates. "I've been trained in home care. I know what I'm doing. You're just a girl. What do you know?"

Draya discovers that if we refuse a certain caregiver, the agency is not obliged to fill that shift with another. But if a caregiver refuses to work with a client, the agency must find a replacement. At sixteen, Draya takes charge, and devises a method. She will drive away the caregivers she doesn't like until an acceptable replacement takes their place.

Unaware of her tactics, I invest inordinate amounts of energy trying to build relationships between Draya and the home care staff. She will not enlighten me until five years have passed.

Where some caregivers are part of the problem, others become part of the solution. We welcome their unceasing patience, gentle skills, and willingness to learn Draya's preferences. But for me, an introvert, they all consume my energy. Exhaustion is my norm. Soon I am no longer aware that any other state exists.

YEAR TWO

Concurrent action plans are unavoidable.
   Task 1. Home Renovations
   Task 2. Managing the System
   Either task would be enough to tip someone over the edge, but both at the same time? Yet there is no choice. This is not a ride from which we can disembark. We are instructed as to the kind of environment Draya needs to live as a quadriplegic, but how do we afford it? At some point, the insurance claim will be settled, but this could take years. We are overwhelmed when Draya's aunt takes a loan against her house and deposits the money in our account. Renovations begin.

   Contractors rip the bathroom and porch off our one-hundred year-old house. Standing like a blue sentinel in the driveway, a rented Port-a-Potty welcomes our reluctant attention as we survive a chilly March. Water to the washing machine is gone as well. Laundromat trips are wedged into an already unbearable schedule. A basement is dug. Walls erected. Demolition powder whispers its breath over every surface. Dusting apples, dishes, books and chairs, anything exposed, becomes automatic. Each evening we blaze a new trail through the day's construction so Draya and her chair can escape her room and come to view the progress.

   Draya celebrates her seventeenth birthday entertaining friends in her new addition—a large bed-sitting room, with private accessible bathroom and a separate ramped entrance. This offers reprieve but no real rest.

   In the midst of this ongoing chaos, we employ the method of hit-and-miss to understand the workings of Alberta's Community Care System. Who holds the power? Who can make decisions? How emotionally overwrought do I have to become before they'll provide more home care support? How sick does Draya have to be before they'll believe something's wrong and not just chalk it up to a complaining teen?

Our small town medical team has little experience dealing with quadriplegia. When their efforts are ineffective, some blame it on the patient. As a mom, I am torn—take my daughter's side or theirs. I opt for the first. "They" are not pleased. As one doctor writes, "Mother chose to support the patient rather than rehab."

We become experts in pressure sores, injury related illnesses, and equipment malfunctions. Professionals give their input, but we are the ones who must learn to navigate the world of spinal cord injury. I become adept at packing wounds, catheterization, and modifying off-the-rack clothing. Rick reads equipment manuals, learns to adjust and repair her wheelchair, her track lift, her hospital bed. Jake sets a healthy tone as he persists in treating Draya as the big sister he still loves to annoy, while helping where he can. We invent gadgets as needs arise. Draya's determination and mind for design teaches us to never say never.

Progress continues. Draya's power chair arrives. Now she can go from A to B at will. One day I look out the window to see her steering full speed down the street, towing her brother on his skateboard. Another day I am recruited to start a race: Draya in her power chair, Dad on our new riding mower, and fourteen-year-old Jake on the old one.

Ready ... Set ... Go! The men are first off the blocks. Draya quickly overtakes and passes the finish line, the neighbour's fence, leaving the mowers in the dust. Shouting in triumph, she throws her arm in the air, forgetting she has biceps controlling the up motion, but no triceps to control the drop. Everyone chortles as her arm overbalances and her fist drops onto her head.

It is a joyous moment as we begin to see the return of the rambunctious, unpredictable teen we knew Before. Capital B.

I thank God as I begin to see evidence of His hope in the After. Capital A.

YEAR THREE

Year One was little more than a flailing of reaction as crisis overlapped crisis. Year Two saw gaps in the chaos, moments to inhale, and not just gasp. Year Three finds us able to breathe enough to think, plan, and begin to act with forethought as we settle into a new normal. I find relief in moments of stability, accepting that tomorrow is up to God.

Draya, however, is ready to advance. Increments are small but evident.

Neighbours hold a fundraiser. The result is a top-of-the-line, bells-and-whistles computer with internet. Now Draya can interact with the outside world at will. Her natural creativity draws her to graphic design, and she spends hundreds of hours teaching herself to build websites. A decade later Draya will be poised, ready to provide when small businesses begin clamouring to advertise on the Internet. God was surely guiding her.

Mother and daughter. Oil and water? It often is, but we didn't have that luxury. Taking new ground meant teamwork. Sometimes I lost my temper, sometimes she lost hers. We learned to close our mouths and silently finish the task at hand. Separating, each of us would regroup privately and put the moment away, knowing that soon she'd need my help again. We couldn't indulge in fighting, pouting, or lecturing. Forgive and forget was our unspoken constitution.

How Draya managed to handle those years with such maturity astounds me, but handle it she did. We remained two soldiers on the battlefield, tackling a common foe on two different fronts: her body, which rebelled at being paralyzed, and the medical system to which it was inextricably linked.

For one year the county provides a tutor until a nearby town donates a handi-bus to our cause. Now Draya can not only attend her final year of school, but if we drive her, she can hang out with friends. It is a milestone year—Grade Twelve Graduation. In our community the Grad party is held at a local farm, supervised by several courageous parents. Rick drives Draya to the party, leaving her in the hands of her friends. At midnight I arrive to locate my daughter. The kids are more than a little tipsy, groggily celebrating while fathers supervise from a distance, holding car keys for designated drivers. I find Draya slouched, partially slipping out of her chair, as she and her friends party hearty.

A lecture begins to bubble to my lips, but in that moment, I realize I now have two distinct roles. In one, I am, of course, Mom. But in the other, I am Draya's arms and legs. My brain cannot register an opinion on anything an able-bodied daughter would normally keep separate from her parents. It is a careful, crucial shift in our relationship. She has to trust me enough to allow me access to her world and I have to facilitate her ability to make the mistakes teens need to make.

Draya has to accept new terms, as well. In the past, she'd dealt with consequences in private, and adjusted her behaviour accordingly. On this night, she realizes that is no longer an option. Arriving home, I use the lift and get my daughter into bed. Once she lies down, her stomach rebels.

"Sit me up, Mom. Quick!"

I prop her up, my arm hooked through hers to lean her forward. With towels and a basin balanced on her lap, she heaves and spits and heaves some more.

An hour later, she is still wretched, but sober. "I'm so sorry, Mom. You shouldn't have to hold me up and watch while I puke. I'll never do this again."

True to her word, she hasn't.

AFTER

Progress was steady. We still staggered at times, but the learning curve had levelled out, and regular living began to take precedence. We understood which rules we could stretch, which we could break, and which we had to carefully adhere to.

Today, disability is at the bottom of Draya's list. When a problem arises, she pays enough attention to address it, and quickly moves on. Her limitations don't define her. She defines them.

Draya is married. She and her husband run a graphic design business from their home. Draya's skill and knowledge are the result of that first computer our community raised money to purchase. She is busy and active and loves her life.

I rarely think back to those early days, but once in a while something stirs the memory.

Last Sunday a friend pulled me aside after church.

"I was at the hospital to visit Thomas and his mom yesterday."

"He just turned four, right?"

She nodded. "He's been fighting cancer for over a year. I wish there was something I could do. Yesterday his mom told me he'd thrown up on his blankie. I took it home and washed it and brought it right back. Doing laundry doesn't seem like much though."

Not much, I thought? You're wrong. Sometimes it's everything. And more.

Needing Mom

ALLISON AKGUNGOR

> Researchers at the University of Wisconsin-Madison found that stressed children had increased levels of the hormone cortisol. Hugging their mothers could significantly drop those cortisol levels and release oxytocin, the warm and fuzzy neurohormone. A phone call to Mom showed the same hormonal changes.
> —Health News column, *Homemakers Magazine*[1]

I CLIP THIS SHORT ARTICLE to keep. This brief description of research provides a scientific explanation for what I have experienced both as a mother and as a child. I wonder how many people still feel the need to turn to their mothers, even as adults, to benefit from this biochemical relief.

At a reunion with nursing classmates, I am interested to learn that several of them are in regular, even daily contact, with their grown daughters by phone or by text message. Their daughters are busy working professionals, some with their own children, some living a continent away. I am reassured that my own frequent chats with my adult daughter are not out of the norm. Perhaps this is a secret ingredient enabling today's young women to carry on "doing it all." I think back to a time when I most needed my mother.

* * *

I am the most stressed I have ever been, waiting here in this hospital room for my husband to return from yet another test. I have been here every day for the past two weeks since his admission just after

New Year's. It seems the turn of the year to 1974 has dramatically ended our run of good fortune of a happy marriage, a healthy baby, and a new house. My husband has been experiencing headaches, dizziness, difficulty swallowing and a loss of balance. There are many, many tests. Today I have timed my visit to correspond to when my husband will return to his room, but he is not here. A nurse explains that the pneumoencephalogram has been delayed and my husband will not be back for a couple of hours. I try not to let my nurse's mind race too far ahead into a minefield of horrible possibilities. I come to learn that the "waiting to know" is even harder than the "knowing."

I wake every morning to my almost one-year-old daughter calling "Mama" from her crib beside my bed. She is oblivious to the crisis surrounding her. Her bouncy curls, bright smile and arms around my neck never fail to lift my spirits.

My baby and I moved into my parents' home immediately upon my husband's admission to hospital. My mother and aunt (who has extended her Christmas visit) are both here to look after my daughter, freeing me to spend my days with my husband. Often one of my parents or their church minister drives me to the hospital.

I have been coping so far, but today unexpectedly finding him gone is too much. I cannot bear standing here in his empty hospital room. I cannot sit. I feel too apprehensive, too agitated to wait here alone. I start to take off my coat, then put it on again. I realize what I must do. I have to find my mother.

I know where she might be. I remember that she was planning an afternoon train trip downtown to return a Christmas gift to Birks. If I leave the hospital right now, I might catch her. I emerge from the Neurological Institute, high on the side of Mount Royal, overlooking downtown Montreal. I trudge through the slush-clogged intersection at Pine Avenue and head down the hill. It is a long, cold walk down University Street, edging the McGill campus, but it helps to translate my anxiety into activity. How casually I have walked up and down this street so many times before. I pass Wilson Hall, home of the nursing school I graduated from eight years ago. Across the street is the High School for Girls, the downtown high school I commuted to by train for four years.

At the bottom of the hill, I finally reach Birks, and push my way through the heavy revolving doors. This is not just any Birks but the elegant flagship department store in downtown Montreal. It was built in the late 1800s, in the era of wealthy English merchants. This is still the place to come for the finest of gifts. It has marble pillars and a mezzanine overlooking the main floor. Glass and mahogany display cases hold emerald and ruby necklaces, gold and silver bracelets, watches from Switzerland, the finest bone china, crystal, and silverware.

I move to a spot where I can watch the door hoping she will soon arrive. As a child in the 1950s, I delighted in a rare visit downtown with my mother: the adventure of the trip on the commuter train, clutching my ticket while watching for the conductor to come punch it, the ride through the dark tunnel under Mount Royal. I often worried that the blackness would never end. If I looked closely out the window I could see the rock walls encasing us. Despite my fears, we always emerged safely into the wide, bright concourse of Central Station. We would make our way to St Catherine's Street and to Birks. I was always a bit intimidated by Birks' large revolving doors and knew I had to move quickly not to be separated from her.

When I was very young, my mother selected a silver pattern for me called London Engraved and every birthday I would receive a small silver teaspoon in the distinctive turquoise Birks' box. It was one of the many ways she tried to prepare for the future she hoped for me. On those long ago visits, we would find my pattern and peer through the display case at all the silverware pieces.

The last time I was in Birks was when my fiancé and I came to choose a wedding ring. It did not take long to find the gold wedding band that seemed right for us. We left it to have an inscription engraved: ACA to AAM 1971. Instead of the expense of an engagement ring we chose a six-week honeymoon, travelling in a secondhand station wagon through Europe and his homeland of Turkey.

As I wait, I observe the people around me pouring over display cases just like my mother and I used to do. Today, a sales clerk carefully unlocks a case and brings items to the counter top for closer scrutiny by a young couple. How valueless all these things look to me today. I move to another location pretending to look at china serving dishes and silverware patterns. My vision blurs.

My mouth is dry. I am almost nauseated. Anxiety overwhelms me again. Where is my mother? I move closer to the door. When I finally see my mother's familiar figure come through the revolving doors, I rush to her and am relieved to feel her arms about me.

"Oh, I'm so glad to find you. The test was delayed. The nurse said he wouldn't be back for two hours. I couldn't stand it. I couldn't stay there alone waiting, worrying about him."

"Oh darling," she says as she hugs me to her. It is only now, so many years later as mother of adult children myself, that I consider how she must have felt. So caught up in my own anxiety, I could not think then of the anguish she too must have been experiencing.

We proceed with the mundane task of returning the gift. I am grateful for the distraction. I watch a salesclerk fill out the return slip, fold it into a small metal cylinder and send it off in the pneumatic tube system that winds its way through the store. I am still as fascinated as I had been as a child to see it fly back in a few minutes with the correct cash refund.

"Well, that is taken care of. I was going to stop in at Eaton's. Do you want to come with me?"

"Okay. Yes." We head down St Catherine's towards Eaton's, my arm linked through hers just as we had done when I was a small child. Her closeness brings the same comfort. I stay with her until it is time for her to catch the train home and for me to head back up the hill.

I return to the hospital feeling less anxious and more hopeful. Maybe there will be some progress, some answers after today's tests. My husband has already been through x-rays, blood tests, and CAT scans. I walk towards his room and see a bed being pushed down the corridor towards me. I breathe a sigh of relief to see that it is my husband finally returning. He is taken into a nearby ward. The neurologist in charge of his case stops me and motions me to a chair in the corridor. The doctor stands looking down at me.

"With the test today we have been able to see something the other tests did not reveal," he explains.

"What is it?" I ask.

He pauses and then replies "It's a tumour."

I have a momentary hope. "Can you operate?"

"No, it is too deep. In the brain stem. It is impossible to operate there. We can try radiation. There is some evidence that it might help. We will start him on medication to relieve the swelling around the tumour, which should reduce his symptoms. At least temporarily."

The neurologist, in his white lab coat, goes on to recite statistics, percentages, survival rates but I can hear no more. I can wait no longer. I must see my husband, touch him—touch always our primary means of communication.

"Can I go to him?" I ask. The doctor nods and I am soon standing by my husband's bed. I gently place my hand on his arm and quietly say his name, the name only I call him. He is groggy from sedatives but opens his eyes briefly and grasps my hand. A nurse comes to check his blood pressure and informs us he must remain flat for a few hours following the procedure to avoid severe headache. I pull over a chair to sit as close to him as I can, rest my hand on his arm, feel his warmth, let him sleep, watch over him, somehow protect him. I will not allow this new truth to intrude between us, though I know now we are caught in something from which we cannot escape.

In the days that follow, we move quickly to inform those who must be told. We send a telegram to his family in Turkey. This is followed by difficult phone calls, complicated by time differences, operators, and language barriers. My mother-in-law's brother, who is a physician, arranges to come with her to Canada. He speaks English which she does not. They arrive and stay with my parents. My mother is a welcoming and compassionate hostess, not letting language barriers faze her. I am so relieved his mother has arrived here in time to see her eldest son and that she has the support of her brother. Such a difficult trip for her to make. She meets her new granddaughter for the first time, holds her in her lap, but cannot smile. Throughout this time, my parents are always a supportive presence. I do not have to worry about my daughter. My mother or my aunt care for her when I am away. I do not have to think about meals or transportation. My own loving family fills in around me. I hardly notice all the things they are doing, so focused am I on my husband. My husband has always loved the sun. It reminds him of the warm beaches of Turkey. When possible he moves to where the sunlight is coming in. One day as I arrive at the door of his room, he is silhouetted against the bright February sun streaming in through the window. It is so bright I cannot maintain my gaze for long. It strikes me how this is like staring death in the face. We cannot stand it and turn away. It is too painful. On the advice of a psychiatrist friend we do not tell him he is dying. Instead we hold out the hope that the radiation treatments might have some effect. I accompany him up elevators and down long corridors for the treatments.

One morning I arrive to find his room empty. A nurse runs to explain, "He had a choking spell during breakfast. He stopped breathing and was resuscitated, but has lapsed into a coma." I have been trying to be here at mealtime to make sure his food is pureed and easy to swallow. But I wasn't here this morning. My husband's mother and I stand on either side of his bed in the intensive care unit, his strong young body lies between us. Neither of us can say anything but we are united by a grief that goes beyond words.

A few days later my husband emerges from the coma. I am so happy to have him return but discover he is unable to move or speak. I continue my vigil, wanting to be by his side every moment I can. He is transferred to a private room. I play tapes of classical music we had recorded to use when I was in labour less than a year ago. It is music we both love. We cannot converse. It is enough to hold his hand, to pace my breathing to his, to be together.

On the night of February 17, I am called back to the hospital after being there most of the day. My husband's breathing has become irregular; this is the stop-and-start pattern that signals a person is close to death. His skin has taken on a grey tone. I know it will not be long. I am with him when he takes his last breath. It seems that he has waited until I could be here. The kind young resident doctor, who is about my husband's age and has cared for him over the past six weeks, certifies his death.

Though my husband and I had purchased a house only six months before his death, I never sleep there again. My daughter and I remain in my parents' home for the next three years. I reserve my outpouring of grief for the shower where the water drowns out my sobs and washes away my tears. I am able to gradually resume my nursing career part-time while my mother looks after my daughter. Time with my daughter is more precious to me now than ever. My greatest concern is the impact of her father's death on her but she is never without someone nearby to love her. My parents never hesitate for a moment in offering us their home and their hearts. They break our fall off the edge of our previous life and provide us with a soft landing. It is only now, as a grandmother myself, that I appreciate fully the personal freedom my mother so generously relinquished to give us support.

I have never stopped needing my mother. Though she has been gone now for over twenty-five years, I still pull the comfort of her love in close around me when I most need it.

My daughter, wife to a loving husband, mother to two little daughters of her own, still calls on me when she is most in need. Trying to balance the demands of her professional work life and the needs of her young family can push her to her limit. When she phones, I mostly listen. Our conversations often end with her saying, "I always feel better after talking to you."

Today when my phone rings it is her husband calling. He explains that my daughter is feeling very ill, probably the flu. He is taking the children out so they don't disturb her but asks if I will come to stay with her. He doesn't want to leave her alone. Within ten minutes I am on my way. I don't do much—a cool cloth on her forehead, sips of ginger ale and some Tylenol. I am relieved to be with her and she relaxes when I am nearby. I stroke her hair, just as my mother used to do to soothe me and she falls asleep. I don't often see my daughter asleep anymore. Her face is turned to one side. There is something about the line of her jaw that is so much like her father's that it could be him lying there. My hand slides gently down her cheek. I caress them both.

With a simple gesture, a comforting tone of voice we tap into a powerful biochemical wellspring that binds us together, helps us carry on, generation after generation, needing and being needed.

NOTES

[1]Seltzer, L. J., T. E. Ziegler, and S. D. Pollak. "Social vocalizations can release oxytocin in humans." *Proceedings of the Royal Society B: Biological Sciences* 277.1694 (2010): 2661-2666. Web.

Nesting Dolls

NANCY SLUKYNSKI

STEPPING FROM THE CHILL of the approaching winter into the warmth of a boutique in Ukraine, I lower the hood of my woollen coat as the door swings behind me. The shop's shelves are filled with handcrafted beauty—ceramics, wood carvings, oil paintings, woven baskets, and painted eggs. Amidst it all, I spot her. She has wide, blue eyes, full bright lips, and rosy red cheeks. Delicately painted flowers in robin's egg blue, cobalt, magenta, and gold encircle her round face and belly. I cannot pry my eyes away. I slide off my leather gloves and with my cold fingertips gingerly twist the first doll open. The wood squeaks. I open another and another until there are five dolls all lined up in a row. The painter's deliberate strokes create slight differences in each doll's eyes, lips, hair colour, and dress. Each one is exquisite. I pay a modest fee, board the crowded local bus, and carefully carry my matroishkas home with me. The year is 2004.

* * *

The year is 1947 and winter whips across the Prairie. The cold winds leave long ribbons of textured snow along the landscape. It is the day my mother is born. My Grandma, Jennie Shewchuk, is in a small country hospital in Portage la Prairie, Manitoba. The daughter of Ukrainian immigrants, Grandma is the oldest of three siblings. She is thirty-five years old and about to give birth to her fourth daughter. My Grandpa wonders if this time it will be a boy.

Two years later in that same hospital, my Grandma will give

birth to her youngest, another daughter. Still later, she will miscarry another child.

This is all I know of my Grandma's birth experiences when, sixty-two years later, I am eight months pregnant with my second child and curious.

"Mom, what was it like when Grandma gave birth?"

"She never really talked about her births. All that I remember her telling us is that the doctor used forceps when your Auntie (the eldest) was born."

She pauses. "I do remember her telling me though that when she brought me home from the hospital, there was so much snow. To get home, your Grandma caught a ride with someone fortunate enough to own a car and then Grandpa met them with a horse-drawn sleigh where their long driveway connects with the highway. A car never would have made it to the house with all of the drifts."

I imagine my Grandpa's quickened heartbeat on his way to meet his new baby as he tightly grips the reigns of the sleigh. I imagine sunlight sparkling off the glittering landscape, the air cold and stinging.

The small farmhouse still stands where my Grandma and Grandpa raised their daughters. I recently visited. There was a faint and familiar scent of borscht, which was always boiling on the stove when we arrived for our annual summer visits: us four grandchildren, fourteen hours sardined in a white Pontiac on the flat, flat highway from Fort Saskatchewan, Alberta to Manitoba. Then, I was too young to have any interest in my Grandma's birth stories, intent instead on raiding the pea patch or capturing garter snakes and frogs by the creek to store in Mason jars and place on my Grandma's kitchen table.

My mother asked me, not long ago, "Did you know that your Grandma hated snakes?" Not wanting to interrupt the innocence of our summer fun, saying nothing to discourage us, she quietly endured them slithering in her kitchen.

My Grandma loved to give away bouquets of dahlias from her garden. She smelled like the sweetness of cooked onions and had at least twenty sets of cutlery in her kitchen drawer. She exuded incredible strength and warmth when she wrapped her arms around me. She had muscular, working hands.

When my Grandma was twenty years old, her future husband, Alec Shewchuk, had already heard about her through the Ukrainian immigrant grapevine. One fall weekend, he had learned that she would be travelling to Winnipeg to buy a winter coat and would be staying the night in his adopted city of St. Boniface. He made sure to meet her in person. Not long after, he knelt on one knee in the soil she inherited from her late father and proposed. He was ten years her senior and, like her parents, had been born in the village of Kamin-Kashyrskyi in Volyn Oblast.

They married in 1932 and lived on her family's homestead where they grew their business and their family. She and my grandfather made a modest living selling strawberries and garden vegetables. To ensure steady income, he also washed dishes in the corporals' mess of the nearby military airbase. Their cellar was stocked each autumn and they made sure that their children never went hungry. By the time my Grandma passed away at the age of 86 years, she and my Grandpa had pre-paid all of their funeral expenses and had chosen their shared tombstone. Etched into the granite above their names is a cornucopia overflowing with apples and pumpkins and other signs of a fruitful harvest.

As I feel my second child shift within my belly, I realize that there is so much more to know about my grandmother. Now, I wish I could ask her for her stories.

* * *

When my mother was twenty-four years old, she had settled a very long flat distance west from her farming community in Manitoba to a small town in Alberta. She was far from her sisters and parents. It was December 1971 and she was in labour for the first time. The chilling winds of the winter were whipping once again.

When I was first pregnant at the age of thirty-five, my mother told me that labour pain is bearable and forgettable. She gave birth to four of us between 1971 and 1977: two daughters, a son, and one more daughter. She has told me that her first was the most difficult, having accepted an episiotomy and a drug to induce labour. My mother has shared her frustration with her first birthing experience, her naïveté and blind trust in the doctors, and how she wished she could have avoided any interventions. She recalls that while in hospital during the days after delivering her first baby, the nurses would direct a heat lamp at her incisions to speed her healing. She laughed, "What did we know?"

I had learned a few years earlier that after my older sister was born, my mother had miscarried twins, noticing blood and two embryos in the toilet. She was not aware she was pregnant. Never having faced such a situation, she simply flushed the toilet. "Maybe I should have taken them to the hospital," she told me. She is a woman who gets on with things.

The rest of her birth experiences were drug-free and without complications. This, however, cannot be said about the rest of her life.

After I was born in 1973, followed by my brother in 1975, my father's mental health began to falter. He was a young constable with the Royal Canadian Mounted Police, stationed in the booming industrial town of Fort Saskatchewan. In the early years of their marriage, with three young children aged five, three, and under a year, he was mourning the loss of his own father. The combination of personal and occupational stress caused my father to suffer a mental breakdown. During a paranoid and delusional panic attack, he returned home from work one day and frantically instructed my mother to load everyone—three children and his visiting mother—into his Pontiac. He insisted that a bomb was planted in our house and we needed to flee. After packing his .38 Special revolver under the front seat, he sped us to his sister's house in a nearby town, where everyone, aside from my father, planned through the night how to get him to the hospital.

For the next four months, my mother visited my father daily, mother-in-law and three preschoolers in tow. As a new driver, she drove on the back roads. She was still breastfeeding my brother. Most days my sister and I ran around the wide grounds of the hospital and had picnic lunches with my Baba, Dad, and Mom. My mother was also meeting with the psychiatrists who were attempting to stabilize my father's condition.

Before my father was released from the hospital, his RCMP supervisors visited him and brought with them dismissal papers. Despite being heavily medicated and not yet mentally stable, my father was required to sign. Once released from the hospital, my father returned home. Delusional, he ingested three bottles of pills, one for his wife, one for his sister, and one for his brother. He thought the act would save them from cancer. By some miracle, he survived.

My maternal grandma told my mother, by rushed long-distance telephone, that she had a vivid dream of my father holding a baby in his arms. In it, his face beamed in a bright smile. My mother had three children under five and, now, a mentally ill, unstable, unemployed husband who needed care. At the time, she did not yet know she was again pregnant. My Grandma was known for her premonitions.

My mother's doctor suggested an abortion. He knew about the crisis that had ripped through our home like a tornado. He thought adding a newborn into the mix would be too much stress for both of my parents.

"Doctor," my mother insisted, "this is a human being. If I cannot look after him or her, I'm sure someone can." She made her decision. Before the baby was due, my mother prepared for the hospital stay by sewing herself a nightgown and housecoat, stitching together carefully cut pieces of Fortrel fabric. Later, the doctor shook his head in disbelief at her composure when he saw her smiling and calm, newborn baby in her arms, dressed in her handmade housecoat. My mother boasts that her doctor did not make it in time to "catch" my younger sister. My father was in the delivery room though, beaming at the birth of his fourth child.

Although not a regular church-attendee, my mother insists, "God is in the driver's seat." She often quotes her mother, "*Sho bude, te bude*. What will be, will be."

My father's rollercoaster mental health never did improve nor could it be cured. His diagnoses over the years included personality disorder, manic depression, and schizophrenia. He endured years of anguish and suffering, frequent stays in mental institutions and shock therapy. Sometimes it was difficult to know who he was, under the weight of his illness. During that time, my mother acted as his advocate, accompanying him to psychiatric appointments, us children in tow. My eight-year-old vocabulary grew to include "lithium" and "Haldol." In our home, plastic bottles filled with intriguingly colourful pills were stored far out of reach. Witnessing his roughshod regime of medications, my mother became a major sceptic of the medical system and especially of the pharmaceutical industry. Her medicine cabinet today is filled with vitamins, cod liver oil, and tea tree oil. I have adopted her apprehension of pills, knowing from experience that there are always side effects.

It became difficult for my mother to live with my father and his unpredictable, sometimes violent mood swings. I remember one outburst at dinner time when he picked up a bowl of boiled, buttered green peas and smashed them onto the floor. They rolled in every direction. My mother wanted some sort of normalcy for us at home. In 1981, my father decided to move into an apartment of his own in Edmonton. My youngest sister was four years old. When my father was well enough, we spent weekends at his apartment or passed time with him at the mall, swimming pool, or bowling alley.

"Did you worry about our safety?" I asked her recently.

She shrugged her shoulders. "What could I do?"

As much as my mother could, she fostered our relationship with him and he remained a part of our lives as children. I could see in her furrowed brow that it had been a dilemma for her, constantly unsure of his mental state and yet not wanting to sever our contact with him. We were potentially a part of his healing, I imagine. Perhaps we were anchors for him. Perhaps we were ties that held the two of them together, even at a distance. It was a complicated time for all of us, living under a never-breaking cloud of uncertainty.

After losing his job with the RCMP, my father worked in a grocery warehouse but for my mother this did not spell financial security. She knew that somebody needed to put food on the table. Rejecting offers of government welfare and Christmas hampers, in 1978 with a one-year-old baby, three other young children and a husband to care for, my mother started a home-based catering company. She nourished and sustained our family by feeding others.

I doubt that initially she had any idea of the eventual success she would achieve—of the scope of events her company would cater. Back then, it was a matter of survival. Through her love of cooking, she contributed to our community at countless birthdays, baptisms, graduations, grand openings, office meetings, dinner parties, weddings, anniversaries, retirements, and funerals. She hired people whose lives and stories would intertwine while they peeled carrots, assembled cabbage rolls, carved roast beef, sliced watermelon, and scrubbed pots. Among countless others, she would serve several of Alberta's Premiers; Fidel Castro's brother, Raúl; the Japanese leaders of Mitsubishi Company; and the Prime Minister of the Netherlands—who asked for her pickled egg recipe.

Christmas was a time when our house was perpetually warm and sticky. The windows dripped with condensation while turkey carcasses boiled in three enormous stockpots. I hated going to school in December, every day hearing my high school classmates say "something smells like turkey"—not expressed with any mocking—more so with longing and anticipation. For me, the smell of turkey is a reminder of the hectic pace of Christmas catering, of my mother shovelling snow, scraping ice off the delivery station wagon, peeling potatoes, chopping onions, mixing gravy, baking desserts, all well before we woke for school. At the end of the school day, we, at times grudgingly, pitched in where we could, usually with dish duty or unloading supplies from the station wagon. Sometimes I sat on my bed while hiding a novel in my oversized textbook, feigning study.

My siblings and I argued about who was doing more. In retrospect, I know it was my mother who did the most—by far.

* * *

Seasons pass. Snow falls and melts. Vibrant tulips push out of the ground, like encouraging miracles when the grass is not yet fully green. On lush landscapes, yellowed leaves scatter and snow falls again.

* * *

The year was 2002. My younger sister was now working full-time with the catering business. My older sister was at her home with her husband raising their toddler son. I was away studying in a Master's program in England. My brother had graduated from university and was working as an engineer-in-training. He was in love with a woman who he had recently introduced to my mother. We were all following our own paths.

On a frosty evening in February, my mother and younger sister returned from a run to the city for groceries and supplies. Just before the ten o'clock news, a lone RCMP officer walked on the crisp-snow-covered path up to her door. He entered and stood in the sunroom. I am not sure which solemn words she was able to comprehend in the moment: "…Your son, Alexander, m'am … collision with train … fatal accident…."

The loss of a child must be the most painful to bear. How did she cope? Is all pain bearable and forgettable? She is a woman who already had a lot of experience getting on with things, often with grace and calm. At the funeral for my brother, she accepted hugs and supportive words from friends and family. It was a reflection of the support she had extended generously to others over the years. In the days that followed, books on grief and grieving were stacked beside her couch. She read them after putting in long hours serving her clients, not taking any time off. After a rushed departure from my university residence in England, I remained in Canada. For several months we mourned together in her kitchen while making sandwiches for her clients. She quoted the Bible and often stated, "All good things are from above".

A few months after the accident, a colleague of my late brother had an idea to rebuild a playground in Alex's memory. The playground that was suggested was serendipitously the very one that we played on as children. During those warm summer nights we played "kick the can" as the setting sun cast long shadows. We swung on the end of a giant steel rocket, hanging upside down from our tanned knees. From her back door, my mother sang out to us, "*Ki-ids* … supper time!"

My mother became the spirit and force behind the playground redevelopment project as we channelled our energy into rebuilding. She taught us how to transform our pain into something that benefits others. She taught us a very powerful form of healing.

My mother lives in the same house and during the long days of summer, the laughter of children playing in Alex's Playground can be heard from her kitchen window.

Pain takes on many shapes. With grace, gratitude, and generosity, strength morphs to match it. This, I have witnessed.

* * *

The year is 2008—thirty-seven years since my mother's first child was born—seventy-one years since my grandmother gave birth to her eldest. I am newly married and excited to be pregnant for the first time. I have moved with my husband John over 300 kilometres away from my mother and sisters. As I prepare to give birth, my foremothers' gifts of confidence, faith, and strength are now transplanting into my own story. My mother, in particular, has taught me to trust nature and my own body.

I am in my second trimester and my longtime friend, a yoga instructor, recommends that John and I watch *The Business of Being Born*, a documentary about how interventions in birth have become increasingly more common in North America and how the rate of caesarean sections has grown to over 30% of all pregnancies. Until that point, John, who has a degree in biochemical engineering, had been sold on the idea of epidurals and elective caesarean sections.

"We are smart enough to invent a way to avoid pain, why would we not use it? Besides, I love you so much, I don't want to see you go through that," he said.

After watching the video, his perspective shifts. What would my grandmother have said if she had seen the video? I picture her sitting at her kitchen table after a long day of cooking and cleaning and gardening, sipping tea, elbow resting, saying "oi yoi yoi" and shaking her head, as she did to indicate disapproval. In a long distance telephone conversation, I tell my mother about the documentary and she says, "See! What did your mother tell you?"

Although John and I both acknowledge the necessity of medical interventions in certain cases and respect the decisions of others, we decide that we will try to avoid them within reason. Upon recommendations from friends, we decide to hire a doula. After first interviewing two other women in two different coffee shops, we meet Deborah. She tells us that she is a mother of two and training to become a midwife.

With down-to-earth warmth, she explains, "I am not here to judge or tell you what you should do. If you would like, I am here to support you in the ways that you need. Birth is a profound experience. I want you to feel informed and empowered."

John and I walk away from the meeting in agreement. She is the one.

During a pre-birth meeting we sit with her in our living room drinking sweetened lemon tea. She shares a sample of a birth plan—a one-page document intended to communicate our vision for the delivery to future hospital staff. Our requests include that I not be offered any drugs unless I specifically ask. Another request is that my movement not be unnecessarily restricted by continuous fetal monitoring or intravenous lines. I also wish to be free to eat and drink during labour.

At the obstetrics clinic at Calgary's Foothills Hospital, I have my fifth visit with my obstetrician. I present our birth plan to her. I notice she has not addressed me by name during this rushed visit. She reads it over. "Yep, it looks alright," she says, pauses and, with a condescending tone, adds, "You know that in the end you get a baby, not a hero biscuit." In that moment, I can't find the words to express my surprise and anger over her slight. When I recount her comment, John is livid.

It is now late November, a week before my due date and my nesting instinct has kicked in. I compulsively clean and organize the freezer, the cupboards, our closets, and the cabinet under our bathroom sink. John has asked me to pick up a can of paint for some touch-up jobs in our condo. While on this errand, I call him from my cell phone. I am in the washroom of a Lebanese restaurant during the lunch rush.

"John!" I say with a loud whisper from the washroom, "I think I've just lost my mucous plug!"

After returning to my table to finish my lunch, I silently sink my teeth into the honey-soaked baklava, my head buzzing with excitement. It could still be days but birth is imminent.

That night we go to bed early. We want to get as much rest as possible. I drift off to sleep with one of my hands touching John's, the other resting on my belly.

As our bedroom fills with a glimmer of light the next morning, I glance over at the clock radio beside our bed which now flashes 6:00 a.m. I can feel that the sheets are damp.

"John!" I nudge him awake. "My waters have broken!"

His eyes flash excitement, like Northern Lights. We phone our mothers.

"It's starting!" we report excitedly.

"WOW! Are you kidding me?" His mother cannot contain her delight.

"Well, this is it," my mother states, a surge of excitement pushing up through her calm.

"I love you!" we hear from both.

We promise to call with news.

In this moment, an ethereal image comes to me of my Grandma at her kitchen table with the light of the morning streaming through her farm house window, her hands wrapped around her steaming cup. Her face is wrinkled and weathered but still soft and beautiful. Her brown eyes are twinkling.

"You can do this," I hear her whisper to me warmly.

John takes some photos of me lying on our bed—the last morning of that giant round belly—with the sun rising on Calgary's downtown skyline in the background. He then makes a short video for the baby-to-be, sweetly describing the morning, the view outside our condo, his desire to meet him or her. His voice is brimming with excitement.

After breakfast, we call our doula.

"Call again when your contractions become closer together. Or if you need anything at all," she reassures us.

Despite having purchased all the necessary provisions in the previous weeks, I do not have my hospital bag entirely packed. I start to gather what I think are the essentials—pyjamas, a CD player, massage oil, popsicles and an accompanying ice-pack. We are not really rushed but we do have it in mind that we should leave for the hospital soon. A few weeks earlier I had tested positive for Group B Streptococcus. The risk of infecting the baby during the delivery is low but the consequences, including brain damage and death, are high. We have already decided that I should have intravenous antibiotic treatment which will need to start before my labour progresses too far. Mid-morning, hospital bag in hand, I waddle out of our nest and we set off.

While en route, my cell phone rings. It is my friend who has recently birthed her first son.

"Did I catch you at a bad time? You're not on the way to the hospital are you?" she jokes.

"Well, as a matter of fact..."

We laugh excitedly and she assures me that it will be a good experience. She repeats to me what her midwives had said to her: "You birth like the person you are." I hold onto these words tightly as we drive toward the hospital. Although the morning sun is beaming, the air outside is cold and the winds of early winter have just begun to stir.

We push open the heavy double doors of the maternity ward and are directed to a tightly-packed triage area. The nurse instructs me to slip on a green hospital gown and lie on the hospital bed—one of three in a crammed space with only a fabric curtain to provide privacy. She hooks some straps around my belly to monitor the baby's heart rate and my contractions.

"We'll need to take a reading for at least twenty minutes," she informs.

I listen to a Morse code of long and short beeps from the machines, pained moaning coming from the bed on the other side of the curtain, some retching, and the conversation of the nurses at the foot of the beds. I anxiously strain to listen and decode their jargon. *What are they saying? Who are they talking about? Is it me?*

The curtain slides open and a young intern appears. She introduces herself and then asks me about the color of the amniotic fluid.

"I can't really recall," I tell her. "Nothing stood out to me."

She does a brief internal swab. "You are two centimetres dilated. And I can see the baby's hair," she tells us, smiling. She seems a bit excited. John and I lock eyes, both grinning. I picture a mass of dark locks, like his.

She leaves and returns.

"There was meconium detected in the amniotic fluid, a sign that the baby is possibly in distress. We'll get you started."

"What do you mean 'get me started'?" I surprise myself with my assertiveness.

"An induction," she replies, matter-of-factly.

"Could you please tell us the likelihood of complications proceeding without an induction compared with the risks of the induction?" John asks.

She stammers with uncertainty and then leaves to fetch the head obstetrician. An older dark-haired man with a slight Scottish accent appears. He seems relaxed.

"Your baby does not appear to be in distress based on the fetal monitoring. There is however a very low chance of infection from Group B Strep so I would recommend that you go home and return to the hospital every four hours for a dose of intravenous antibiotics. We could use a saline lock so that you do not have to stay attached to the drip. Does that work for you?"

"Yes," I answer, relieved. I am grateful that my labour will follow its intended path and pace.

I put my own clothes back on. A nurse searches for a vein on the top of my hand and slides in a long needle, setting up the saline lock for the intravenous antibiotic. Clear liquid hangs in a sac from a metal pole on wheels. I drag this pole beside me as we take the elevator to the first floor to wander through the busy halls. We find a quiet corner with interesting sculptures and take photos beside them. Consciously, I hold the pole outside of the frame of the photo.

After returning to the busy maternity ward, a nurse removes the IV. We are able to leave the bustle of the hospital. While driving away, I call Deborah with an update.

"Why don't you go and have an early dinner. Maybe some carbohydrates," she suggests. "You will need the energy."

Rushing into and out from the cold, we are wrapped in the scent of garlic, tomatoes, basil, and parmesan in the humid warmth of an Italian restaurant. John asks for a table for two.

"And could you make it quick? My wife is in labour."

In what seems like seconds, a steaming bowl of tortellini with tomato cream sauce is placed in front of me. I savour every warm bite and am grateful for Deborah's advice to eat, knowing that I will need the strength to make it through the very physically demanding road ahead.

After dinner, we decide to go to a nearby mall to do some last minute shopping. There is still over an hour before we are expected to return to the hospital for the next dose of antibiotics. As with the restaurant, I would never have imagined having contractions in a mall. John picks out a tiny green onesie and we return again to the hospital. It is late now and the whole hospital seems to have sighed, the dull roar of the daytime activities abated. The nurse gives me a slightly stronger dose of antibiotics so that we can wait six hours to return, rather than four. It is nearly midnight when we arrive back home.

"Come to bed," John says. As much as I try, I cannot sleep, anticipation enveloping me.

The city outside is still and dark. In the warm cocoon of our condo, I watch the snowflakes swirl under the street lights far below and play a CD by the Cuban band, Maraca. I play it twice, all the way through, continuously dancing salsa in the middle of the winter's night, swinging my hips rhythmically. I flip through the pages of *Baby Names* and jot down some ideas on paper, even though we already have a shortlist. I send an email to close friends to share our news.

A few hours later, John walks into the living room and asks how I am doing. He is bleary-eyed but excited. The sun will not yet rise for a few hours but it is time to return to the hospital. The empty road is relatively smooth, for which I am grateful, since even slight jostling is uncomfortable.

For a few hours now, my contractions have been close to five minutes apart and about a minute long. However, once we arrive at the maternity ward, they slow down. We are told that all the rooms on the ward are full. The halls of the hospital and the triage area are both places that I instinctively know are not conducive to labouring. Yearning for some privacy, I find a stairwell that is dusty, but at least far from the hospital hubbub. I climb up and down the stairs, my rhythmic steps echoing loudly.

We call Deborah again. Her sweet voice is tinged with anger.

"It's been almost thirty hours since your water broke. Tell the nurses that you are going home. If they hear that, they will certainly get you into a delivery room. You should *not* be labouring in the stairwell!"

She is right. When John announces that we are planning to go home, the nurses quickly offer to find us a bed. They assign us a room typically reserved for midwives and their clients who require or request hospital facilities. The young, blonde nurse who is waiting in the room smiles warmly. We present her with a copy of our birth plan and her smile widens. I sense her support and am grateful. Outside the windows of our spacious room, the sharp peaks of the Rockies spread out in the distance as the midday sunlight falls all around. Quite suddenly, the muscles in my belly begin to tighten sharply and I stop mid-sentence to focus on my breathing.

My Grandma and Mom's voices float into my mind once again between these first very intense contractions. "You can do this!"

John makes another call to Deborah. "We are in a room now; I think you should come as soon as you can."

The nurse shows us the way to the shower after I tell her that I would like to spend some time labouring there. After another, much stronger wave of contractions, I disrobe and start to run the water. Nausea threatens but subsides. John helps me into the shower. Time seems suspended as my belly tightens and waves of contractions become more powerful.

Twenty minutes pass before Deborah quietly announces her arrival. She scans the scene in the shower room. John is holding one showerhead on my back while I am taking sips of warm water from another showerhead mounted on the wall.

Standing and swaying in the shower, I feel clean and safe and soothed—most of the time. Sporadically, the water temperature shifts from comfortingly warm to spine-chillingly, teeth-grindingly, toe-curlingly cold. Unable to speak during my contractions, I wave my hand frantically, signalling to John that the water pipes suddenly seem to be glacier-fed. I stay under the stream of water—when it is warm—until my fingertips are like prunes. Throughout, I breathe through each contraction, moaning, groaning, and surrendering to my body's instincts.

I feel three strong heaves downward during one of the contractions. It is a wild, wild feeling like my body is knocking towards the earth. I start to moan slowly, deeply, unconsciously, "...oh baby, oh baby, oh baby...."

"I feel like I need to push," I softly but intently say.

"Listen to your body," Deborah quietly encourages. "Reach down and see if you can feel the baby's head."

My shrivelled fingertips search and find the top of a skull between my legs, hard and foreign. "I can feel it!" I am awe-struck.

"Stop pushing!" Deborah instructs. "I am going to find the nurse."

My body feels full of strength and resolve. Suddenly there are many voices in the room, all saying that I need to get out of the shower. I listen closely for Deborah's or John's, not recognizing or trusting any others. My eyes are closed. Through all of the noise, I hear Deborah reassuring me. "Nancy, it's okay."

A green gown is draped over my wet skin as I get up onto the bed. The doctor checks my cervix and says, "Okay, it's time."

As I kneel, knees digging into the mattress, the intense urge to push returns, fierce and untamed. I growl deeply. I bear down, using the earth's pull to augment my push. I rest briefly and ask for someone to please bring the grape seed oil from my bag and some warm compresses. The doctor applies pressure on my perineum with the oil and compresses, the heat soothing stretched skin.

While surrendering to my body's involuntary rhythm, I feel completely in control of the decision to submit. Resistance and strain, resistance and strain, resistance and strain; after the third push, our baby wriggles and jiggles and fumbles out, still connected to me by the umbilical cord, screaming, face and eyes pinched tight and fists shaking. This moment feels paradoxically climactic and calm.

I flip over onto my back and our baby is placed on my belly, inching around, head bobbing, seeking my breast. Since nobody else has made an announcement, I exclaim in sheer delight, "We have a little girl!"

* * *

We are now alone with our daughter. John says, "That was incredible, Nancy. What a privilege to see!"

We discuss her name. We agree on Emelia for her first name, which carries the meaning "industrious and hardworking." Until then, we had not narrowed down any middle names. John tenderly holds our swaddled daughter while I shower and dress. While combing my wet hair, the name comes to me.

"We should call her Faith!—Emelia Faith."

Her name speaks of our trust in her arrival. It honours my mother and grandmother whose faith and determination have rarely been shaken. And most importantly, it is a wish for her.

After a cautious drive home from the hospital the next day, Emelia and I glide peacefully in the rocking chair. She is asleep in the crook of my arm, bundled in a soft flannel blanket. In the afternoon light, I gaze at her with amazement. I try to drink in every detail of her small curled-up body in my arms. Mesmerized, I can barely pry my eyes away. In the background, across the room, I spot the nesting dolls, lined up in a row on our bookshelf. I smile, making a mental note that I have a perfect gift to pass onto Emelia someday.

When I purchased the wooden dolls, I had always thought of the largest one as the momma: when I opened her up, I saw her daughter and granddaughters within. Now though, I see the dolls in a completely different light. When I open the first one, I see her mother inside of her, and then her grandmother inside of her mother, and so on—a sort of matrilineal matroishka. Within her, the momma carries those who have come before and those yet to appear.

Traces[1]

JESSICA KLUTHE

SHE DANGLES THERE. A sort of crucifix over my doorway. I don't have much. A name—three syllables. Ro. Si. Na. There is no song to help me feel her, no voice to remind me of hers.

There is no scent, no texture. No time of day. She died in 1969, sixteen years before I was born.

It was late fall the first time that I really saw her. Everything was wet, rotting. Branches like raw knuckles. The Nanking cherries, instead of letting go, held on tighter—solid black raisins for the birds to peck. The crabapples exploded, burst and shrivelled far below the once-bright sky, their skins deflated red balloons. As I ran up the front steps, my breath clung to the air, a blurry stream. I yanked open the door and knew that the furnace was on; I smelled lint and hair and whatever else had collected in the heat vents since spring.

I was in the basement digging out my winter clothes when I found her. I had hauled out all of the boxes and bins from under the stairs and tried to squeeze myself into my former hide-and-seek spots to look for the partner to a mitten. My parents' crawl space was a collection site for objects that didn't have year-round positions, relocated hall closet and junk drawer items like rubber boots and tobacco tins full of fence-board nails.

I found the photo inside a box that also held a *Company's Coming* cookbook, a brown velvet pincushion, and an oil lantern. The picture was a copy, enlarged from a smaller print, distorted in length. I blew off the dust and watched the tiny particles sway

201

in the air before they found new surfaces to land on. And there she was—Rosina. She is wearing a long dark dress, cinched in at the waist. Her hair, mostly white, is pulled back from her face. Deep circles surround her dark eyes. Her hands are wrinkled like crushed paper. With one hand she holds on to a wooden chair, the other rests on her hip. She stands there on worn stones, in front of an old stucco wall, almost smiling.

Only this one photo of her was ever taken, or at least that is what everyone says. Nanni Rose keeps a copy in a cabinet, between gold-rimmed teacups and the dishes that are never used. When she speaks of Rosina, she glances toward the cabinet. If we are sitting at her kitchen table, sipping thick espresso out of tiny cups, she will peer over my head at it. If we are in the backyard, she will look toward the house. On holidays, when Nanni pulls out the wine glasses or platters, she will pause there a moment before returning to the pots boiling on the stove. Sometimes she will say, "Come. Come. I will show you," but it is hard to get a clear view through the cabinet's crystal doors. She taps on the glass with her finger, and I peek in. Before asking me when I plan to have children, she always mentions that Rosina was an *ostetrica*, a midwife. She always nods before I answer. *She delivered hundreds. Hundreds.* It's always hundreds.

This was as close as I had ever been to Rosina. I took the photo out of the frame and turned it over to see if anyone had printed on the back. No year. No place name. Nothing but *Rosina vecchia*. Old Rosina.

I wondered what existed outside the frame. Another chair? Did the stucco wall belong to her house? Where did she live and with whom? Who stood behind the lens? I packed up the box, except for the oil lantern and the photo, and sat a while on the basement floor before filling in the hiding places with boxes, and hauling my winter clothes upstairs. I played around with the lantern; it wasn't the kind you take camping. The glass was thin, and the handle wasn't made for function. It was probably bought at one of those estate auctions, along with that box of glass negatives, those slides of strangers who stare at us with piercing eyes, backwards, their clothing more visible than their faces. I stayed there, trying to light the lantern and imagine her.

But the frayed wick would not catch long enough to make a steady flame.

* * *

She runs, alive with the night, shocked that it is happening so soon. Shadows spread across a worn path. The bright moon flashes between the trees and collides with the glassy light of the lantern in her hand as she goes. Her shadow rushes over the bony silhouettes of the trees on either side, lost to the darkness, to be lit up again in a stride. She had thought she would have at least another two weeks, maybe three, but when her neighbour tapped on the door just as she started to fall asleep, she knew.

"I'll come with you," she offered.

"No. No. You stay here. Rest. It's late."

She knows the ground well, even in the dark. She slows down around the spots where rotting roots have left holes and takes wider strides over a nettle patch; her legs are bare beneath her gown. There's a rush that comes with a night birth. A baby slips in to the world while neighbours are asleep in darkened houses and wayward husbands slumber somewhere under the stars. Nearby female relatives—aunts, sisters, mothers, and cousins—are awake and alert, ready to assist the midwife, to welcome new life. The exhausted mother pleads for rest in the seconds between the contractions that attack her body, force it to twist into a knot around her belly. She spits out the name *Gesù!* and belts hard *ahhhs* from her throat after she swallows strings of vomit.

When a flickering light in the window comes into view, Rosina runs faster, snapping the brittle grass as each foot smacks the ground. She feels dizzy; the tall trees look like deep green smudges, but the stars stay in place. She concentrates on planning her movements, imagines what could happen. What she will do if there is too much blood. If the water has not broken. If the cord is tangled. If the baby is crowning, or if its legs are pushing through first. *She's done this hundreds of times. Hundreds.*

She plunges her hands into a pail of water on the porch, splashing moonlit water onto the wooden steps. As she yanks open the door, heat from the fireplace flashes against her cheeks. In the corner, coffee boils on the stove, preparation for the long night ahead.

The scent of dark beans and blood curls in the air. In haste she lets her bag slump off her shoulders and fall to the floor. The bag is teeming with herbal remedies, homebrews in corked jars. Puffy aloe leaves, cabbage, and containers of clover. Cotton cloths, pressed and folded. Forceps, scissors, and sewing needles.

An oil lantern, hanging from a ceiling beam, spills pale yellow light across the floor. Women stare at her. They shuffle to make space and then look to her for direction. One says, "Come. Come. We've been waiting."

With her hands on the labouring woman's sticky thighs, her hip hard against the bed frame, Rosina presses the woman's legs apart and counts the number of beats between shudders. She instructs the others. You, hold her legs back—farther. And you, rub a damp cloth on her neck and lips to keep her cool. And someone, open the window and let the breeze in. Rosina's heart thumps deep in her chest and an ache throbs behind her eyes, making it impossible to keep track. The others count; she trusts their heavy whispers. The woman has been pushing already and is soaked in sweat, and shaking. Her hands, balled into tight fists, are white, and her veins, bright purple lines, are thick with blood. Rosina takes the mother's hands into her own. Damp skin sticks to her palms. She uncurls the woman's fists, reminds her to breathe, and with two fingers to the wrist feels her pulse. Rosina brushes away the black curls stuck to the woman's forehead and neck. She steps back for a moment and looks at the mother—two round breasts atop one round belly, swollen feet and fingers, puffy eyelids and lips, back arched, pushing everything she has forward. She is ready. The bed sheets are stained with bright blood. Some women speak to Mary. Some ask Mary to speak to God. *Let the surges stop. Let the baby come.*

After a night of labour—the entire house heaving together—a baby is born. Sunlight creeps in beneath the brown velvet curtains: a too bright, unwelcome rising. Daylight reveals lines of brown blood, tiny dry rivers, following the cracks of the floorboards. The women stare at the ground, following the rivers with their eyes, tracing the flow. The mother cries out to Mary, Mother of God, and a still infant never wakes to see the morning.

Rosina swaddles the tiny body in a thin white sheet, creasing the folds. After brushing eyelids closed, she pulls the top edge over the baby's blue face. She kisses the child's forehead and then crosses it with her fingertips. She rests the baby girl in her weeping mama's arms. Whispering gentle instructions, Rosina tells the woman to stay in bed for a least one week, to let her body pull back together. To eat a cupful of chicken broth and drink water, a teaspoon at a time. She peels off a cabbage leaf for the woman to tuck into her dress against her breasts to prevent cracking. First, she instructs, squeeze out the unneeded milk. She'll be back in a day or two to check in, to make sure there is no infection, no more bleeding.

Without letting her voice break, she whispers, "God bless," and then leaves the house. She puts her hands into her apron pockets and nods up at the bright morning sky as she follows the dusty path back home.

* * *

Later I sat at the kitchen table and watched my older sister, Melissa, put in the filter. Measure out the grounds. She moved around the kitchen until the coffee had brewed. The women in my family could glide through the kitchen, from sink to cupboard, oven to stovetop. They could double or triple a recipe without missing an ingredient. They spoke in pounds and ounces, thyme and oregano.

"Don't worry about it," they would say to me when I tried to help.

"You'll just have to marry a man who can cook."

Once, we had a family reunion inside a wood-panelled community hall that smelled of cellar. Next to the table, among too many open bottles of Coke, were rows of lasagna in oven-wide silver pans. I guess no one had specified what to bring. The pans were filled with the same long, scalloped-edge noodles, sliced eggs, and globs of tomato sauce. Nanni snuck up behind me and, with her cheek against mine, whispered, "Pick the best one." I spotted hers right away. I had watched her make it dozens of times. Her final touch: fresh Parmesan shaken through the fingers.

Melissa had practically lived with Nanni—Rosina's granddaughter—for the first years of her life. Nanni and Nonno always tell the story of waiting in line all night at Toys "R" Us for the release of the Cabbage Patch dolls. Was it 1976? Or the next year? They elbowed young parents as they rushed through the doors to the big green display. The doll came with a birth certificate.

Melissa was the first one of her friends to have one, and they were just as proud as she was.

"I didn't have dolls. I dressed up zucchinis," Nanni always finishes. "Cradled them in my arms. Tucked them in at night."

"Yep. Yep. So'd my sisters," Nonno always adds. "Zucchinis."

After the Toys "R" Us story, the table would grow quiet. Family members would move the food around on their plates, or inspect their cuticles. Mom would change the subject. Nanni and Nonno were the ones in line at the store because Mom had been too busy growing up; she had Melissa at seventeen with some man who wasn't my dad.

In a way, I was jealous. Melissa had been part of Nanni's inside world while spending entire days with her. She collected all of Nanni's secrets over pound cakes, and all the stories about Calabria—the Old Country—while picking peas or peeling apples. She watched Nanni brush her hair. Fold towels. Tie back the tomato plants with strips of old pantyhose. I was told watered-down, second-hand versions of stories, and only when I asked. Melissa would tell me things like Nan didn't say yes to Nonno until they moved to Canada. That she was promised to another man, and he immigrated at the same time too. That the man lived in Edmonton and he sometimes went over there for dinner or for a barbecue. Nanni was still young when she took care of Melissa, and so her memories were still ripe.

I had gone over to my sister's house that afternoon to find out what she knew about Rosina, what Nanni had told her.

"I don't think I know much more about Rosina than you. When I opened the email I recognized the picture. Her slight smile. Reminds me of Nan. Glad you scanned it," Melissa said while pouring the coffee and pushing sugar cubes across the table. "I think I will print it out and frame it."

Something. Tell me something.

"You know, I used to spend every day with Nan, and she would tell me that she used to spend all of her days with Rosina. Even though Rosina was Nan's grandmother, she was like a mother to Nan. She was closer to her than anyone else," Melissa said.

I thought about the Cabbage Patch story, and the way Nanni treated Melissa like a daughter. I imagined Nanni tucking that yarn-headed, freckled doll into bed next to Melissa, so she could wake to find it. Wake to be a little mother.

"What else do you know about Rosina?" I asked.

"I can't really remember. When you're a kid, you don't really listen to all those stories, you think they will always be there. You can always ask to hear them again and again. Each time only remembering a few things."

I needed to know about Rosina because I sensed that somewhere inside my belly was a baby; I didn't yet have the kind of words I needed to tell anyone about it, or the courage to find out for sure. I needed her—matriarch, midwife, mother. And Melissa was my way into Rosina's world.

I had almost told Mom about my missed periods earlier that morning, but she would have been too practical. Before I was ready to know for sure, she would have made me find out. Find out if I needed to grow up too fast. Melissa, at twenty-nine, was almost like a second mother. She was someone I could go to with questions I didn't want to ask anyone else: how to kiss, how to get over a heartbreak, how to have sex. And now, I was nineteen, just two years older than Mom had been when she was carrying Melissa and I needed to know how to deal with this situation.

Melissa tapped her hand on the table. "I do remember one thing. Nan told me that she used to sleep in Rosina's bed with her, just like I used to sleep with Nan. Nan would kick Nonno out, and I would get to spend the night in their room. Nan used to sleep with Rosina, partly because their place was so small, but also because she wanted to. Nanni always wanted to be near her, like a little shadow."

I thought of Nanni's stories. She would wake up in the night when Rosina was preparing to leave for a delivery. Nanni would sit up on her knees, careful not to let the bed creak because she didn't want to wake anyone else. She would peek through the window, squinting into the night until her grandmother, delivery bag in hand, had disappeared into darkness. In the morning, she'd ask to hear all about the baby. And sometimes, in the days that followed, she would be allowed to go with Rosina to check on a new mother or to bathe a baby, check its skin colour and its little thump, thumping heart.

Melissa put her hand on her shoulder and pulled it forward, leaned her head back and looked up at the ceiling. I took the opportunity to really look at her—at the dark curls that fell over her shoulders, at her brown, deep-set eyes—we looked alike despite the ten years between us, and despite our different fathers. She didn't say anything for a while until, with her perfectly arched eyebrows scrunched together, she asked, "Why are you suddenly so curious about Rosina?"

I shrugged, then lied. "Just because I found her picture, I guess."

My sister let the silence move across the kitchen. I leaned toward the baker's rack piled with recipe books and pretended to be reading the titles on the spines. Eventually, she spoke of the only line that connected them. And now a line—however faint—that connected me.

"You know when you lose a baby more than once, they start to look into your family history."

"Oh yeah?" I responded, feeling myself flush. I reached for a recipe book, *Slow Cooker Meals*, and fanned through the pages.

"They didn't find out anything really," Melissa said. "I guess sometimes women just lose babies. For me that was the first time I really thought about her. You know, Rosina was a midwife and she gave birth five times just like Nanni and Mom. And here I was, losing baby after baby. I just thought about her. I don't know why. It's important to know about your history, at least the medical stuff."

My sister was looking right at me.

I stared down to watch my sugar cube dissolve. Pieces of the cube floated on the milky surface, then sank. I told her about the box with the lantern and velvet pincushion, told her the story about Rosina dashing through the night, the bony trees and open field.

"I think I've heard that story before."

"No. I wrote it after I found her picture. I imagined it."

"Are you sure? I think I've heard it before."

NOTES

Me, Myself and My Mother

SONIA NIJJAR

> *A woman is her mother.*
> *That's the main thing.*
> —Anne Sexton, "Housewife"

MY MOTHER WAS BORN during the oppressive summer heat in a city nestled on the banks of the Ganges River. Minutes after her birth, a baby wrapped in a pink blanket was gently placed into my grandmother's arms. As the child began to cry, my grandmother watched, silently. The nurses in the room read her indifference to the girl as remorse over the birth of a daughter, not a son, so they told her "A second one will come," but my grandmother calmly shook her head.

"This is not my baby," she stated, holding the crying child out towards the confused women.

Twenty minutes later, only thirty minutes after my mother's birth, my grandmother lay in her bed nursing her child with whom she insisted she was sacredly connected. The nurses apologized profusely as my grandmother watched her baby and smiled.

* * *

When I was five years old, my grandmother gave me a doll with a painted red smile. I gave her my middle name, "Jeniffer," with two f's. My mother sat the doll at the top of my closet so as not to ruin her white bridal dress. In those days, I would pull the heavy metal doors open, look up at Jeniffer, and explain to her why we couldn't play.

By the next year, I had forgotten about the beautiful, lonely girl. At a small kiosk in the middle of an unpopulated mall, my mother stopped in front of a lacy, satin-lined carriage. In an instant, she was at the register paying an amount that caused her to look at me before she placed a finger to her red lips—a warning to keep the price hidden from my dad. Without words, I remember, I followed her out the doors, watching her carry the new box against her hip in the way she would carry a laundry basket.

During the ride home, my mother looked over to me and said, "Jeniffer needs a home too."

I nodded, turning away from the box.

I don't know what happened to my doll. Sometimes I feel as though I should look for her, to save her from her carriage or maybe from herself.

I don't know where to look or what questions to ask.

* * *

I watch a reflection in the mirror. The girl in it is familiar, in an unfamiliar way, so I watch her. I want to be connected to her. I want to be sacredly connected. I wait.

* * *

Graduating at the top of her class, my grandmother's daughter was a popular teacher. Wrapped elegantly in a pure white sari, red lips and smooth olive skin, I imagine my mother silencing every room she entered.

I look at her gripping a plaque and smiling into the camera. Dark eyeliner frames her light brown eyes, so much like mine. My mother stares at me; I stare at her, I stare at myself, I stare at someone. She seems to be telling me something, so I listen. As I wait for her words, I can imagine the sound of applause coming from the audience sitting, standing, in front of my mother's teaching stage.

The sound of an ovation fades and then there is silence. I adjust the frame and walk away.

* * *

My mother's teaching career ended after a short two years when she was married at twenty-four.

I look at her hands folded over a heavily embroidered, traditional bridal lengha. The bright red of her outfit gives me an uneasy feeling and I tell myself that she shares my discomfort. Her makeup is done so as to emphasize her eyes, which no longer resemble mine. I try to listen for her but my mother is silent. I am left silently looking at her.

After a while, her excessive gold jewellery pinches my own skin. I nod at my mother before leaving her.

* * *

For their honeymoon, my parents travelled to the northern Indian state of Uttar Pradesh with my aunt and uncle.

I hold a photograph that she has carefully framed from that time. My parents are in a different part of the world—a different world altogether. I look at my mother as she pumps water from a well into my dad's hands. Half of her body is bent over the handle of the pump, and her long dark hair hangs loosely over her eyes. I stare as if waiting for her to express agony over her task, to which I would nod and say, *exactly*.

I wait, but I only feel the water flowing out of its pump, I only hear it pouring into my father's hands. I imagine the photographer laughing—maybe it was my uncle—as he clicks and captures a moment that has become a part of my mother. I see she is preoccupied; I see her red lips parted by a white smile that I cannot understand. I continue to stare, waiting for her to look back at me. She doesn't. I tell myself her laughter has no sound.

I stare at the pump and imagine the friction as my mother pushes its handle up, and down. Up and down. This is enough to cause sparks, I tell myself. The sparks will come, I tell myself. And then she will tell me, "Stay away from the fire."

I hold the frame at a distance before reluctantly setting it down. I avert my eyes. And then I wait for the fire.

* * *

My mother had her first child at twenty-six. In India, she was a respected teacher. In Canada, a wife and dutiful daughter-in-law.

For several years, my mother supported her husband while he completed his education. He went to class in the mornings while she tearfully said goodbye to her son and went to work. In the evenings, she would rush home to make dinner and hold her baby. On most nights, the child's blue duvet was already tucked neatly under his chin. My mother would stand and watch him sleeping, her eyes glistening with tears.

The next morning, from his crib, her baby boy would watch her sleeping and squeal with excitement at the flutter of her eyelid. My mother has told me, "This kept me alive."

* * *

I was born twenty months after my mother had her first child and two days before her twenty-eighth birthday.

There are days that I look at a picture of her with her second-born child, and she appears as she did at twenty-two, gripping her plaque, smiling into the camera. Her royal blue blouse and short haircut give her a scholarly look. This woman is confident, proud.

Shifting my gaze, I become aware of the child in her arms. This woman is my mother. Maybe I am her plaque.

I return the frame wondering if I am seeing her at all.

* * *

On Mother's Day, I find my way inside my grandmother's darkened closet and shake open a bottle of what I believe to be my favourite Flintstones Vitamins. After chewing and swallowing, I stumble out of the room, swing the door shut, and collapse onto the carpeted floor.

Some time later, I wake up and watch white-coated doctors murmuring around me. The tubes extending out from my body are blue and I hear the sound of a vacuum coming from them. I laugh at this noise, and the doctors laugh with me, tickling my sides. I see my mother running towards me. She screams, "I thought I would die!"

Later, I am told that the painkillers are not Flintstones Vitamins, and that swallowing them could have killed me. I am only three, but the remorse is overwhelming. I must save my mother. I cannot let her die.

* * *

I have tried to look for her. I have stared into her eyes that are so much like mine, trying to find her. "How was your day?"

"I've been up since your dad left to work," she would say. "You know, you walk in with your boots, the flat ones I don't even like anyway, and then there is dirt on my floor. I clean it, you don't even see it."

I watched her, then. Her milky skin blending with the cream of the walls. The red bridal bangle she wears and has never taken off—the same one that I, now, wear—the exact hue of the décor inside the house my father built for her. I watch as she polishes her vases, beautiful and empty. And then I watch as she moves out of my sight.

* * *

I sit on the stairs of my parents' large house, my mother unaware of my presence. Her dark hair is pulled back, her eyeliner uncharacteristically smudged. Holding a wooden ladle, my mother stirs a steaming pot of soup with one hand, and with the other placed on the granite countertop, she holds herself up. The familiar sound of her red bangles clashing together with every stir unsettles me as I keep myself hidden from her view.

For a few minutes, the only sound comes from the stove where liquid bubbles. It fills the air. It fills my mother. I realize the soup has finished boiling when my mother gracefully bangs the edge of the ladle against her pot to prevent the liquid from falling on her immaculate tile. Lifting her hand from the countertop, she cups it underneath the ladle and slowly walks towards the kitchen sink. I realize that she has not turned down the heat of the stove, but I remain, in our shared silence, and I watch knowingly. I hear the raging bubbles of soup that I am certain will boil over, and without words, I try to tell my mother to hear it too. She continues washing the ladle, inspecting it in the sunlight from the window in front of her. This familiar action unsettles me further as I urge her to listen to me, to let me save her.

A few seconds later, the liquid rages uncontrollably, and finally my mother turns her head towards the gas stove. She drops the ladle in the sink and runs to the pot that is already overflowing, its contents burning on the surface of the stove. Turning the knob quickly, my mother's hand finds its place on the countertop.

Her heavy breathing breaks the silence between us. She is tired and I see it. I watch her back, interpret her stillness as a revolt, and I don't move. We are in solidarity, my mother and I. Through our silence, she tells me, "Stay away from this heat."

The phone rings as I slowly descend from my hiding place, feeling my mother and I are both free: finally, together. My mother lets out a cough before answering the call.

"Hi. Are you coming home for lunch? Yes, it's ready. Yes, see you soon."

She gives me a half-red smile, turns around, and stands motionless. I mirror her stillness.

Seconds pass before she turns to the sink and fills it with rushing water.

I grab a mop. My mother is not free.

* * *

In a bright, airy suite overlooking the Atlantic, my mother places an elaborate ornament around my neck. I look ahead at the camera pointed to capture what I'm told is a sacred moment between mother and bride.

The jewellery pinches my skin. My mother tells me, "I have never been so happy."

We stand in silence—the kind brought on only by uncomfortable truths. I'm happy too.

Voice

STEPHANIE WERNER

6:30 A.M. I HEAR A VOICE: "Mo-mmy!" I can't answer. Not for the first time, I have laryngitis.

Losing my voice is an occupational hazard of being the mother of three small children. Between the nagging, cajoling, repeating, and of course, the yelling, my voice gets a workout every day. On top of that is the fact that my kids use me as Kleenex, which means that I catch whatever viruses they bring home from school.

I try my best not to talk, but by 6:45 I am yelling, "Don't wake up your sister!" in a hoarse stage-whisper that fades in and out like a bad radio signal. Three-year-old Sophie ignores my pleas, and turns on the overhead light, waking six-year-old Claire.

Later, Claire repeats "What?" three times. My voice cracks as I repeat my request, which she then ignores.

"Lis-en–oo me!" I squawk.

* * *

There is a part in Disney's version of *The Little Mermaid* where Ursula the sea witch says to Ariel that as payment for a spell to make her human, "What I want from you is ... your voice."

Ursula's own voice is gravelly and low. Ariel is a natural Soprano, whose voice lifts up into the octaves and snakes out of her mouth like glowing green smoke.

"Aaah-Aah-Aaah-Aah-Aaaah…"

Until the green smoke is captured by the Sea Witch in a seashell necklace.

Without her voice, Ariel loses her power and her sense of self.

Early in the story, the mermaid is fearless: she takes on sharks and swims up to the forbidden surface. After she loses her voice, Ariel becomes helpless, almost failing to woo the prince in the agreed amount of time. Instead of taking charge, she just waits for him to "kiss the girl" and break the spell.

I feel Ariel's pain: without my voice, my strength as a mother seems impotent. Why should they listen to me when they have the ready excuse that they can't hear my voice? They know I can't intervene in an argument in another room. I also can't call them for dinner, or even complain about my situation. Like Ariel, I am silenced.

* * *

I tuck Claire into bed. I mouth "I love you" to her.

"I don't remember what your voice sounds like, Mommy," she says. She has only missed hearing me speak for one day.

I think about family members who have died and what we forget first and what we remember longest. I wonder how long it will be until my daughter forgets my voice when I die. I think about my grandmother, who died eight months ago. Before her death, I hadn't spoken to her in almost three years. She had Alzheimer's, so phone conversations were difficult as she couldn't remember who was calling. But even though I haven't heard my grandmother speak for over three years, I can still hear her voice in my head. The cutting consonants of her German accent: Bs became Ps, Ds became Ts, all the syllables clipped with her blunt scissor-tongue. All my life I knew her voice, but it was only when I was about ten or so that I realized she had an accent.

I remember when I had that realization; she was listening to her voice on tape.

"Nah," she said, "Dat's not me. I don't haf an accent like dat."

"Grandma, that is you. It's not an accent, it's just your voice." But I realized once I had said it that she *did* have an accent.

Nevertheless, she refused to listen to the offensive tape. To her ears, she sounded just like everybody else. Something was wrong with that tape.

I remember lying in the dark on a mattress on the floor of Grandma's craft room. Light spilled under the folding door. Voices rose like waves crashing over each other in an incoming tide, Grandma's voice always rising above the rest. She had what could be politely called "natural projection." The more excited she got by the card game, the more annoyed at Grandpa's cheating (or losing if they were on the same team), the louder she got. Her laughter would roar over all the rest: "AH-HA-HA!" The inevitable snort would get everyone going again.

English isn't my mother's first language, either. She is French-Canadian, but she learned English when she was young. I never really could hear her accent either.

Friends would comment: "I didn't know your Mom was French" when they heard her voice for the first time. I would think, *How can they tell?* Even now, I only notice my mother's accent when she sings. She'll belt out a Melissa Etheridge song and drop the H's and change TH's to Ds.

I remember Mom losing her voice when I was a child. It was a big thrill for me, at age five or six, to get to answer the phone for her and be her "voice."

My mother doesn't have the loud voice that her mother-in-law, my German grandmother, had. But I do remember her yelling at me when I was younger. As she screamed, her voice would crack. It was a sign to me that I had made her lose control. The shards of her voice breaking were a signal of my victory.

* * *

"Aah-Mum-mum-mum … Te-te-te. A-oh-ah." Eleven-month-old Charlotte has pulled off my breast during a feeding and smiling up at me. "Ah-ta-ta-ta. Ah-ra-ra-ra."

My third, and youngest, daughter clearly enjoys the sound of her own voice; she experiments with the sounds she can create like a DJ sampling vinyl, and just as repetitive. She reminds me of Claire at that age, also a chatterbox, even before she could speak. Once Claire could speak there was no stopping her. She created an ongoing narration for anything she was doing, and being endowed with the same "natural projection" as my grandmother, her voice carried through most of the house. At age two, I would put her in her room with toys while I nursed her baby sister. I could hear her playing across the hall even with the door closed.

"Now you go in there," she would say, "I'll just get your mommy."

Or, one time: "Here, chicken, chicken, chicken!" That was a mystery, what was she doing in her room by herself that had anything to do with chickens?

When her "quiet time" was over, I came in to find an entire box of Kleenex shredded all over the floor.

"What is this?" I asked.

"I was feedin' the chickens, Mommy!" Claire replied in her high voice.

Claire could speak in full sentences by the age of nineteen months. The only sounds she could not pronounce were Ls and Rs, which were in her name. When you asked her name, she would reply: "Cweah," which nobody could understand, so I taught her to spell it. Then she would say "C-EWH-A-I-AWH-E, that spells CWEAH!"

Claire has so far inherited my grandmother's ability to carry a tune. Grandma always used to sing when she cleaned. Even if there was no music on, Grandma would still sing or hum to herself. I can remember hearing her singing from the kitchen: "*Que sera, sera ... whatever will be, will be ...*" she only knew the refrain, but would repeat it, humming the parts she didn't know in-between. Claire used to make up her own songs too, singing about whatever it was she was doing to a made-up tune. Now, she can hear a song once, and then repeat the chorus. Over and over. She really still loves the sound of her own voice.

My second daughter, Sophie, has a voice at home, but has only recently started to use it when we are out in public. Her shyness made it easy to take her places as a toddler. She wasn't the type of child who would speak to strangers, or yell and scream in public when she was little.

Her quiet temperament also means I can't always hear what she is up to, until it's too late: "Sophie, why are you standing naked in the bathroom with water all over the floor?"

"I wanted to play in the sink."

I will hear her calling me: "MO-MMY! I'M ALL DONE!" And I know now from experience that this means she's ready for me to help her wipe her bum. But usually I don't even realize that she's in the bathroom until I hear her calling. Claire, on the other hand, still announces her bodily functions before she uses the bathroom.

Sometimes I wish Sophie had more of a voice, that she would speak up for herself when we are at the park. When other kids take her toys, she will just look at me, mute. At home, when her sister does the same thing, she can say something and stand up for herself. But it's as if her voice gets lost once we are out in the world.

* * *

"There's something about that voice. Too beautiful to be real," says Prince Phillip in Disney's *Sleeping Beauty* when he hears Briar Rose singing in the woods.

As a mother of three girls, I watch a lot of princess movies. Princesses in Disney movies always sing like the larks they attract to sit on their fingers. Their beautiful voices also attract princes who hear them singing and seek them out for a duet.

When she was a teenager, my sister took voice lessons as part of a musical theatre group. She may sound like me when we are talking, but according to her, she is a Mezzo-Soprano when she sings, and I am more of an Alto. I've never had any lessons, but I can carry a tune and Michelle and I have even harmonized on occasion.

Once Michelle and I went on a road trip to the mountains. We took a hike up to Parker Ridge in Banff National Park where you can see the Saskatchewan Glacier and part of the Columbia Icefields from the top of a moraine-covered hill. On the way down, we sang "Closer to Fine" by the Indigo Girls, our voices carrying down the switchbacks: "*I went to the doctor, I went to the mountains, I looked to the children, I drank from the fountains...*" and our feet (mine in hiking boots, hers in trail runners) kept time with our singing on the narrow, gravel-covered trail.

I rarely talk to Michelle on the phone, and when I hear my voice recorded, I sound eerily like her. Even my parents have a hard time telling us apart. Instead of potentially hurting our feelings by asking who was calling, Mom asks "What's up?" and then figures out it is me based on the context of the conversation.

I'm not sure what bothers me more: the fact that I sound like my sister, or the fact that my voice isn't unique because we sound so alike. As if I don't have a voice of my own. Like my grandmother, I also hate the sound of my voice. When I hear myself on tape now,

I find that I sound too nasally. Definitely too loud. All my jokes fall flat in the recording, my laughter is obnoxious. Sometimes, I even snort. The sound of my own voice is as annoying as nails on a chalkboard, and makes the hair on the back of my neck stand up.

* * *

A few days later, my voice has returned, only slightly more gravelly than usual. I can almost sing Sarah McLachlan again, but I still fade out on the higher notes. My daughters can hear me. I miss the interesting sounds my voice makes when I have laryngitis, but relish the return of my voice's power. Sometimes I need to be heard—especially by my three little girls—even if I can't always stand the sound of my own voice.

Our Dead Fish

M. ELIZABETH SARGENT

O UR GOLDFISH had been a birthday present for our two-year-old, Molly, and had come complete with bowl, fish food, water conditioner, and net for transferring him from one body of water to another. The friends who presented him to us also purchased one for their little boy, but their goldfish died within the week of causes unknown. On the occasion of his death, we warned our daughters that a goldfish life is short and sweet so not to expect that ours would be able to attend their high school graduations. They sprinkled several teaspoons of fish food into his bowl and ignored us. They were captivated by his untiring circular slither along the inside of the glass.

Our second grader, Hannah, named the fish, although she solicited Molly's approval for the name first. Hannah had recently filled out a form for school which asked "Child's name?" She had written "Hannah," as we would have expected. The form then asked "Name child likes to be called?"—and she had written "Debbie." That had been news to us and to the teacher. But so it was that Hannah decided to call the fish Debbie. (I shall continue to refer to Debbie as "he," however, not only to register my conviction that Debbie was no lady, but also to distinguish him from my daughters.)

Debbie was not very interesting. He performed no tricks. He routinely dirtied the water, and we routinely cleaned it, scrubbing fish slime off the few shells we had put in the bottom of the bowl. The girls learned not to douse him with food three times a day and instead to scatter a few grains of fish-food on the surface of his water every morning. Occasionally Molly would press her nose against the glass bowl and watch Debbie's activities close up. I only noticed him if I was alone in the kitchen late at night, reading or writing quietly, and heard the primeval, muted glub glub of him opening his mouth near the surface of the water. At those times, I felt he was good company.

Remarkably, Debbie was just several days past the eight-month anniversary of his joining our family, when my husband—searching for the fish food in the cupboard above Debbie's bowl one February evening—accidentally knocked a tightly closed jar of popcorn salt, butter-flavoured, off the shelf. It crashed into Debbie's watery den, dislocating his shells, displacing water, and distracting him beyond all measure. Debbie whirled round and round the salt jar and also around my husband's fingers as he groped for it guiltily. My husband apologized several times to the fish, but Debbie didn't give him a second glance.

We made sure no salt had gotten into the water, cleaned up the counter, made as many comforting noises as we could without feeling too ridiculous, and went up to bed. When we came down to breakfast the next morning and fumbled as usual for boxes of cereal, jugs of milk, and jars of wheat germ, Debbie was neglected in the rush. Hannah somehow ate enough to keep her alive until noon, slid into her jeans, sweatshirt, and jacket and made it out the door and to the bus stop on time. Her father and I waved from the door and then walked back to the kitchen to join Molly and finish our coffee.

Molly was not in her chair. She was standing with her nose pressed against Debbie's bowl. "Move!" she shouted.

My husband looked stricken.

Molly turned toward us. "Debbie's not moving, Mom," she said.

"Oh dear," I said. I took a closer look. Debbie lay very still near the bottom of the bowl beside a pink and gray shell. "Poor Debbie. Maybe he needs his water changed."

The water didn't look particularly filmy, but I thought I'd give it a try. As I ran the tap water to get it at room temperature instead of freezing, I talked soberly about how short-lived goldfish were and how bored Debbie must have been by now with swimming in circles for so many months in the same bowl, with the same few sea shells, in the same kitchen.

Molly stood on a chair beside me at the sink. When we transferred Debbie into clean, conditioned water, he took heart, gave a flip of his tail and swam twice in a circle.

"Hi, Debbie!" Molly screamed piercingly. He then rolled over and floated to the surface.

Molly moved closer and stared. "Move," she said, but with less conviction. She stroked Debbie's belly with her little finger.

"Molly," I said as gently as I could, "I think Debbie's dead. I think Debbie was old and tired. And perhaps, he had a heart attack," I said, glancing at my husband. He looked as remorseful as one can while eating toast. It was understood, of course, that no mention would be made to the children of the popcorn salt fiasco.

Molly, meanwhile, was across the room trying to put on her shoes. "Time for school, Dad?" she said, apparently having worked through her grief and already thinking ahead to her two hours of nursery school down the street.

While she was gone, I flushed Debbie down the toilet and cleaned out his bowl and put it away. It didn't seem right to bury a fish in the ground, earth not being its natural element.

I didn't think about Debbie again until Hannah came home from school that afternoon. Molly piped up without warning, "Debbie died. Hurt attacks today."

I was unprepared for Hannah's reaction.

"Debbie *died*?" She ran to the kitchen to check, then ran back. "How?" and her voice broke, and she came into my arms, sobbing and talking at the same time. "Where is Debbie? What happened to her? Can I see her?" Molly looked on with big eyes: she looked as if she thought perhaps she hadn't reacted enough to Debbie's passing, hadn't taken in the full seriousness of it, especially since technically Debbie had been *her* fish.

I held Hannah on my lap and patted her back and tried to explain. Hannah was offended at the toilet episode until I reasoned with her that Debbie would be happier in water than in dirt and also that he could float eventually back out to the streams with fellow fishes. One could think of it as a kind of burial at sea. Gradually, the storm subsided. I comforted Hannah with statements I didn't believe myself, such as "Debbie had a good, full life for a goldfish."

I was sure even goldfish had a right to expect more.

At any rate, all at once the clouds cleared, and Hannah was busily addressing store-bought Valentines to the children in her class and to her schoolteachers. There was one relapse when she came over to me with a sad face and handed me an envelope marked "Debbie."

"Open it," she said.

Inside, there was a picture of an ear of corn holding a heart: the printed message was, "When is an ear of corn like a question?"

"Turn it over," Hannah said.

On the back it read, "When it is popped." Underneath, in red ink, Hannah had printed, "To Debbie, my dead fish. Love, Hannah."

I didn't smile.

Hannah said, "I almost did these Valentines yesterday. I was thinking of it, Mom, but I didn't have time. I was going to give this one to Debbie and now it's too late."

"That would've been nice, sweetheart," I said, "but you know Debbie couldn't read."

"I know, but I could've held it against the bowl and she could've looked at the picture." I didn't tell her that I doubted Debbie would have wanted to be reminded of popcorn in any form.

Hannah walked out of the room. I heard her open the bathroom door.

"Hannah," I called. "What are you doing?"

"I'm going to flush Debbie's Valentine down the toilet. Then maybe she'll find it."

"Absolutely not," I ordered. "Get back in here." Even crazed with grief, a child cannot be permitted everything.

She came obediently.

"Now, Hannah, that Valentine would get all soggy and Debbie would *never* find it. Plus it could clog up the toilet." I paused and spoke more gently: "I think it's a nice idea you want Debbie to know you miss her, but this isn't the way to go about it."

Molly said, "I want *my* Balentines."

I welcomed the distraction. "Now why don't we get Molly's package of Valentines and she can draw on hers while you finish yours?"

I began to feel capable and sensible as the two girls got busy, though I still felt I hadn't handled Debbie's departure well. The loss of a fish was clearly a greater trauma for a seven-year-old than I had realized. Perhaps Hannah needed some kind of ritual to help her feel a part of Debbie's last day and to help her accept it. I meditated on possible courses of action as I started to scrub carrots for dinner. But about twenty minutes later, Hannah called out, "Mom, I'm all out of Valentines and I still don't have any for my speech teacher, Miss Winkleman. And I really like Miss Winkleman."

"Well, make her one," I said. "Homemade ones are nicer anyway."

"Okay." A minute passed. Then Hannah came bounding in to me at the sink. "I know what I'll do!" She was happy, excited, full of a good idea. She held up a used-looking envelope. "Miss Winkleman's first name is Debbie. I'll give her Debbie's card!"

"But sweetie, it says 'My dead fish' on the back."

"Oh, that's okay. I'll cross that part out." She bounded back into the living room and then called out a few minutes later, "I'm all done, Mom! I bet I have all my Valentines ready before anyone else in the class!"

"Me, too," Molly said.

Late Born

Motherhood at Sixty-Two

FAYE HANSEN

ROSANNA DELLA CORTE MADE HEADLINES in Italian newspapers in 1994 when her son was born. Rosanna was desperate to have a child and seized in vitro fertilization like a drowning woman grabs a life raft. She believed it would ease the pain of losing her first son in a motorcycle accident. It would please her husband and preserve the family name. She was sixty-two years old.

In a three-minute phone call, I acquired two children and became a mother again on June 21, 2010. A month later, I turned sixty-two.

That summer day, the phone rings and my son's girlfriend Jessica asks me, "Can you take the kids for a few days? They're at daycare."

"Of course," I respond. "I'll pick them up after work." I mentally shift my plans. I will have a weekend with Mary and Daniel instead of a grown-up summer weekend of sleeping in, coffee on the balcony, meeting my new man William for a walk in the river valley, a drink, dinner; a respite before another week of work.

Two minutes later, the phone rings again. "This is mumble, mumble from Social Services," a strange voice intones. I don't get her name. The words "Social Services" have drowned it out. "Have you agreed to look after Daniel and Mary?"

"Yes," I reply. "Their mother just called me. What's this about?"

Someone, perhaps a neighbour, has phoned social services. An unannounced visit has determined that Jessica's home is unsafe for small children. Alternative care is required or the children will be "apprehended."

I feel myself turning an abrupt corner, leaving my old life behind and moving into unknown territory: my son is ensnared by drugs, a young woman I don't really know is the mother of my grandchildren, a baby and a two-year-old in a household with few resources, shaky jobs, social housing, and intergenerational addiction in the mother's family. I need to pick up my grandchildren.

The windows of the daycare on 118th Avenue are covered with fading cartoon characters smudged by a layer of grime. The front door is open two inches with a bunched-up mat acting as a doorstop to allow a tiny breeze into the sweltering interior. A little boy in a highchair cries and mops at his runny nose with his sleeve. The television blares before a row of small children perched along an old wine-coloured couch. Daniel and Mary rush over to hug my legs. They are filthy and tired-looking. Mary's skirt is two sizes too big, held up with a big safety pin. Daniel's big brown eyes gaze up over bluish sleepless bags. I think of ragged Oliver Twist whispering, "More please." A daycare worker reports that Daniel and Mary arrived around two that afternoon, as they do most days. "They're usually the last to be picked up," she states, in a flat accusatory tone.

"How can this be?" I wonder, knowing that Daniel is enrolled in full day kindergarten. "Where are their backpacks?" I ask and hear that they come unencumbered by sweaters or snacks or a special toy. They come to me with nothing, given over to my care without a qualm. No permission slip required.

I have no experience with daycare, having chosen to stay home with my own two children, one of whom is their father, until the youngest reached school age. Having put off having my own children until age thirty-two, I had the luxury of choice provided by a good education, savings, and a supportive husband. Jessica has had two children before reaching the age I was when I married.

Should I have anticipated that phone call? Whenever I had picked the children up for visits, they were waiting on the doorstep, ready to leave, clean, smiling, and eager to visit. I wasn't invited in. I had never had a cup of coffee with their mother but I chalked it up to her feelings of intimidation, remembering the beginning of my relationship with my mother-in-law. Shy country girl meets accomplished European sophisticate. But that's another story.

Looking back, I recall how quiet they had typically become when I was driving them home on Sunday evenings. We would sing along to "Teddy Bear's Picnic" and suddenly I would find myself doing a solo: "At six o'clock, their mommies and daddies will take them home to bed because they're tired little teddy bears." I would glance into the rear view mirror to see that Daniel had reached across the gap between the car seats to take Mary's hand. I thought, "How sweet," recalling me and my brother squabbling in the backseat of an old Hudson Hornet. It didn't occur to me then that this skinny little five year old was offering comfort and assurance to his little sister. The unspoken, "I'll look after you" instead of the spoken, "Grandma, we need help."

The "few days" stretches into a week. Daniel's sixth birthday is approaching. I cobble together a birthday party. There are gifts but no Mom and no neighbourhood friends. I overdo presents so I can begin to fill the gap left behind: some clothes, some toys, and some books. We have a chocolate cake laden with candles and sparklers and Neapolitan ice cream. We play the games I organized at my children's birthdays. Pin the Tail on the Donkey, Hot Potato, Musical Chairs.

Jessica shows up the following week, loaded down with a Superstore slab cake, a bicycle with training wheels, guilt, and her Mom—"Kohkum" to the kids—and Kohkum's boyfriend. I leave the apartment to give them privacy and fight with myself while I walk in the river valley, chastising myself for leaving virtual strangers in my home but knowing that Jessica shuts down in my presence. After an hour has passed, I return to over-sugared, over-stimulated children huddled with their mother on my leather couch. Kohkum and her boyfriend disappear. It takes numerous attempts and many promises before a crying Jessica can tear herself away from her weeping children. I replace her on the couch, repeating, "It's okay, it's okay," endlessly in a singsong voice as we rock side to side with our arms around one another.

Mary whimpers for Mommy in a little voice that stabs my heart with a pain so acute that I feel sick. That night the whimpers turns to screams as the night terrors begin. Her eyes are open but she is not conscious of my presence. Nothing, no words, can comfort her. I sing. I repeat her name, over and over and attempt to rock her in my lap but she kicks, flails, and screams. When she is exhausted, she collapses on the soggy pillow, again whispering "Mommy,

Mommy." Then she rolls over to face the wall and is asleep. I, on the other hand, don't sleep.

That Monday morning, I begin my relationship with Social Services. I leave frantic messages and receive no response. I show up at offices. "The case worker is in a planning meeting," a young woman posted behind a glass partition tells me. I attempt to describe my problem through the small circle cut in the glass separating me from the inner workings of social services. I'm met with repetition, "She's in a meeting. She's not available."

"I'll just sit here until she's free," I respond.

"She is completely booked for the day," I'm told.

"I'll just sit here until I see her," I repeat, dredging up some rarely used backbone. I plunk down on a brown vinyl chair and begin to read the posters and pamphlets left for my edification. There appears to be a support group for almost everything, everyone except me.

A slight shift is apparently made in the social worker's schedule. She pokes her head through a three-inch opening in a secure door and asks me what I want.

I don't shriek, "I want my life back." I'm rational and ask what is to happen to Mary and Daniel.

She looks blank. According to her, the kids have been removed from their home and come to live with me. It's a "family arrangement." In her opinion, the case is closed.

The word "dumbfounded" does not suffice.

It takes me nearly a year to work out a reasonable relationship with Social Services, aided largely by the "Kincare" worker assigned to me. That's what I've become. Kincare is the modern term for extended family, paralleling foster care for unrelated children. I know that in the early days of Alberta's settlement, kids were taken in when a mother died or a father deserted the family. It was expected of relatives. I learn more than I ever wanted to know about the workings of Child and Family Services. I read legislation, which sets the rules. I sit for twenty-five hours of interviews to see if I will be accepted as a Kincare "parent." I submit a Criminal Record Check. I let someone snoop through my house. Is there a lock on the medicine cabinet? Do I have guns? Does the fridge hold nutritious food? I ask friends to write references.

We pretend that there are other alternatives to the kids remaining with me.

No one explains the alternatives. I remember the case a number of years back of the young First Nations' boy, Richard, found hanged when he was sixteen. The subsequent investigation revealed that he had been in numerous white foster homes before he put a rope around his neck. A rope where loving arms should have been.

I begin to reconfigure my apartment to accommodate my expanded family. I install bunk beds in my writing room and move books from shelves to make room for a baby doll and Spiderman. I visit second hand children's stores to acquire clothes, games, and all the accoutrements I thought were well behind me. I need Raffi CDs, plastic drinking glasses, plastic mattress covers, and knowledge of the current fad in toys. I place step stools in front of the sinks and buy toothbrushes and hairbrushes.

I soon realize that I cannot maintain my sanity in my sweet little co-op apartment overlooking the North Saskatchewan River. I buy a house that is close to a park and acquire a mortgage. I rummage through my old trunk of keepsakes to try to find Halloween costumes and favourite children's storybooks. We relocate in time for Christmas—a new family in a new home.

I also acquire a partner, William, and ask my sweetheart if he would like to move in with us. He submits to his twenty-five hours of interviews with social services too. He is found acceptable and moves in. I think of pioneer women with a bunch of kids on the farm, facing futures after the early death of husbands. They cast about, picking a father for their children, a source of income, entering marriages of convenience. I'm thankful that our partnership is one of love and that he is willing to take us all on.

We attend a Christmas Kincare party put on by Catholic Social Services. The gymnasium of a community centre is draped in decorations and filled with the shell-shocked. Grandparents, aunts, and uncles with unexpected families are picking up the pieces and trying to act normal.

The guy at the next table is in year seven with three grandsons. He's given up on the children returning to his daughter. "It never lasts," he says. "She cleans up for a while but it always falls apart." They're his for keeps. He says that there are one million grandparents across Canada raising grandchildren. A woman leans over to me, "Thank God for Grandmothers, eh?" I can't find any statistics which confirm or deny this astounding figure.

I realize that in my innocent suburban days, raising my own children, I saw only one family model, the one I tried to create and maintain. Father goes off to work in the morning and Mommy stays home with the little ones. Nice bungalow, holiday trailer, a pet cat, everything but the white picket fence. I spent years trying to pull off the Dick and Jane family of my Grade One readers, eventually giving up when the kids left home. My suburban dream was supposed to morph into a grandmother whose grandchildren visited on the odd weekend and then went home to another suburban house while I used retirement for its intended purpose: to travel, read, put my feet up.

I know that in many cultures, extended family members raise children. In China, in Africa, in the Philippines, grandmothers have taken in their grandchildren and other orphaned children in the community, without the resources that Social Services provide me. In the U.S., African-American grandmothers in vast numbers jump in to prevent grandchildren becoming wards of the state. In Edmonton, live-in Filipino nannies care for other people's children, cook meals, and clean house. They receive room, board, and small paycheques, some of which are sent home to support their own children, often left in the care of a grandmother. I dream about winning the lottery so that I can hire a nanny. I imagine a clean house, empty laundry baskets, and the ability to go out in the evening.

I think of Rosanna, the Italian mamma so determined to have that child in 1994. I wonder what she is doing now. This year, in 2014, she is eighty, if she is still alive. Did she get to raise her bambino? Did she sometimes sit in the bathroom with the door closed, wondering what on earth ever possessed her to fall for in vitro fertilization? Or does she now have a handsome seventeen-year-old, of whom she is proud? One who is looking after her? I think about her and her son during the long gaps between hearing from mine.

As Daniel and Mary and I approach one year together, the Temporary Guardianship Order (TGO) becomes a Permanent

Guardianship Order (PGO)—there's a whole new lingo associated with this life. I begin to do the math; my job plus my grandchildren equals insanity.

When my first child was born thirty years ago, I tried working part-time, teaching for one year before giving it up to become a stay-at-home mom. When I was teaching, I worried about my baby being cared for in a dayhome. When I was with her, I worried about my students in the care of another teacher. I knew that I wasn't giving either important job my best efforts. Too much to do. Too tired all the time. I remained at home until my second child, born three years later, started Kindergarten. Now his daughter is ready for kindergarten and I'm taking a day off work to walk her to her first day of school and walk her brother to his Grade Two door.

I turn sixty-three. I've tried working and looking after my six- and four-year-olds for a year. I have one abiding sensation. Fatigue. I begin to research early retirement. I've been called "a saint" this last year. I'm not a saint. I'm simply another descendant of Alberta's pioneers. We step up to the plate, do what needs to be done, and try to refrain from whining. My grandmother adopted a little girl after giving birth to her own daughter and seven sons. She wanted more female energy in the family. My mother took in a little girl when the child's mother was committed to a mental institution. When I wrote to her of my situation, she responded, "Of course, you did it. You're your mother's daughter."

I'm reticent about telling people that I'm raising my grandchildren. I suspect that it's shame about the reason. I don't think that anyone would want to admit that a child of theirs, either male or female, could not look after his or her own children. My shame is probably nothing compared to a parent's despair that contributes to the endless cycle of addiction, shame, and guilt.

Most people don't ask why I am raising Daniel and Mary. I find that Canadians are generally polite, nosy but polite. According to Social Services, it's much more common for the maternal grandmother to parent grandchildren. As there are so many more single daughters with children, this makes sense. Of course for every woman with a child, there is a man with a child but this doesn't translate into parenting. So, I'm an anomaly. Paternal grandmother of Mary, raising her and her brother as their mother.

My mind less often shrieks that I want my old life back. The resentment usually strikes when an opportunity falls into my lap that I previously would have grasped and run with. When I was sixty, a friend said, "There's a $399 all-inclusive to Cuba for a week. You need to decide by end of day." I phoned my cousin and we went. "Want to go to China?" my friend Susan asked the next year. "I need a roommate for double occupancy rates." I went. Sometimes I want to stomp my feet, throw a plate, swear. But who would listen? And what difference would my wants make? None. Nothing. And who would take care of Daniel and Mary?

Sometimes my longings are more mundane—a book launch at a bookstore—but bedtime is 7:30 p.m. I stay home. Evening dances to practice the steps William and I were learning at dance lessons. Babysitting is nine dollars an hour. Often, it's just the fantasy of being alone in the house or the car. My sweetie offers me an evening out each week. I am eternally grateful and choose a meditation class nearby. I'm told that it's supposed to relieve stress.

I also worry: what if this doesn't work out? What if I get sick? Die? What if my William finally comes to his senses and decides that this is more than he signed on for?

But then, I realize that if I wasn't in this situation, there would be no one reaching up to take my hand and whisper, "I love you." I wouldn't burst with pride when Daniel decodes a three-syllable word for the first time and gets a certificate for best Cree language at the end of Grade One. I wouldn't find love notes on my pillow and be offered masterpieces to stick to the fridge door. I wouldn't get another chance to dedicate a doorframe to height measurements and marvel when the training wheels come off. I couldn't celebrate that Daniel now begins a sentence without asking permission to speak. "Grandma can I tell you something?" Occasionally he even tells Mary to "shut up" when she goes overboard. He used to do anything to keep her from crying: he offered toys and hugs, remembering his old role of being the responsible one in the house. Now he acts like a normal seven-year-old and Mary acts five. I rejoice in the normal.

And I wouldn't be able to watch myself grow millimetre by millimetre, patience contracting and expanding, fatigue set aside with a smile, vulnerability and fear examined and replaced by openness to whatever the future brings.

I create a mantra, put a stress reduction tape on the bedside table. I say prayers and find a psychiatrist. I cross my fingers and hope. I join a support group. Then I count the years. I'll be seventy-six when, hopefully, they have finished high school and I can declare them grown-up. Or at least beyond my control. Then, I'll pick up the pieces of the life I had planned—travelling, sitting in the sun reading, cooking, gardening, enjoying the gift of empty time—and start my retirement. Or perhaps not. My dream may shift again like clouds in the sky.

I hope Rosanna is sitting in the Italian sunshine, proud of what she has accomplished with her baby born when she was sixty-two. Maybe I'll look her up sometime and we can share a nice glass of Chianti and talk about our children.

Sleep Little One, Sleep[1]

NAOMI MCILWRAITH

"SLEEP LITTLE ONE, SLEEP" say the words on the bronze plaque that now marks the place where James Thomas Calvin Meakes has lain for nearly eighty years. Absent for seventy-eight years, Grandma's searing loss and Baby James's headstone only become real the summer of 2013, when Mom and I attend the 125th Anniversary of the Stone Church, a few short miles west and south of Wishart, Saskatchewan. With the help of the organizing committee, we search the cemetery to find where he was buried. We drove here with the bronze plaque carefully wrapped in thick towels and packaged snugly in a box. Our precious cargo is stored securely in the trunk so that we can get help locating Baby James's grave.

Twenty-five years ago when Mom and Grandma last visited the graveyard, Grandma pointed and said, "That's where your brother is buried. There, where the lilac bush is growing." Now, so many years later, it's a cold July day, and we're all wearing a couple of layers of fall clothing as we study the map to locate little James's resting place just a few inches west of the ever-expanding lilac bush, in between Big Fred's and Mrs. Marshall's graves. Mom's deep brown eyes sparkle with a mix of sadness and joy that is layered with wisdom gained from a lifetime of caring for others, as she reads the handwritten words on the parchment map of the cemetery: Baby Meakes (James and Lucabelle). The words and Baby James seem so far way, like looking through a snowstorm or glancing in the rearview mirror at an image obscured by eight decades of life and death, love and loss. Grandma and Grandpa tried to leave their heartache behind them when they left first for Regina, then Winnipeg, and later for Edmonton. But Mom has never forgotten their sorrow and she returns today to honour both their grief and wee Baby James's short time on earth. Like the Stone Church standing nearby and the granite marker she now lays, Mom's commitment to observing these memories and honouring their lives is formidable.

On a desperately cold night in February 1935, Grandma Meakes went into labour with her first child. Great Grannie Sabiston served as midwife and a young doctor came by cutter from a good long way off to help in the delivery. Far more experienced than the doctor, Great Grannie Sabiston advised him that the baby was breech and needed to be turned. This Grannie Sabiston and the doctor did, but the doctor's use of forceps left Baby James with holes in his cheeks and unable to suck. Grandma Meakes fed him with an eye dropper until he died in her arms less than two weeks later. Mom wouldn't be born until July 1939, but Baby James's death at eleven days after his birth and Grandma and Grandpa's subsequent grief surely shaped my Mom's future as a neonatal intensive care nurse to premature and sick newborns, and as a foster mother to children needing safer homes than their biological parents would or could provide.

* * *

What does it mean to mother from an Aboriginal perspective? Mom inherits and therefore bequeaths to my natural siblings and me our Aboriginal legacy through the social history of the Hudson's Bay Company's fur trade with Cree and Ojibwe peoples of Rupert's Land and, as Mom and I learned more recently, through the French trade with the Indigenous people further east in what are now known as Ontario and Quebec. Most HBC records of unions between company employees and Aboriginal women fail to name the women. A hundred, two hundred, three hundred years later, let me invoke my Mom's name: Lavona Lillian McIlwraith (*née* Meakes); my Grandma's name: Lucabelle Meakes (*née* Sabiston); my Great Grandmother's name: Grannie Lillian Sabiston (*née* McLeod); my Great-Great Grandmother's name: Annabella McLeod (*née* Thomas); my Great-Great-Great Grandmother's name: Mary Thomas (*née* Bouvier); my Great-Great-Great-Great Grandmother's name: Marguerite Bouvier (*née* Lariviere). Grannie Sabiston had ten children; one died in infancy. Grandma Meakes had five pregnancies, but Mom is the only one to have survived. Fortunately, Grandma and Grandpa Meakes adopted my Auntie Ruth, a sister for my Mom. Mom herself sailed through four pregnancies without complication and went on to become a nurse and a foster mother.

Because of the unmitigated heartbreak of racism, only in recent years have Mom and I been able to speak about our Métis heritage and how that factors into her exceptional life of service to babies of all colours, including many Aboriginal infants and youngsters. My mother's story exemplifies a concern for all children, not just her own. Her tenacity in overcoming the challenges so many mothers face is like a mountain's timeless ability to weather nature's erosive forces.

Mom's interest in becoming a foster mother began one hot August night in 1981 when firemen came with their screaming trucks to respond to a small fire behind the garage of a house two doors south of us in West Jasper Place, Edmonton. A sordid collection of adults had come and gone from that house, but now all those grownups had drifted away like smoke and downriver like whisky. One small child of about eighteen months remained, wandering around the back alley and wearing only a soggy diaper. Naturally, Mom took the little girl with long curly light brown hair into our home to change her diaper and we called the police. The policeman said not to change the child's diaper until he arrived because he needed to check for signs of abuse. The officer and Mom discovered that the little girl was actually a boy. We also found cigarette burns on the child's arms, rope burns around his wrists, and bald spots on his head. These discoveries were bad enough, but when the friendly policeman sat on the couch an hour later saying, "I know this kid. We apprehended him a couple of months ago," the betrayal was as clear as the wounds on this little boy's arms and head. Adults and a system designed by them had failed this boy. Adults and their adult structures, even in the late-twentieth century, had not protected this boy from unimaginable abuse. Mom and Dad did not foster him, but the officer did apprehend him. We wonder to this day about that little boy and the rest of his story.

* * *

My younger brother was eight that year we found the little boy wandering in the alley and Mom, knowing she wouldn't have any more children, advertised a number of baby items in the *Bargain Finder*. Having already sold the crib and several other baby accessories, Mom had but one small infant chair left to sell. A woman came to the door to buy it. Mom had bought it in the early 1960s and all four of her natural babies had sat in it, so she advertised it for $1.00. The woman who came to the door insisted on giving Mom $4.00 and explained that Paramed Health Services (PHS) would reimburse her. Mom had been considering taking a break from her job as an NICU nurse and the woman's comment piqued her curiosity. She asked about PHS. The woman explained that she was a homemaker with PHS, and that she received babies into her home for emergency placements. Social Services had so many babies needing homes and so few homes in which to place them. Mom looked further into PHS. She talked it over with Dad and my siblings and me, and proceeded to apply to be a PHS homemaker.

Within two weeks, Mom, my sister, and my brother went to the Camsell Hospital to pick up Baby Lilly. The plan was for Mom to use her technical skills as an NICU nurse and her gifts of compassion and love to nurse the baby to health in preparation for heart surgery. Born with a number of congenital ailments, Baby Lilly had already undergone kidney surgery. At five months of age, though she had received the attention of many concerned professionals, she languished at nine pounds. She seemed unable to gain the necessary weight required to qualify for the heart surgery needed to repair her torn septum. Over the next six or seven months, between Mom's expertise as an NICU nurse, her whispers of "Sleep little one, sleep," and her and Dad's abundant love and care, Baby Lilly reached the fifteen pound mark and gained the strength she needed to get through heart surgery. Baby Lilly survived the surgical trauma and returned to our home for several months until she was strong enough to return to her biological mother. And then, with the singular maternal devotion she has always shown, Mom resolutely ensured this baby's wellbeing by teaching Baby Lilly's own mother how to help Lilly eliminate and to prepare her for bowel surgery.

Not long after Lilly was returned to her own mother, Mom and Dad took in another child—Baby Jackie—from the Royal Alexandra Hospital's neonatal intensive care unit. Rather than suffering from a congenital weakness, she was dealing with the outcomes of having been prenatally exposed to a concoction of "T n' Rs" (Talwin and Ritalin) and other street drugs. One of the neonatologists at the Edmonton hospital where Mom still worked as an NICU nurse was very concerned about Baby Jackie's mother, who was high during the delivery and whose body was a roadmap of the pitted and potholed intersections of the sex-and-drug trade. Her case had to work its way through the legal system. Another foster family was originally selected, but on the morning of the baby's discharge from the hospital they opted out, so Baby Jackie was brought to my parents' home, where she would remain for the next eighteen months. When a final legal decision was made not to return Baby Jackie to her biological mother, Mom phoned the neonatologist. She asked him to appear as a witness in court where he testified to the track marks in various places on the mother's body during Baby Jackie's birth. Mom and Dad were in no position to adopt Baby Jackie, but they could love, shelter, and protect her until a younger couple could adopt her. From the day she was born until she was eighteen months old she benefited from Mom's professional nursing skills and her personal mothering gifts. Late one Saturday morning in February 1988, Baby Jackie's adoptive family came to take her home with them to the West Coast. In time, Jackie would grow into an adult burdened with the challenges of prenatal drug exposure.

For the eighteen months that she lived in my parents' home, Jackie had an older foster sister, Baby Jill. This girl had been apprehended by Social Services and was brought to my parents' home after being left alone with her six-year-old auntie in an apartment in Edmonton's inner city. Neighbours in the building, hearing a baby crying and crying, had called the police. Baby Jill, nine months of age, was apprehended and her Auntie Judy was returned to her mother. On a cold Grey Cup Sunday in November, 1983, Social

Workers brought Baby Jill to my parents' home. This was to be a short-term placement, but more than three decades later, Jill remains a valued member of our family. To my parents goes all the credit for keeping my beautiful foster sister alive. She will always be vulnerable to predators who capitalize on her gullibility, and even as she matures her road remains rough and her future shaky. Jill's identity as a marginalized, colonized Aboriginal woman is an essential part of her own story, and my parents' abiding commitment to love her, shelter her, and keep her safe in our family is an integral part of their story.

My parents never weakened in their commitment to love and protect Jill and the other foster babies, despite everything conspiring against Mom and Dad, including the Alberta provincial government's lukewarm support throughout three decades of fostering. To this day, Mom remains resolute in her support of Jill, now a mother herself to six children, five of them in care. How, in the space of seven years, did Jill birth six children with four different fathers and have five of them apprehended? I remain insistent that Jill is my foster sister and not my biological sister. But why, especially when we are the only family Jill has ever known? Because my mother has never consumed alcohol and is not responsible for Jill's Fetal Alcohol Spectrum Disorder (FASD).

Jill inherits a history of colonization, residential schools, alcohol as a coping strategy, sexual exploitation, marginalization, violence, and abuse that has crippled so many Aboriginal women and communities. Her own beginnings in that inner-city apartment and subsequent abuses experienced as an adult in other inner-city apartments speak to a disability not of her own making: FASD. Each of Jill's six siblings also has FASD and their mother died young as result of the occupational hazards associated with the sex trade. Authorities tried to keep Baby Jill connected to her family but with little success. After one home visit, the driver returned Baby Jill to Mom and Dad and said that he would file a report because the only adult present when he picked Jill up from the home visit was an unconscious, unknown man. When my own grandma took Baby Jill's bottle to the sink to clean it, she noticed curdled milk and the smell of alcohol. Perhaps this man had tried to get Baby Jill to sleep with an additive to her milk.

So very different from the hopeless strategy of trying to silence a baby with alcohol, Mom never swayed from her resolve to provide safe lodgings, healthy food, and good medicine to vulnerable babies. When Jill jumped out the window and ran away in March of her thirteenth year, this did not weaken Mom's awesome persistence in mothering her. When we called and looked for Jill for hours the day my Dad died only to have her show up high, this did not discourage Mom in her mission to mother her. When the police called Mom into a domestic fray between Jill and the father of her last three children, this did not dampen Mom's tenacity in parenting Jill. Off Mom went to the rescue. Now, as Jill tries to raise her youngest child with his father and with the unsteady support of Social Services, Mom continues to coach and council Jill and her partner, drive them to the food bank, and help them access other necessities. My foster sister lives at the very margins of an affluent society where bitumen and banknotes lubricate the ball bearings of a global economy, and yet she and her children—her family—are left struggling for minimum subsistence.

Much preferring to be respected as a mother or a nurse or a foster mother, Mom occasionally experiences racism and does not like to identify as Métis; regardless of these and the other daunting challenges she has faced much of her life, she has taught me the remarkable lesson of what it's like to mother from an Aboriginal perspective: *Never Give In*. Mom and Dad decided to continue to be foster parents with Social Services after PHS closed its fostering services. They took several foster parenting classes, including workshops on FASD. When Jill was only three or four years old, the Government of Alberta attempted to coerce my parents into adopting her. This would have meant an end to all social, medical, and psychological supports. One tactic used was to threaten to remove Baby Jill from my parents' home and send her to a reserve in Saskatchewan where, though she had biological and communal ties, she had never lived and had never been acknowledged. Dad, from his ten years spent on reserves as a kid, had gained a deep awareness of the source and the consequence of non-existent or dubious supports. When my father was growing up on a reserve in east-central Alberta, another child unrelated to my father had been running with a loaded shotgun; the unthinkable happened, and the child died in my Grandma McIlwraith's arms. Perhaps this catastrophe, which happened in the mid-1940s, motivated Dad's own gritty dedication to Baby Jill's welfare and the safety of all the children he parented. Later in the mid-1980s, in an effort to protect Jill and to keep our family intact, he broke every rule in the book and called the *Edmonton Journal*. When a picture appeared in the newspaper of him holding Baby Jill in his arms, with an accompanying article explaining why he wouldn't let them send her back to the reserve, Social Services threatened to prevent my parents from ever fostering again. My parents experienced the usual obstacles most married couples face, but this is the only time my mom refused to talk to Dad for three days because she was afraid Social Services would close their home to foster children. Even so, their union was as solid as hard igneous rock. The provincial government, unable to wear down my parents' astounding concern for powerless children, caved in and let them continue fostering.

Deep in thought recently, Mom wrote a note to me:

> I learned a lot about myself taking on the fostering role, and soon after Baby Lilly came it became clear that part of my decision and later need to continue in the work was the bond that Ruth and I have and how my Mom and Dad opened their hearts to her. The fact that your father didn't hesitate to continue fostering says a lot about who he was, in particular his actions on Baby Jill's behalf when he called the *Edmonton Journal*. He became "Mr. Mom" in the truest sense of the word, so I could continue nursing.

Her combination of technical expertise as an NICU nurse and her innate compassion links back to that headstone she laid that cold day in July 2013 to commemorate her brother's and her parents' memories.

Over breakfast in early December 2013, as the *Edmonton Journal* lay between us, Mom and I sat and read an article together, wrestling to comprehend the horror described by Karen Kleiss and Darcy Henton in the *Edmonton Journal/Calgary Herald* series: "Fatal Care: A Special Investigation." Very quietly, Mom said, "Baby Lilly could have died in our home." Remembering Baby

Lilly's serious and congenital kidney, bowel, and heart problems, we have a justifiable and visceral response to the six-part series. As important as we recognize the series to be in its exposure of systemic failure and government secrecy in not properly investigating and reporting these deaths, we also know that many children survive, even thrive, in foster care. Whether Jill has actually thrived as a member of our family is a debatable issue, given the pervasive and chaotic effects of FASD on her personhood. FASD is insidious. In combination with government miserliness, it could have defeated my teetotalling family. Supporting Jill's development into a complete adult could have crushed all of us, but it didn't. My parents' marriage did not disintegrate as many others' have. Instead, my parents have passed on to us a kind of wisdom that is difficult to put into words. All tolled, between their four biological children and all their foster children, my Mom and Dad parented for forty years of their adult lives. Mom washed cloth diapers for thirteen years, and she didn't quit working as a nurse until she was struck with multiple sclerosis. Now a great-grandmother, she councils the young moms in our family who have babies with runny noses, rashes, or other more serious ailments. Mom will help these young moms decide if it's time to take their baby to the doctor or to the hospital. She is filled with the most incredible joy when she shops for onesies and other baby clothes and when she knits or crochets a blanket for a newborn.

* * *

"Ever kind and ever true" reads the epitaph on my father's tombstone, here in Edmonton. "Sleep little one, sleep" reads the epitaph on wee Baby James Thomas Calvin Meakes's headstone, near Wishart, Saskatchewan. As the sun peeks through an opaque sky and as the graveyard grass and all the countryside surrounding us take on the most amazing hue of pale pink quartz, Mom smiles with the might of a lifetime of love. Precisely because my father was ever kind and ever true, precisely because my mother chose a good man whom she could trust to raise a family with, precisely because my mother whispered the words "Sleep little one, sleep" to countless babies in her calling as a mother, a nurse, and a foster mother, I am filled with hope that the world is a safe place. My

The Estrangement

NATASHA CLARK

SHE'S BENT OVER, hands on her knees; breasts thrust out; ass adorned with a homemade bunny tail, pinned to a black leotard atop black pantyhose; homemade felt bunny ears on her head. She looks at the camera, her bottle-black hair poofed out, dry and light as a cotton candy wig but feeling like fine steel wool. I haven't felt her hair in twelve years but my childish hands memorised its yarn as I picked out the silver ones for her.

"Call me Jane," she said to nine-year-old me. "Or Blackie."

"Why?" I asked. I didn't ask why "Blackie." It's a nickname she gave herself, thinking it mysterious, sexy, and vaguely threatening: how she wants men to perceive her.

"So no one will think I'm your mother."

She isn't really. She wasn't old enough to be a mother.

She isn't old enough to be a grandmother, either, and she wants everyone to say so on Facebook. So, she's bent over in a homemade *Playboy* bunny costume in her non-ironic, entirely earnest profile photo. Though her lovely, straight teeth belie her impoverished upbringing, "Smiling gives me crow's feet," she says. Rather, she widens her eyes, like a frozen highway deer—a deer-bunny—mid-sprint. Her mouth is slack and affected.

An early gastric bypass operation paid for her slim thighs, trotted out in their sheer casings. The doctors performed the most invasive variation of the surgery upon her, though she didn't actually meet the weight requirement; her family physician lied for her after she lied to him about the efforts she had already fruitlessly expended to lose weight. She hadn't actually exercised, given up weekly cases of beer and menthol extra-light cigarettes, or increased her consumption of fruits and vegetables. Also, because her knee gave out a few times a year, she rarely left the couch or bed.

This was some of the story she told to *The Dini Petty Show*: single mother, welfare, bummed knee, depression, suicide attempts, no support. I don't know what she expected but I doubt it was Richard Simmons in white polyester short shorts.

"He's like a happy little coconut," she says to Dini, straining positivity when she's thinking something like, "Fucking brillo-haired faggot spaz." She fake-laughs in a fake living room. Her public persona strains her until there will be no energy later to consider how to navigate to *Phantom of the Opera* with her complimentary tickets, Toronto a city so expansive and expensive with possibilities she'll never know. Thousands of pairs of Canadian eyes are upon her and the red lipstick and heavy TV face powder feels as oppressive as pretending to have a middle-class brain. She hates trying to fit in. Richard explains to her that she shouldn't let her weak knee keep her from exercising from a sitting point. After having her join two other people on the talk show stage, he gets excited about the chair-ridden arm exercises he has them perform.

"One! Two! One! Two! Up! Down! Come on, Jane! See! You can do this!"

She laughs in embarrassment. Later she tells Dini, "I would love to do Richard's work-out videos at home but I don't have a VCR." She knows they will give her one. She feigns surprise and gratitude which her entitlement schema prevents her from genuinely feeling.

She didn't, and doesn't, really want a step up. She certainly wasn't there to mime seventy-year-olds' exercise regimes in a Toronto television studio. She wanted attention.

It's hard to get attention when you are one of eight children. I can't imagine what it was like to be the oldest of five girls, responsible for the cleanliness of their shared tiny bedroom and the possible subsequent temper of a punch-happy alcoholic father. Or to have shared a three-bedroom, one-bathroom, no-basement bungalow through six-month Northern Ontario freezes. I don't know how it would have felt to be called, like my sisters, into my grandfather's bedroom to "rub cream on his feet," when I knew this meant he was going to touch my privates again.

I do know what it's like to want attention, to *need* it. Though it was just the two of us in a cloistered and sparse apartment, I rarely found my mother in my daily searchings. She pushed my sofa cuddles away as though I had cooties. I'd cry alone in my room from nightmares. I usually managed to dodge objects thrown at my head. We rarely went anywhere besides the grocery store, the bank, the dentist and doctor, or did much besides watch The Cosby Show. These are the generous things I can say about our time together. We are Cat Stevens' "Cat's Cradle" and a soap opera plot line saddled together through the misfortune of one drunken night.

She thinks grudges have me blocking her on Facebook and refusing her access to my children. They don't. As a middle-aged woman with four children, a divorce, little formal education, a major faith transition, and a tiny and delicate support system, I have wanted to give up at least fifty-six times. I understand disadvantaged struggle and I know her story: severely abused in childhood; teenage mother; little-to-no help from a spouse, friends, or family; poverty. People do the best they can and she did.

The real issue is that without an umbilical cord bridge, our paths would never have crossed. She is not someone I'd choose for a friend, nor would my friends. We have little to discuss, nothing over which we can relate. Sometimes I wonder if she will one day get the number of pills right and I'll get a phone call at four a.m. I wonder if she'll have my attention then. I wonder if I have to lose her to love her and if, to love her, I have to like her.

But my mother may not even need this from me. As consistently surprised as I am by her, I can't help feel it possible that she just wants to borrow a hundred bucks.

Mud Bath

BETH OSNES

I TOLD DESIREE I had to get her out of town just for the night. I had to get her out of a desperation that neither of us understood. I had to keep her from hurting herself anymore. She had been home alone on a day off from the "at-risk" high school program she attended and had begun obsessing about her boyfriend not calling and losing her make-up in her messy room, and about less immediate problems, such as her mom dying just two years ago and her mom's abandonment of her even when she was alive, due to alcohol and violent lovers. When I got home from taking my little kids on an outing, I discovered Desiree had trashed her room and cut herself on her arm and across each of her cheeks. Desiree is our teen-aged foster daughter. She doesn't have many ways of coping with the storm inside her heart. Cutting herself is one of ways she tries to reign in the dark clouds and perhaps to let out some of the pain. When I walked in the house and realized what she had done, I didn't know what to say. I don't know the psychology of cutting or the correct response. She had a look of infinite sadness; like a saint revealing her wounds. I took her head in my hands and kissed her forehead. Since my husband was working late at the theatre, I called my sister-in-law in Denver who recognized the tone in my voice and, without question, agreed to take my two little kids for the night. I told Desiree to pack a bag, and after a few more calls, we set off into the mountains.

Desiree's mood lifted as we drove up the canyon road and talked about old movies we had seen and movie stars we liked. She was thankful to be going away. We didn't speak about what was bothering her. She usually confided in me with specific problems, and since nothing in particular was up, I sensed this was a much deeper demon of discontent. We went to a 1940s relic of a resort in Idaho Springs with mineral baths. The brochure claims that the Native Americans believed these were healing waters from the great earth spirit. I was drawn there more out of instinct than logic. I yearned for some comfort and healing for her that was bigger than me. The hotel is built directly over the remains of gold and silver mines. Now they form a labyrinth of chances for relaxation and rejuvenation in the form of hot mineral baths, massage rooms, and mud treatments.

After checking in and putting our bags in our room, we went down the narrow stairs into the underground dressing room. Beneath the low ceilings we began to undress. Through the corner of my eye I watched Desiree untie her *Nikes* and take them off. She unbuttoned her baggy black pants and peeled them off. Up over her head she pulled her black t-shirt with some band's logo on it. She carefully undid all her jewellery. Each these items she stashed in the locker provided is a social signifier identifying her with some larger group. Between us there was a growing easiness that happened when the outside world did not interfere. We laughed about how creepy and old-fashioned this place seemed to be, as though it survived forgotten by the progression of time. Indeed, even the other patrons seemed caught in a time-loop—resembling middle-aged women from an old black and white movie. There were signs up saying that bathing suits were not allowed in this portion of the resort. So wrapped just in white towels, we walked into the cement showers to wash our bodies in preparation for the communal baths.

We entered the dimly lit steam tunnels as if travelling into the heart of the earth through its arteries. Along the sides of this narrow deserted mine were small deep pools that had been carved into the rock, each full of dark bubbling spring water, naturally heated by the earth. A quiet decorum was enforced by generously-weighted women strewn on slabs of wet rocks who shushed any giggling, of which we were both guilty. All traces of female competition were wiped away by the overall enormity of the other patrons and the fact that no one sported a more fashionable bathing suit than anyone else. The egalitarian uniform of the birthday suit prevailed. Approaching an empty pool, we silently slipped our naked bodies into the earth's heated waters. It took us a while to get used to the temperature, but slowly we immersed ourselves up to our necks. I watched Desiree slowly dunk her head and I was glad for the touch of the water, hoping it would sooth her cuts. Comfortable just being together we soaked in the baths for over an hour enjoying prolonged silences.

Once the heavy air of the tunnels weighed too much upon us, we left the caves and sneaked around exploring the skinny corridors of the resort still wrapped only in our towels. We came upon a room labelled the "mud room." It was dark and closed up for the night, but not locked. We cautiously went in and surmised the room, shutting the door behind us. High along one wall, two long horizontal windows let in only the faintest moonlight sneaking through the leaves of a tall tree outside. Our eyes could barely discern the layout of the space. We spied showerheads along one wall, and to our left we saw the glistening wet mud. We could not resist dipping our toes into the tiled pit of whitish mud that was filtered from the mineral water. Throwing our towels aside, we began squeamishly by stepping into the thick mud. It squished between our toes and cooled our skin. In the darkness, through our giddy squeals, we both reached down to touch it with our hands, feeling the grit within the silky goo. Led by a sensual child-like curiosity, we rubbed it on our legs, then up our thighs. Reaching down to grab more of the stuff we drew circles of mud on our tummies. Freed from self-consciousness by the darkness, we plastered our breasts, our necks, and our faces, until we both looked up and regarded each other with eyes now acclimated to the dim light. We stared, not moving. In that moment we were transformed by our masks of mud, out of time, out of context, like ancient tribeswomen conjuring the great earth spirit for the healing of a wounded soul. Locked in each other's eyes, the separation between us dissolved. Unable to sustain the gravitas, we both fell into uproarious laughter dispelling the magic of that moment but not losing its gift. We showered off the mud and left.

That night in our hotel room, my foster daughter and I drew abstract pictures of each other with pastels and art paper I had brought along. Later, we fell asleep in our shared double bed. It's been over ten years since that night.

I wish I could say that that trip cured her. I wish I had a different ending to this story. I don't. She grew up, left us, moved to the West coast, worked some, met a guy, had a child, and then died of a meth overdose just a few months ago. At the small ceremony we had in my backyard after her death with some family, friends, and neighbours, we burned small offerings of Chinese ceremonial money and each said something about her life and experiences we had shared with her. I shared this story.

This remains. Those things happened. People remember. It might be just these memories and the connections that endure as Desiree finds what I hope is her final healing.

Nevermom

JULIE GOSSELIN

I NEVER PLAYED WITH DOLLS, never wanted to have a dollhouse, or a baby carriage, or an Easy Bake-Oven. Instead, I had Barbies. Many, many Barbies. They each had an interesting career: pilot, racecar driver, adventurer, shop owner, doctor. They had friends. Some were Ken. They did not marry. They had no children. They were successful, smart, and happy. In Grade Two, I had to complete an essay on the career I wanted as an adult. I wrote that I wanted to be Wonder Woman, but if I did not develop godly powers of strength and endurance by the time I reached adulthood, I would settle for being a police officer, an astronaut, or prime minister. It all seemed interchangeable to me.

My parents divorced when I was ten. The following years were not pleasant. Parents do not separate from their partners because they get along well. That part doesn't change after divorce. My mother entered and exited relationships throughout the rest of my youth. I remember hearing her cry at night in her bed after every breakup. The worst boyfriends, as far as I could tell, were the ones that came back, only to leave again. My father had more relationship success. He eventually formed a stable stepfamily, entering a common-law relationship with a childless woman. She was a good partner to him and eventually became a very engaged stepmother, but even that relationship faced challenges. I watched my parents attempt to raise me together while living apart, watched them navigate their anger for each other, watched as they deconstructed and reconstructed our family and their respective sense of self. They muddled through years of confusion. It taught me one important lesson: married or not, you are always trapped in a relationship when you share a child. From my youthful perspective, I concluded that if I did not have children, I'd always be free.

* * *

I met George[1] while I was still completing my undergraduate degree in psychology. He was already successfully established in his career. He'd very recently separated from his wife. He had two young daughters, ages five and seven years old. As our relationship developed, I gave little thought to being a stepmother until it dawned on me that I had become one. I am pretty certain I had that "deer caught in the headlights" look when I finally clued in. When I realized that they had started to expect me to be there when they got home from school. When his youngest daughter decreed that I was the only one who could be trusted to pull out baby teeth. When his oldest daughter stopped asking when their mother and father would get back together, and instead developed the fantasy that we could all live together under the same roof. When they introduced me to new friends as their stepmother and I found that I did not mind. In fact, I did not mind at all.

* * *

Wintertime. I have been living with my stepfamily for the last four years. As we do every night after completing homework together, we are eating dinner as we talk about our day. The girls mention an anecdote involving their mother's boyfriend, David. I have just referred to David as their stepfather, a label they both immediately deny with vigour. Brenda and Karen are adamant about the fact that this man is their mother's boyfriend, not their stepfather. Their father cannot resist asking them if they feel the same way about me. He looks at me and winks. I know what he is doing. He thinks they will say something cute and funny, and this will make for a warm happy family moment. I can feel myself squirming in my chair, picking at my food, avoiding eye contact with either girl. After a drawn out moment of silence, in which the girls exchange a look, they simultaneously reply that his question is unfair, like comparing apples and oranges. I exhale more loudly than I had intended. I realize I have been clenching my fists under the table.

I look at my half-empty dinner plate, my appetite lost.

The girls soon finish their supper and ask to be excused. They rush out the front door merrily to join their friends playing in the street. George takes the leash and motions for the dog to follow. I pick up the dishes and start cleaning the kitchen. As I occupy myself with the minutia of our evening routine, I cannot help but wonder what makes my relationship with the girls different from David's. Both David and I are actively involved in the girls' lives, spending comparable amounts of time driving them to soccer, sharing meals, and going on family weekend outings.

* * *

The relationship I developed with each of my stepdaughters evolved in very different ways over the years. With Brenda, his youngest daughter, things unfolded with ease from the outset. Memories of my first two years living with them included many moments with Brenda in my arms, on my lap, holding my hand. The first time I met her she climbed on my lap and never really left. At the same time, the relationship I developed with his oldest daughter Karen was always marked with the same kind of ambivalence I had felt toward my own stepmother during my adolescence. Initially, we were able to bond over some aspects of our family life: braiding her hair in the morning before school, lazy Sunday afternoons spent doing crafts together or playing board games. Still, I could feel Karen gauging me, assessing whether or not she should let me in. Her smile held some measure of sadness that always struck me somewhere deep in an unresolved part of my own experience as a child of divorce.

There were times during her teen years when Karen hardly ever spoke to any of us—and only when she needed to communicate practicalities. She was like a shadow in our house, barely ever seen and only when she needed to leave her bedroom to go to the bathroom or the kitchen. Her footsteps were light. If I accidentally crossed her path, she averted her eyes and scurried away. The most painful encounters were the ones where she looked through me, like she could negate my presence from her reality. I had spent years forging a place in her life: making dinner, preparing birthday parties, helping with homework, playing with her and her sister.

Now I found myself slipping into a realm where I'd lost my footing and my voice. Karen had a complicated and painful relationship with her own mother, a reality that I convinced myself was somehow related to the resentment she exhibited towards us in general, and me in particular. At the same time, I never felt the same kind of tension in my relationship with Brenda. As a result, I felt that I wasn't simply a stepmother to the girls, but two stepmothers: a different person and parent to each of them.

I was a stepmother, not because I took care of my partner's children or because I disciplined them or provided them with affection. I was a stepmother because they had confirmed this identity through their words and their behaviour. As a stepmother, I was at the mercy of my stepchildren's avowal of my identity. I was a stepmother because my stepchildren allowed it to be.

* * *

After seven years of cohabitation, my stepdaughters' father and I announced that we were separating. I remember feeling anger and sadness at the mess we had created. I was also frustrated and unsure about what the future would hold for me and the girls. We had spent years developing a relationship that connected us as a family. I suddenly saw my membership card revoked, as I was shown the door. I wondered how other people outside our family would now see us and our relationship. Was I still a stepmother? Did I have any right to the title? Although I had been working both as a researcher and a clinician in the area of divorce and stepfamily adjustment for a number of years, our story made me realize just how poorly equipped I was in terms of points of reference. I was suddenly acutely aware that step-motherhood can be an isolating experience, despite not having felt that way during the years I spent with George. Perhaps that was a testament to the connections we built over that period of time. As I left our house to move in with a friend, I felt abandoned, confused, and alone. It felt weird to shed this motherhood like a worn jacket, to become single and childless again. It felt wrong.

When I left, I extended an invitation to both my stepdaughters to maintain a relationship. Initially, Karen and I had a few strained conversations. It was an effort for both of us and over time our relationship dissolved. Years later, I continue to meet Brenda for regular dinner dates. Instead of telling me about her day, she now tells me about her week. At Christmas, we bake cookies together like we used to do when I was still with her father. When I married my new partner Vic, a few years ago, she proudly stood by my side as a bridesmaid. But what *is* this relationship? Who is she to me now? And who am I to her?

* * *

When I think about the end of my relationship with George and how it affected my connection to my stepdaughters, I instinctively feel complicity with others mothering at the margins: foster mothers, non-custodial mothers, mothers who have lost contact with their children, and mothers of children who have disappeared or passed away. Working as a clinical psychologist has afforded me the opportunity to speak to a number of these mothers and to observe their own struggle in defining their identity and their connection to their (lost) "child."

* * *

Springtime. Two months before our separation. I am sitting across from a very pregnant woman in my office. She has been referred to me because she is exhibiting symptoms of complicated grief. While she is due to deliver her fifth child in a week, she appears sullen and listless. About a year ago, one of her sons drowned while at day camp. She has been severely depressed ever since. She tells me about a recurring dream that she has every night: she awakens to sounds coming from outside her bedroom. When she goes to investigate, she finds that her deceased son is waiting for her in the hallway. He smiles to her. She runs to him and hugs him ferociously while her sobs wet her face, her clothes, and her son's body. She wakes up from her dream her face wet with tears. She says to me in a broken whisper: "All I want to do is sleep."

* * *

Summertime. I have been separated from my partner for two months. I have moved in with a friend who agreed to rent me a room in her house. I am struggling with bouts of insomnia. My bedroom is too quiet, the bed too large for me, and the air is too dry. When I finally fall asleep, the dream is always the same. I am in an unfamiliar place. I look around and see Brenda. I take her by the hand. We need to find out where we are and where to go. Suddenly, I realize that Karen is walking behind us. I am unsure about whether I should also take her hand, and so I simply move forward—hoping that she will follow. Their father then comes into the picture and wants to follow us as well. I try to run away from him, still holding on to Brenda's hand. Karen tries to follow but soon gives up. Their father is relentless in his pursuit. My hand firmly holds Brenda's as I try to run faster, away from him. I steal a car, but he manages to get into the backseat. I enter a building and try to shut the door to keep him out, but he puts his foot in the doorway, preventing me from closing the door. I finally wake up, drenched in sweat, frustrated and exhausted. My first thought is for Brenda, who I miss profoundly. My second thought is for Karen, who I haven't heard from in a long time. Guilt and anger clench my throat as I lie flat on my back, tears silently streaming down my face.

* * *

Later that same summer. I am working with a female patient who is experiencing difficulties in her relationship with her daughter while caring for her own dying mother. She struggles with her grief as she prepares to say goodbye to her mother, and finds the estrangement with her adult daughter difficult to bear. She wonders if she can still consider herself a mother, if her daughter wants nothing to do with her. She wonders out loud if she'll stop being a daughter once her mother is gone. Suddenly, she looks straight at me and asks: "What will I be left with if they both leave me. Who will I be?"

* * *

Looking back on the time spent in my stepfamily, I recognize the role played by my intense desire to offer my stepdaughters a positive maternal experience, to protect them from the pain I had suffered as a child who felt caught between divorcing parents and new stepparents. However, this was not mere generosity on my part. Investing in my stepdaughters was allowing me to learn so much about myself: namely, I was surprised to discover, with some elation, that I had a capacity for parenting. My own struggle for differentiation and autonomy had left me very wary of having children. My relationship with Brenda, to a large degree, represented an opportunity to repair that attachment injury. Meanwhile, my relationship with Karen was a reminder that even with the best of intentions some embraces eventually fall apart. The girls had reconciled me with the concept of maternity—a gift laced with both apprehension and yearning.

Now that I am no longer part of their daily family life and I have been replaced by a new stepmother, I struggle with the same longing and grief of any mother who has had her parental relationships redefined through shared custody arrangements or the loss or rejection of a child. But, my grief goes unnamed and unrecognized. I am an invisible mother whose pain is socially ignored. For a number of months after the separation, my dreams were my only connection to my stepfamily. I was losing not only a husband but a whole family. In the aftermath of my separation from George, I wondered what I would be left with. What would be left of my relationships with my step-daughters?

* * *

Summertime. It is the day after George and I have decided to end our relationship. I am sitting in the kitchen as Brenda and Karen enter the house. Their father has explained the situation to them on the way home. Karen goes straight to her bedroom and shuts the door behind her. Brenda enters the kitchen, visibly shaken. Her face is red and she is standing straight, rigid, both fists clenched at her side. I am composed. I have been preparing myself for this moment.

"Is it true?" she asks.

"Yes, it is." I motion for her to come to me. She sits down with me. Her head sinks and her hair covers her face. This is something she has always done when she is upset. She is a private child that does not share her grief with others easily. I see small pools of tears form on the surface of the kitchen table.

"Just because my relationship with your dad is over doesn't

mean that ours has to be. I love you and as long as you want me in your life, I will be there. I promise."

"But you'll be gone. And things won't be the same," she replies angrily between quiet sobs. I can sense sadness and resentment in her voice. She has been through a family break-up before, so she speaks from experience.

"That's true, but it doesn't mean that we can't agree on how and when we will see each other. If you want me to, I will make it happen." She nods, but her face remains hidden.

* * *

Summertime. It has been over a year since I separated from George. I am sitting with Brenda at a table at a downtown patio restaurant. We are having lunch together. The day is sunny and warm. I turn to her.

"You sent me a Facebook request to confirm that I am a member of your family?" I ask her. She smiles and nods.

"Yeah ... I was a little unsure, because there were only so many categories to choose from. I didn't know what to put down, so I chose 'sister.' That seemed to make the most sense." I smile back to her, grateful for her resourcefulness in the face of limited options.

* * *

There is no clear social script to help define the role of the stepmother, and the existence of a stepmother outside the stepfamily remains absent from the public discourse. And so, we are left with the only reference point we can find: sisterhood. A term that unites us as women across generations and a decade of shared family history. One that has a long history of representing solidarity between women, united in their beliefs, their values and their commitment to their community. It is a basic link, but as good a starting point as any to forge a new social script.

* * *

Brenda didn't use the term step-mother often when I lived with her father, and she doesn't use it now. It was always only a term we used to define our relationship for others—when I was introduced to new friends or teachers. While I'm no longer publicly acknowledged as a stepmother, I'm left with a daughter-sister-friend. Her behaviour toward me affirms the affection, respect and value she has for our bond, and I feel secure that I hold a special place in her life.

When Brenda was little, she always made two gifts at school when they had craft assignments on holidays (one for her mother and one for me). Once, while on a work trip, I arrived at my hotel and opened my suitcase only to find a card that she'd carefully inserted between layers of clothes. On the front, there was a picture of Wonder Woman with rainbows in the background and a text bubble exclaimed: "I am proud of you!" The card reminded me of the pictures I used to draw as a child—of female superheroes and career Barbies.

Now, Brenda continues to remember my birthday and she finds other small ways to privately recognize me. I only need to look around my office to find countless mementos and gifts that she has offered me: a Wonder Woman bobble-head she brought back from her first high school trip to New York; a little gnome figurine she found that reminds her of an old inside joke we shared years ago; a small painting of two young women embracing—with the following inscription: "May we always be connected in our travelling journeys and may you always know how deeply you are loved."

NOTES

[1]Names have been changed to protect anonymity.

What I Need Is a Wife

MARITA DACHSEL

WHEN I'M OUT SOCIALLY with a group of women, inevitably the conversation drifts towards how difficult it is to find balance in our lives—work, children, home, partner—as if balance were something achievable. More often than not, someone exclaims, "what I need is a wife" and everyone laughs and agrees. I've done it—the laughing and the agreeing—but I'll be honest: I've considered it. Not just in passing, like during those nights out, a little drunk, a little giddy, but seriously considered it.

From 2006-2012, my family and I lived in four different residences in three cities in two provinces. During this time, we had three kids and I was pregnant for the two provincial moves. Because of the nature of my husband's work, I spent many stretches of time solo-parenting with very little outside support.

My first year in Edmonton, a city I had not even visited before we made the decision to move there, was difficult. I hadn't experienced winter for a long time—twelve years in Vancouver makes anyone soft. We didn't have a car, I was pregnant until February, and then we had a newborn and a toddler. We lived in a small, 850-square-foot house, and, what proved to be the most challenging that first year was that I didn't know anyone. I hadn't realized how crucial my support system in Vancouver had been, how much I had taken it for granted. It'd been a long time since I had to make new friends and I was out of practice. After a few false starts, I eventually found some great people, life-long friends, but it took time to find them. Those early years of parenting have been called "being in the trenches" and that description felt apt.

During those six years I was also researching the beginnings of Mormon polygamy, specifically the lives of the thirty-four wives of Joseph Smith, founder of The Church of Jesus Christ of the Latter-day Saints, for my book of poetry *Glossolalia*. I learned a lot about American spirituality, Mormon culture, and 1840s America. I learned about sacrifice and martyrdom, about revelation and inspiration, about creation and mythology. Many things surprised me, but what surprised me the most what how the ideas of polygamy changed not only how I viewed motherhood, but also my own roles as a wife and mother.

A key question I wanted to answer for myself while researching early Mormon polygamy was what would I have done in that situation? I understand why modern women who have grown up in polygamous communities choose polygamy—it's their culture, it's all they know—but what about the women who first agreed? What would I have done if faced with that choice?

I don't know if it was some kind Stockholm Syndrome—Joseph Smith working his magic through space and time—but part of me bought in. During those lonely, dark days of my first Edmonton winter I would imagine having a sister-wife, someone to share the load of my solo-parenting, of housework, and to be a companion.

When I looked at pictures of polygamous families, from pre-1890s Utah to present day, I'd feel a pang of longing—all those siblings, all those mothers, all that love. Of course the polygamy of my fantasies was nothing like the kind that makes the news—the Fundamentalist Church of Jesus Christ of Latter-day Saints (FLDS) women with their poofed-up hair and pastel prairie dresses, its systemic abuse, and child brides. Instead, my imagined polygamy felt similar to when my real sister or best friend visited. I have a clear memory of one evening when my husband was putting our eldest to bed, my best friend and I were in the kitchen cleaning up after supper, gossiping and laughing. I thought *yes, this is it*. If I could have a sister-wife who was a close friend, I understood how it could work, how, in some respects, it made perfect sense. We're told over and over again that it takes a village to raise children—so why not a village in my own home?

Mormons believe in pre-existence and eternal families. While I have a hard time understanding the logistics behind the Mormon

tenet of eternal families, I can't help but look at my own, especially as it is now, with an eight, six, and two-year-old—young
children who are still affectionate, trusting, and loving—and wish
to capture this time, let it be like this forever. But, of course, when
I speak of my family, it is the one I have created—my husband, my
children. My original one—my mother, my father, my sister—are
family, but not *my* family; note the lack of possessive. After a
particularly wonderful day and I announce yet again that I love
my family, it is my insular one I am referring to, the one I helped
create. These are who I would want to be with for eternity—if I
believed in an afterlife.

As a child, I was told that family was the most important thing
in life. I have a large extended family on both sides, but I barely
know them. What kind of lesson was this when our tiny quartet
was the only kin we had in the expanse of the Americas? How
could I trust that family was most important when both my parents had left theirs?

But I did trust and the lesson has stayed with me.

Those long dark months in our first winter in Edmonton, when
my longing for a sister-wife was most acute, it wasn't really because I wanted someone to do the cleaning and cooking, and it
definitely was not because I wanted another sexual partner for my
husband. It was because I wanted to feel like I belonged to something greater than myself—a larger family, something important.
Mormon polygamists believe they are living as God wants them to
live, that polygamy is part of a higher order. Those who will talk
candidly admit that it's a difficult life, but that they are devoted
to it because it is an important part of their faith.

Perhaps what I really was longing for was not a helpmate, but a
sense of belonging, or even more. What I desired was faith.

This is what I believe in: there is more to the universe than we
will ever comprehend; material things don't matter—people do;
art is powerful; science is an art; family is vital; love is the meaning of life.

* * *

I imagine that sharing a husband in a heterosexual marriage would
be messy, difficult, and emotionally fraught. But do I think my

husband would love me less if he had another wife? No, I don't. I have three children. When my eldest was born, the love I felt for my child was a huge, all-encompassing tsunami. Did I love my husband any less? Did I worry that his love for me was any less? Not at all.

In the days leading up to the birth of my second child, I began to doubt. I looked at my eldest, not yet two, and I was overcome with fear that I was about to short-change him. And then when my second son was born, I worried for him. He was a stranger— would I ever be able to love him like I loved my eldest? Looking back, that seems ridiculous. Of course I am able to love him, and this love never compromised the love I have for my eldest. With my third, these worries never once surfaced.

My hunch is that it would be the same with polygamy. We have enough love in our hearts for more than one parent, grandparent, sibling, child, or friend. Why not for more than one spouse?

One of the many criticisms of polygamy is that women are reduced to being concubines, while the man is creating a harem. That's definitely a salacious way to look at it, especially when considering sects such as the FLDS under Warren Jeffs that regularly practiced marrying girls (some as young as 12) to older men. It's little surprise that for a monogamous, and some would argue sexually repressed, culture fantasizing the thrill of polygamous sex is such a focus.

When the rare polygamist will risk his family's safety and even legal persecution through the social exposure that accompanies opening himself up to be interviewed, journalists more often than not ask, "How does it work?" They want to hear about the sex, the imagined schedules, fantasizing the women as concubines. The public is both titillated and repulsed by the idea of a man with a sexual hunger that can only be satiated by a bevy of young brides.

I've wondered how I'd fare as a sister-wife. I'm a jealous person, but I'm also competitive. Would I do everything I could to be the favourite wife? Absolutely. I can imagine how this could work in the man's favour. Do I admit that I've played this part in my own fantasies? A little role play, even silent and one-sided, never hurt anyone.

But stepping outside the fantasy for a moment, there were times in that sexual wasteland after the birth of our third child where the absolute last thing I wanted was to be touched, to be looked at, to even be thought of as a sexual being. The physical demands placed upon my body by my infant and two other small children were too much to fulfill what the prudish (and during those months I would count myself amongst them) would call my marital duties. More than once I'd thought having an extra wife or two around would be helpful, especially in the marital bed. Outside of those first few months after having a baby, it's been rare, but it has happened that I have gone through phases when I am just not that interested in sex. I think it's normal, like losing an appetite for apples for a while. In those times, I've thought that perhaps if our family had another wife, I wouldn't feel as badly about not wanting to be intimate.

I've considered what it would be like to be polygamous enough that I've asked my husband many times over the last few years if he'd like another wife. He claims he has no interest, no desire whatsoever in being polygamous. I think I believe him. I choose to believe him. I know that I wouldn't want another husband.

* * *

In all the ruminations about polygamy, one must remember that most polygamous families are more than a husband and wives. There are children to consider.

For seven-and-a-half years, I was a stay-at-home-parent, the primary caregiver for my children. I wrote when I could, carving out time, although it never seemed enough. I have had friends and acquaintances, other mothers give me back-handed compliments—at least, that's how I chose to take their comments—that they "could never do" what I do: SAHP three kids. But of course, nobody knows what happens in private. I am not the mother I want to be, that I believe my children deserve. Often I am a better mother when I have an audience. I can't help but consider how much better their childhood would be if they had an additional mother, someone whose heart was softer, whose mind wasn't so often elsewhere.

At times I can picture it: my husband, my children, myself, my sister-wife and her children. Our children, I suppose. A larger family. More love. Perhaps there would be greater peace. Would my children have a happier childhood? Would there be less stress, less yelling? I'm sure there are many sayings that would be appropriate: the grass is always greener; many hands make light work. Perhaps if I had a sister-wife, I'd have time to cross-stitch one of these on a sampler.

Recently my husband was away for a seven-week period interrupted by his return at four different intervals for only one day at a time. It was difficult. My esteem for single mothers, which has always been very high, skyrocketed. And it made me wonder: would I rather be a single mum or a sister wife? Any feminist credibility I have left is sure to be revoked when I state this: I'd rather be tied to a patriarchal institution with at least one other wife, have the financial and emotional stability that a marriage brings, than be a single parent. Perhaps I'm weak and insecure. Perhaps I'm a fool. Perhaps I shouldn't be allowed to call myself a feminist. I do know this: I wouldn't wish polygamy for my daughter. So what does that say about me?

* * *

When I'm out socially with a group of women, inevitably the conversation drifts towards how difficult it is to find balance in our lives—work, children, home, partner—as if balance were something achievable. More often than not, someone exclaims, "what I need is a wife" and everyone laughs and agrees.

I've done it—the laughing and agreeing—but I'll be honest: I've come to hate it. I hate what it implies, because this throwaway line isn't about wanting to explore the complexities of plural marriage or questioning the role of a wife, it's about how wives take care of all the crappy jobs no one else wants to do. Do we laugh at this because this is how we see ourselves? Or because we realize that this is how the world sees us? Are we laughing out of desperation?

Now, after the laughing and agreeing, I've begun to respond by saying that what I really want is the financial means to be able to hire a housecleaner and a nanny. Or, when I'm feeling a little bit cheeky, I'll say, "I don't want a wife, I'd like a second husband." Because what does it say about us that we, too, associate the burden of domesticity with the wife? If we can't stop talking about how we wish we had a wife to clean the toilet, make the lunches, do the laundry, then how will we expect society, and more specifically the people in our lives, to look at us, and the role of wife, differently?

The role of the wife has shifted from the 1950s ideal of the perky stay-at-home-wife and mother, but her public image has not. Even we picture our imaginary sister-wife wearing an apron, making us dinner, cleaning the toilet. We don't know what a feminist wife and mother looks like.

Perhaps once we, the feminist wives of Canada and beyond, create an image that better reflects our own realities, one that isn't holding a feather duster and a diapered baby, one that is more inclusive—ages, faiths, colours, sizes—then the public might stop equating wifedom with female subservience and domestic drudgery. Perhaps then, we'll be able to think of polygamy not as a unilateral sexist and oppressive system, but one that could house complex, interesting, and even progressive women—women like us. While the option of becoming a sister-wife is not the right one for my family or me, I would like to see polygamy move beyond the realm of punchlines or salacious fantasies. It would do us all a world of good.

(Mis)Conceptions

A Meditation on Red

PAM KLASSEN-DUECK

> *The law requires*
> *that nearly*
> *everything be cleansed*
> *with blood,*
> *and without*
> *the shedding of blood*
> *there is no forgiveness.*
> *—Hebrews 9:22*

RED. VIBRANT, erotic, frightening. I want red glasses. I covet red shoes. Dancing in Christian Louboutin lacquered confections. Red is the starry sky of an apple; a story of shame.

I am barren and unwantedly so. Here is a list of synonyms of the physically unreproductive state: not producing or incapable of producing offspring; sterile: *a barren woman.* Unproductive; unfruitful: *barren land.* Without capacity to interest or attract: *a barren period in American architecture.* Mentally unproductive; dull; stupid. Not producing results; fruitless: *a barren effort.* Destitute; bereft; lacking (usually followed by of): barren of tender feelings. Usually, barrens: level or slightly rolling land, usually with a sandy soil and few trees, and relatively infertile.

In this state of *being childless,* the colour red adopts a host of meanings. My red spectrum: baby pinks, coral reds, vermilion. This is what I mean. I stop writing for long periods of time, especially when I feel guilty or anxious. This is not fiction.

In my quest for motherhood as my traditional Canadian Mennonite world upholds it (tweeting #*iamamom* means that you must have at least one living biological child), my life has undergone series of upheavals: an enigmatic move across the country, changes in career, relationship-altering quakes, the spilling of secrets along prayer chains. All for the sake of finding the best doctor with the best statistics to force one damn sperm and one damn egg together. And *stay* fused. Along the way, I have become the subject of ART. Not the kind that imitates life, or vice versa; rather, it's the kind that tries to produce life. ART is an acronym for "assisted reproductive technology": tests, diagnoses, surgeries; fertility charting, Clomid, vitamins; artificial insemination, sperm donorship; shots, suppositories, multiple egg retrievals, ICSI, assisted hatching, live transfers, frozen embryo transfers.

I lived with cued sex, misinterpretations of the body, misreadings of charts, failed cycles. Red and brown and black streamed forcefully.

At first it was me. It is always the woman's fault. My cycles have always been long to begin with, as I noted when I charted my temperatures to determine ovulation. I didn't have the textbook cycles doctors want to see. I ovulate on cycle day twenty-one or twenty-two, not day fourteen. My first infertility specialist misread my chart—too many valleys on that particular month, and not enough peaks—and wouldn't listen to me when I said that I was indeed ovulating, it was just occurring later in my cycle. He knew. He said. He looked. He left. Stacks of unwitnessed graph paper were my evidence—one crown on each chart to witness my body's hard work. Test after test to prove me wrong.

Years later, when my partner was, in fact, diagnosed by one of Canada's leading infertility specialists with severe male factor, I should not have felt relief because then the problem was more opaque than ever. We can do something about female infertility; we can do much less about male factor.

"Sorry, sir. Your sperm won't move. Their heads look odd. They don't penetrate. They don't work."

My partner and I daydream about children and how our lives would change with a baby. I like teaching, writing, art galleries, reading, a geometric skirt, a beautiful room, the glint on fresh fruit. My partner is an electrician and in his workshop he reimagines vintage cars. In feminist studies, perhaps one thinks that only women ask the following question—how can art and family life ever work together? But my male partner wonders about this, too. A good sign? We agree to protect each other's materials and space and time—even if we manage, somehow, to pull a baby down from the sky—and so I have cause for optimism, perhaps.

Feasibly he and I are relieved by our childfree state. We can thread words together, build windows, paint the spare room scarlet, and sculpt car fenders. He brings me red roses. The awful critical voice in my head cries *cliché*. Unlike the biblical Hannah's spouse, he thinks I am his one and only. Other women tried to share him. I have his heart on a silver platter. My luv is a red red rose.

"Don't buy a red car," my husband says. "The cops will be after you nonstop."

Aunt Flow. The Crimson Wave. Bloody Mary. Adultery. War.

I pick at my cuticles until they are raw. I grind my teeth at night. I pull my hair. I tug at my lips until they bleed and I'm too embarrassed to speak. My womb must not be red enough, the doctor says—the depth is lacking. I'm inadequate. The wait for the blood to appear is agony, a passion. Fourteen days. A fortnight. My cycles don't listen to my body, the doctor, or the moon.

When I was hopeful, I saw a trace of watery pink. Hope faded to China red and then a gush of scarlet. The longest wavelength. In the online infertility world, positive use of the word "hope" indicates newbie status.

"*Just have hope,*" tweet the IVF Barbies through ruby lips. The ones who make it to the right side on the first ART attempt, who push their babies in various baby containers along the avenue. We 'veterans,' as we call ourselves, we who have been through so much trying that we've given up, even though we can't give up. We who have endured battles and post-traumatic stress disorder and depression rates similar to those of cancer patients. We who loathe the word "hope" for signifying a meaning that doesn't exist. *It was luck and money.*

I canned Evans cherries last summer which stained my hands red for days. Being of hardy peasant immigrant stock, it interested me to hear a theory that pioneer women bled into their clothing. I bled after my three diagnostic surgeries. During the last one, the nurse,

270

while I was not quite awake, checked between my legs to see if the pad was adequate to hold the flow. I don't know if I could give up any more privacy if I tried. Privacy means: STOP. Don't open my diary; none of this could possibly mean anything to you. The chairs in the fertility specialist's office are slickly red. As I sit in mine, waiting with my legs crossed, I have the impression of sitting in a business-like womb. I'm hoping that the doctor won't see fit to order another transvaginal ultrasound—or a "dildo cam" as they're known in the digital infertility world. A sign in the window, neon red, shouts "Playing Doctor!" Still I sit. A crimson sign to the right reads: EXIT. Red means STOP and the traffic light is broken. The detours disappear. My name has been called. I uncross my legs, stand up, and follow the nurse to a back chamber.

Nothing relieves me. I move to another province and I study the history of motherhood, reading bell hooks and Adrienne Rich and Sara Ruddick and Madeleine Grumet and Hélène Cixous. I adore Adrienne Rich's work but her famous quotation about the "exquisite suffering" of motherhood makes me feel guilty for wishing I could be in the mommy club. I'm not a feminist because of my wish. I shouldn't care about this. My admission: I'm envious of women who miscarry because at least they know what it is like to be pregnant. My graduate readings show me why I feel the way I do, why western society is conditioned to accept only a strict definition of motherhood, why I shouldn't care. But the words do little to numb my desire.

While pulsing through treatments, two-thousand kilometres away from my home, I produce my graduate thesis and earn a master's degree. I create. I write. I attend galleries and listen to music and view films and admire architecture. It's all so much beauty for a Manitoba Mennonite farm girl. I wander through downtown Hamilton and watch the many beautiful people. I want my daughter. I don't know why she won't come to me.

If I wear red shoes, it means that I'm walking through blood. Going home (to remember who I am) would be signified through other means. If I wore red lipstick, it would not mean that I want sex for pleasure. My code has fallen short. I am forgiven, over and over.

Out in Mommyland

SARA GRAEFE

I AM ON MY KNEES, picking up stray LEGO, when the ad comes on. The rainbow flag catches my eye, and I initially mistake it as a Pride message: *"Referendum 74 is not about equality. Gays and lesbians already have the same legal rights as married couples."*

I tense. My wife is working late tonight; I'm sitting up, waiting for her, after a long day on the Mommy-front. Same sex-marriage has been legal here in Canada for almost a decade. Have I just been beamed to another planet?

No, wait—the other planet is being beamed into my living room. On November 6, 2012, Americans residing in Washington State will vote not only for the next President, but also on R-74, a bill to legalize same-sex marriage: *"Marriage is more than a commitment between adults,"* the announcer declares. *"It was created for the care and well-being of the next generation."*

A happy heterosexual family fills the screen in close-up: a white mother and father snuggling their newborn and preschool-aged son. Our own son is fast asleep upstairs, five years old and still blissfully oblivious to the prejudice and hatred towards families like ours. Do his care and well-being not count?

"You can oppose same-sex marriage, and not be anti-gay."

Oh, really? It's just an ad, but the attack feels personal. I'm struck, in this moment, by how my experiences as a lesbian mother are polarized. Most of the time, I'm preoccupied with the daily grind, just like any other middle-class mom in my East Vancouver neighbourhood—wiping noses, kissing boo-boos, and juggling kids and career. Then there are moments like these, where I'm acutely aware of being "other"—situations that demand I perpetually advocate for my family, and for our very right to exist.

Becoming a mom has had an impact on my identity in ways I could have never imagined. I've always known I was queer; I had crushes on other girls as early as kindergarten. I didn't act on them, though, until my university years, when a handful of Women's Studies electives finally gave me the courage to venture out of the closet and embrace my true self.

At that time, in the late 1980s/early '90s, the only lesbian moms I knew were women with kids from previous, straight relationships. Society didn't smile kindly on them: many of these women had been though hellish court battles to retain custody of their children. Fertility treatments, meanwhile, were still in their infancy. I hadn't wrapped my head around the fact that I could still become a mom without a man in the picture, or without a partner, period. Instead, coming out, for me, had heart-wrenching strings attached: I had to kiss goodbye a lifelong, deep-seated desire to bring a baby into the world.

I could not have predicted the huge changes to come. When I first came out, it was unfathomable that same-sex unions could be legalized during my lifetime. By the time I'd met my life partner in 2004, Canada had equal marriage legislation in place, and by 2006, we'd tied the knot ourselves.

Meanwhile, a few short years after grieving my lost shot at motherhood, an older lesbian I'd known back in my small university town—a therapist who'd supported me during my coming-out process—became a mom with her same-sex partner with the help of an anonymous sperm donor. She and her partner were embroiled in a battle with the Ontario government to get both mothers' names on the birth certificate. I was impressed by their advocacy efforts and political gumption. But most of all, the news of their daughter's birth gave me a surge of hope: *motherhood was still possible.*

Next thing I knew, dykes of all stripes were getting pregnant and giving birth. "Do you want to have kids?" became a legitimate question when testing the waters of a brand-new lesbian relationship. The minutiae of queer baby-making was now a hot topic at community parties and potlucks, where we compared notes on the merits of fresh versus frozen sperm, known versus unknown donors, and DIY home-jobbies with the turkey baster versus pricey, highly-medicalized procedures. Women shared the low-down on which fertility clinics in town were most queer-friendly, and which sperm banks had "open-id" donor programs. By the time Amanda and I started our own baby-making journey, the Canadian LGBT community was in the throes of a veritable gayby boom. In 2007, I gave birth to our son, conceived through IUI with anonymous donor sperm. All these years after my bittersweet coming out, it turned out that I got to have my cake and eat it too. I was an out, proud lesbian and a mom.

Parenting a young child has not been without its surprises. In addition to the physical demands of feeding, the sleep deprivation, and the sudden disappearance of my sex life (a.k.a. early-onset lesbian bed death), being a lesbian mom outed me like never before, even though I'd been openly, visibly queer for over fifteen years. Whenever I'm out in the world with Amanda and our boy—be it pushing him as baby in the stroller down the street, taking him to specialist appointments at Children's Hospital, or splashing around together like goofballs in a waterpark miles from home—there's no denying we're a queer family. Sometimes people smile, sometimes people stare, sometimes people spit on the sidewalk after we've passed. Often people are curious and pepper us with all kinds of intrusive questions, like "is he a test tube baby?" or the ultimate zinger, "Which of you is the *real* mom?" Newsflash: we both are.

Before our son came into the world, there was always the option of passing in public by releasing Amanda's hand to avoid a potentially sketchy situation on the street. But now, with our young one in tow, we're no longer willing or able to hide our true relationship. In public, as in our son's private universe, I am without question his Mommy and Amanda his Mama. We don't ever want to cause our boy doubt or shame about who we are as his parents, or about our place in society as a family. No doubt he'll get plenty of those messages from other sources as he grows up (cue that homophobic TV ad). We're painfully aware that, unless the world radically changes overnight, we can't protect him from homophobia forever. I dread the day he first faces a gay slur on the playground or encounters an adult who casts aspersions on his family. But what we *can* do, however, is foster his sense of confidence and self-esteem so that he's equipped to deal with such negative, hurtful messages down the road. We model how we are a family just like any other. And this demands that we are perpetually, comfortably out, not only on the home front, but also in the broader world.

Another surprise has been how new parenthood abruptly plucked me from my tight-knit social circle in the queer community, and unceremoniously dumped me onto the strange, other-worldly planet of Mommyland and its alien culture of baby groups, stroller fitness classes, and playground chit-chat. This is a world which, weekdays nine to five, is disproportionately populated by women—moms and nannies—although there are a few stay-at-home dads in the mix. This is a straight world that presumes heterosexuality.

As a queer mom in these new surroundings, I feel like a fish-out-of-water. Despite being suddenly, conspicuously out in the broader, work-a-day world, here, in Mommyland, without Amanda at my side, I can be invisible. I don't know how many times in casual conversation I've had to correct assumptions about my "husband" or "boyfriend," or pointedly change pronouns to "she" when asked about my partner. And once I out myself in Mommyland, I field those pesky, prying questions: "Which of you carried the baby?" "How did you *decide* who was going to carry the baby?" And: "Who's the father?" which can alternately mean, "Who's the sperm donor?" or "Which of you moms is the daddy?"

There are assumptions, too, that being two moms somehow makes this messy business of parenting easier. People imagine a double dose of estrogen in our household automatically makes us a parenting dream team. I'm tired of hearing words to the effect of, "At least you can hand off your kid to your partner, knowing she has half a clue what to do!" While this last part happens to be true, Amanda and I still face the same struggles as any straight couple parenting together. We get worn down by the daily grind of raising kids and find ourselves locked into the same kinds of petty arguments over parenting styles, division of household chores, and whose turn it is to finally get a break. And in the middle of it all, it's easy for us to lose touch with ourselves as an intimate couple and forget the two people we were together in our lives before motherhood.

There are other queer parents in Mommyland; we're just few and far between. When I encounter my compatriots in this foreign place, it's like a breath of fresh air. We seek each other out on queer family listservs and glom onto each other like long lost friends from back home. And on good days in Mommyland, it can feel empowering to share my queer parenting journey with non-queers, and to dispel myths and false assumptions along the way. In a post-natal group for first-time mothers, for example, my personal story paved the way for two straight women in the group, one who'd conceived with a donor egg and the other with donor sperm, to talk openly about their experiences. But other times, when my resources are low, I grow tired of constantly having to explain our family constellation. Times when I just want to go about the business of parenting, no questions asked, when even correcting the gender of a pronoun feels like too much effort.

As my son has grown, my social interactions in Mommyland have shifted from play groups to play dates, from the playground to the school ground, and from around the circle in Mom-and-me classes to the parental watching and waiting areas outside of our children's extracurricular activities. I'm surprised to discover that, over the course of my son's early childhood, I've gradually become assimilated by the dominant culture. I'm no longer a foreign operative, working under cover; I've since become a double agent. I've come to realize that most of the time, I actually have more in common with my new tribe, straight as it often is, than with my queer friends without kids. I really enjoy and value the company of other mothers, even if I can't always relate when they start chalking up their husbands' shortcomings to gender differences.

The fact is, as a lesbian mom, this is my world now. I'm preoccupied with packing lunch boxes, getting my son to school on time, and ferrying him to and from his afterschool activities. When I'm not teaching my graduate students how to write, I'm teaching my five-year-old how to tie his shoes and wipe his bum. I can't just pack up and go anywhere, on a whim, like my queer buddies without kids. Date nights, like nights out with friends, must be carefully planned, often weeks in advance. And if I do go out, I rarely stay out late any more. All too often, I'm so exhausted by the end of the day that I accidentally fall asleep as I put my son to bed. In other words, so much of lesbian parenthood is just parenthood, period. The only difference is my child has two moms instead of a mom and a dad, or any other family configuration.

Because I feel so at home now, in Mommyland, it's doubly jarring when I encounter a situation that reminds me that I'm still "other," a queer interloper in this heteronormative world. Sometimes it's little things: tense, awkward moments of confusion with customs officers, medical personnel, passport bureaucrats, and other official gatekeepers who hold our family's fate in the balance. "And who are *you*?" Amanda's been asked countless times, as though she's an afterthought, a hanger-on rather than a co-parent. We perpetually cross out and correct "Name of Father?" on important forms, including the one welcoming our son to kindergarten, our family's first point of contact with the school system. We spent a long, stressful week in the maternity ward dealing with post-partum complications, where Amanda was repeatedly mistaken by nursing staff as my sister, my friend, and, unbelievably, my mother (and yes, Amanda *is* older than me—but by a whopping year and a half). While these uncomfortable situations are most often caused by benign ignorance or simple oversight, they still sting. They send us the subconscious message that society does not yet truly recognize or welcome us as a family.

What's more deeply troubling, though, is when Amanda and I find ourselves the target of blatant homophobia. That evening I was verbally attacked in my own living room by the ad from Washington State, I was informed that I had no right to be married, and also sent the message, loud and clear, that I shouldn't be raising children. Or, like the morning I was shocked awake by my clock radio blaring news from Russia, where the Kremlin had just passed more anti-gay legislation, this time mandating that children of LGBT parents be forcibly removed from their families and placed into foster homes. "I'd rather be an orphan than raised by a gay parent," a Russian MP was quoted as saying, his words landing like a punch in my gut. *Just breathe*, I told myself. I looked over at my family sleeping peacefully beside me, our son having padded down the hall and into our bed at daybreak, nestling between his two moms for a last snuggle before a busy day at school. Why is there such hatred towards us when all our son has ever known is love?

Over the years, I've learned to shield myself from homophobic taunts and hateful attitudes. But the words still hurt, even as I let them roll off me. My fight-or-flight response automatically kicks in, flooding me with fear and anger, more so than ever now that I'm a parent. I have become a fierce Mama Bear, determined to protect my brood at all costs. I felt vindicated and relieved on U.S. election night when Americans re-elected President Obama and Referendum 74 passed by a large majority in Washington State. A month later, Amanda and I watched, teary-eyed, television footage of the first same-sex couples marrying in Seattle, just a short three hours' drive from our Vancouver home. As elated as we were to be witnessing this history-making moment, the ugly debate that had preceded it was not far from our minds. The referendum process had drawn hate-mongers out as a stark reminder of how fragile our status as a family still is and that we should never take our rights for granted. As the persecution of Russian gays and their children persists, I am appalled that my own Canadian government, which purportedly recognizes my rights as a queer person, has not taken a tougher stance against the Kremlin.

In order to be a good mother, I cannot live in a perpetual state of anger and fear. Instead, Amanda and I go about our day-to-day business of raising our son, projecting onto him love, confidence, and pride, with the hope that with more and more queers having children, and that with each new generation of LGBT offspring, societal tolerance and acceptance will continue to grow, until the day when no one bats an eye when we're out in the world—and not because we're invisible, but because we're finally seen as a family.

Snow Day

ROBIN SILBERGLEID

I LIKE SNOW. I like fine flurries that settle to the ground like dust motes. I like wet fat clumps that stick to my hair when I get out of the car. I like the steady fall of snowflakes picture perfect as a greeting card in December, when I look out my window and think only of a snow globe. I've been back in the snowy North for four years, and I don't see myself tired of shovelling and de-icing any time soon. I consider it a good birthday when it snows enough to last for a few days. For a girl who grew up in the Windy City, a snow day is a good day indeed.

* * *

The Inuit have an unusually large number of words for snow. Words that describe the weight and texture and amount, the important distinctions that impact daily life, those are the words that describe snow. My own vocabulary isn't as nuanced, but here, as an adult living in a place where it has the capacity to snow from October through late April, I am learning the differences the way I might study the sexual proclivities of a new lover.

* * *

Our first winter after my father left, my mother came into my room in her long underwear and coat, cheeks flushed from the snow. It was below zero—I never understood how the temperature could be less than nothing—but still her hands felt hot as they smoothed my forehead. Later I would think of that year as she spoke of it, "the blizzard of Seventy-Six," when my next-door neighbour dove from his garage roof into a mountain of snow piled in our shared yard, where my friend Becca and I had gotten stuck hours earlier as we tried to build an igloo. Becca's mother plucked us out like daisies and brought us inside for Oreo cookies and juice. Now, I think of that image often when I try to understand what it was like for my mother, divorced with two children by age thirty, as she learned how to survive on her own. She was warm and tender where my father was absent, shucking off her snow gear to sit on the edge of the twin bed with my sister and me. We sucked our thumbs as she read *Are You My Mother?* and *The Snowy Day*. Even in those first months my father was gone—"On a business trip," I was told—I don't think I missed him.

* * *

The week before her official winter break, my four-year-old daughter has a snow day. Last night, when I put her to bed, I said, watching the salt trucks go up and down the major street by our house, "You know, I'd bet you don't have school tomorrow." Now, when I look out the window at the wide expanse of white blanketing our neighbourhood, our unplowed streets, even before I check my email for the official word from the director of the preschool, I know with absolute certainty that we will be spending the day at home, drinking hot cocoa, shovelling the drive, watching a video or staring out the window at the snow, still falling and drifting against our door.

I have been awake for hours by the time she comes into my bed. She asks me to call the Child Development Center and see if it is open. I am crabby from lack of sleep, and despite my deep love for snow, today I wish I could get in the car and drive her to school, so I can stay home and wallow in self-pity. It's hard to be depressed when you need to cook breakfast and entertain a restless preschooler. It's the six-year anniversary of the D&C that ended my first pregnancy, the result of six months of fertility treatment and prayer. It's a day that usually goes unmarked, but today I feel it in the clenched fist of my uterus, in the blood speckling my underwear. I've been trying again for a sibling, pumping my body full of synthetic hormones and vitamin supplements. When I woke at 3:30, my skin slick with nightmare, I took a home pregnancy test. For long minutes, it sat there on the counter, blank as a sheet of paper fresh from the ream, unmarred as snow before it's been plowed, insulting me with evidence of what I already knew. Not this month, no baby to look forward to with the start of the school year in September. If it had worked, I noted the wonderful irony, I would have been due on Labour Day.

* * *

In Billy Collins's poem "Snow Day," the speaker looks out his window and watches his child neighbours play by a fence, "climbing and sliding," whispering to themselves in this world beyond adults. The schools are closed; the children take over the snowy landscape while the speaker stays inside, drinking his tea, a "willing prisoner" in his house. His poem makes it clear that snow days are for children. Kids make snow angels and build forts and sled down the largest hills they can find, while adults sprinkle salt from plastic containers and shove large piles of white into the far corners of their yards.

Getting the car out of the drive is a major ordeal. I think of his poem today, as my daughter asks me to build a snowman.

"It's the wrong kind of snow," I tell her, "this is too light and fluffy to stick. Not good packing snow."

"Try it," she says, "Please." Her voice turns into a grating whine. It's going to be a long day.

* * *

It is almost time for lunch when Hannah and I finally struggle into our winter coats and boots, two pairs of socks and mittens for each of us, mismatched hats and scarves. When I open it, the door cuts through the snow piled on our front stoop like a plow. I shovel a path for us, leading only to more snow. She flops on her back and makes angels while I use her yellow child-sized shovel to chip at the frozen blocks at the end of our driveway. Across the street, my neighbour does the same.

At some point, I know, he will cross the street and volunteer to help me, after I've managed to do three quarters of the drive—the hardest, heaviest parts—on my own. It's a gesture of chivalry from another era, more about appearance than actual assistance. If he wanted to help, he would have shovelled for me when I was gone for a week last winter; instead he let eighteen inches pile up until the woman watching my cats wasn't able to get her truck up the incline.

"My mother," I imagine him telling me, "wouldn't stand for me watching a pretty young girl shovelling snow."

I try not to resent him for not doing work that isn't really his to do. He's not my husband. He's not Hannah's father. He's not even a friend. *Maybe an independent woman threatens him,* I think. *Maybe he needs to shovel for me to put me back in my place.* Instead of saying this I will offer him cookies, coffee with milk. This neighbour turns me into the wife I never was or wanted to be.

* * *

I brought my daughter home from the hospital on Valentine's Day in a rare Texas snowstorm. In her baby book, along with the snapshots of her wearing a pink-and-blue striped cap, is a picture of the snow as it fell against our apartment door. My mother snapped the photo of the snow, almost melting as it hit the ground, while I sat in a rocking chair, in the nursery decorated with balloons, and watched my heavy-lidded five-day-old suck and swallow. I hoped, but did not know, that one day she would be stuck home from school, begging to go sledding, watching me skim the thin crust off the milk as it warmed on the stove for cocoa. I wanted her to grow up surrounded by snow, by the change of seasons and winter days that dimmed before dinner was cooked and on the table. I got her out of Texas as fast as I could.

* * *

After an hour of shovelling the muscles in my lower back spasm and quit. I'm hot enough to take off my hat and scarf. I let the steam rise from the top of my head like a kettle about to whistle. I'd take off my coat, except I know Hannah would want to do the same. Her cheeks are bright red, the back of her hair soaked, and large chunks of ice stick out the tops of her boots. As soon as I get the snow off the drive and onto the area of our yard where grass grows in the spring, my daughter takes her new saucer and slides down. My work spills in an avalanche. "Please," I say, "would you please slide the other direction so I don't need to do more work?" I hear the clipped annoyance in my voice. I know I am sucking the joy out of the snow day I once desperately wanted her to have.

"Come on," I urge her, willing my voice to soften. "Let's go inside and warm up. We can go to the park later, I promise."

"Five more minutes, please, Mommy?" she begs, grabbing a handful of snow and throwing it up in the air, her own private snowstorm that scatters and lands back on top of her head.

I can't help but smile.

"Sure, five minutes, but then we really need to go in. It's too cold to be out here for long."

Frostbite is white, I remind myself, not scarlet. There's a dull cramping in my uterus. I know I'll go inside and pull the test back out from the trash hoping beyond hope that somehow two lines will have appeared, like the lines in the road after the plow has come through and made the world easy to navigate again.

* * *

Those nights when my mother came in from shovelling the snow I saw how strong she was, how capable. In photos from that time her face is pinched, her legs swimming in sweatpants that look several sizes too big. She couldn't have weighed more than ninety pounds. She didn't choose for my father to have an affair and move out. But she did choose marriage and all the possibilities that affords, including children and divorce. By the time she was my age, she had remarried and given birth to her third child, a brother younger than me by eight-and-a-half years. I'm sure she loved my stepfather, although I have often wondered if she married him more for a sense of security than for romance. For a woman who moved from her father's house to her first husband's, being the sole provider, family cook, chauffeur, gardener and more must have been a very threatening experience.

For me, chipping away at the snow at the end of the drive, there is strength and confidence in what I have done on my own. I have been pregnant. I have given birth. I have earned a PhD and landed two tenure-track jobs as a professor. I have bought a house in a charming neighbourhood where my child might walk to the park and go sledding down the hill with her friends. I am single, to be sure, but I am neither lonely nor alone.

* * *

What I've always liked about snow days is the way that the world stands still and watches. Exams don't need to be taken. Papers don't need to be written or graded. It is as if the world is saying, "I need a break." And snow days, I have found, always come at exactly the right time, just when you think you can't possibly keep up with the demands of the planner's red-ink schedule. Snow days ask you to stop and take notice.

As a woman trying to get pregnant, I live too often in the future rather than the present, the blank screen of the negative test. I will see the new doctor next week, come up with a plan for trying again in the spring. If things work then, I could have a December baby, born in the middle of a snowstorm. I can't imagine anything better. For now, I take my daughter outside to sled on the hill. She sits in front of me and we slide, wind biting at our faces. For now, her shrieks of delight are more than enough.

Traps, Stars and Raising Men

DIANA DAVIDSON

MY SON TELLS ME, "We need to build a leprechaun trap." He is seven, in Grade Two, and believes that these mischievous creatures of Irish folklore are somehow akin to rodents. The whole notion of making a trap is confusing for him: one of his grandfathers traps marten, muskrat, and beaver in Northern Alberta. My son has seen the jagged jaws and lifeless pelts of traps. My little boy asks me, "What happens to the leprechauns in the trap? Will they just climb out? Will they die?" I would like to celebrate St. Patrick's Day by reading some Seamus Heaney, having a Guinness, and maybe digging up my "Best of U2" playlist. But leprechaun trap-building has become a thing and so we will participate. It's Wednesday and he is with me for the next few nights. St. Patrick's Day is on a Monday this year so we have until Friday to get the trap to school.

I respond, "Alright." I can't stop myself from thinking: *your Dad would do a better job.* But my son's father, my husband of nearly fourteen years, moved out in December, saying he couldn't be married anymore. At least not to me. So I need to push beyond my grief, my loss, and build something.

I retrieve an empty one-litre milk carton from the recycling bin. I scrounge some green Christmas wrapping paper from a box in the crawlspace, in the house we bought when I was heavily pregnant with my little boy—a house I now have to manage on my own. I can't find any tape other than some heavy book-binding stuff. My son and I wrap the crinkly green paper around flimsy fuchsia cardboard. I press down the pointed vale opening that poured milk onto cornflakes a week ago.

My son loves that I am building something with him. He chatters non-stop. He takes big unwieldy scissors and cuts a hole through the wrapping and the carton. He puts gold stickers on the inside waxy walls and says, "That'll get him Mom!" He makes a ramp from some other scrap of cardboard rescued from the recycling I haven't bothered to take out for some weeks because I can't face the crusted still-there snowbank.

"It looks like a house Mom. This is good." We stretch an uninflated gold balloon over a jam jar lid to make a trampoline: "The leprechaun will bounce right into my trap Mom. It's going to be awesome." We inflate some other gold and green balloons and tie them to the pointy top of the wrapped shiny carton.

My son likes making traps—for tiny plastic superheroes who fight each other, for our beleaguered twelve-year-old dog, sometimes even for me. A few weeks after his dad left, we were lying in his bed, me stroking his hair, his little brain whirling with ideas. "Mom," he said, "We should make a trap."

"What kind of trap?" I ask.

"We'd need rope and a big rock and a candle. We'll put the rock over the door and we'll light the candle and when Dad opens the door, the boulder will hit him on the head and he'll forget about divorce."

"And then what?" I ask, pushing back tears.

"Then we'll be our family."

My only response can be a goodnight kiss.

We don't make the boulder-candle-rope trap. Instead, we finish the leprechaun trap in time for the deadline. We find some green glitter, left over from another long-abandoned craft, and even though it's impractical and most of it will likely will end up in the bottom of his backpack as he carries this contraption to school on Friday, my son and I sprinkle the glitter over the milk carton walk up, jam-jar trampoline, and pneumatic balloons.

The sparkling balloons look like they could carry the little green house up into the clouds.

My son tells me, "Mom—I think my trap will be the best."

* * *

When I was eleven, I became obsessed with constellations and their stories. I may have been working on getting a Girl Guide badge or I may have taken a book out of the library—memory is blurry that way—although I'd like to think now that my astronomical interest was an inquisitiveness about the worlds outside mine. I took a book out of the library titled something like *Crafts and Other Delights*. Buried within this hardcover's well-worn glossy and binding-taped pages, was a two-page spread on how to make tin cans into stargazing machines. I imagine the instructions went something like this: "Take an empty soup can, rinse it out, use a small hammer and tiny finishing nails to punch delicate holes in the pattern of your favourite constellation, and you can have your own tiny universe in your hands." I became desperate to do this.

The difficulty in this project was getting enough cans. Summer was the wrong time to eat store-bought things in my childhood home. Summer was the time of bounty. It was the time to pick beans and peas and saskatoons and raspberries. When I told my Dad I wanted to make constellations out of used tins, he dutifully ate soup every day for lunch, even on those rare prairie days when it was over twenty-five degrees. A careful and gentle man, my father encouraged me. He showed me how to pound a nail into the bottom of a carefully-scrubbed can with one wing of a hammer. But he also had his own work to do: he worked as a crop scientist so summer was his busy season. "Finish the patterns," he told me, "and we'll try them out tonight." I wonder what my father was pushing away when we built our tin can galaxies.

I spent many afternoons that summer in the basement work-room—a misnamed crawlspace where Dad stored tools not used in gardening—and hammered out patterns into cans that once held clam chowder and beef barley. I retreated there and sought out the long workbench and one adjacent wall covered in corkboard as a validation that there was life beyond. I made sure the cans were spotless, using precious well-water that should have gone to sustaining the bushes and blossoms that would become winter's food supply to rinse away a milky film or stray barley bead. I competed with my mom for nighttime kitchen space, space she needed to rinse purple curves of beans and meticulously shelled peas waiting to be blanched and frozen, pushing my own agenda of clean shiny tin cans that could mimic the wonder of the universe. I was collecting the night sky. No one could get in my way.

I can't remember if my father and I ever discussed how my constellation-cans would have been a better winter project than summer one. Winter would have made more sense. In the summer, in Northern Alberta, the sun barely sets. There are not a lot of nighttime hours to put a flashlight inside the tunnel and project patterns onto walls, floors, ceilings. And why would we—when we could step outside at midnight and see the real thing, although made hazy by a still-setting sun or visible swoop of milky way trace?

In summer we could stay up late, since there was no school, and Dad and I could stand outside in our yard, on our hilltop acreage in the North, and look up into the sky and watch the constellations and green-blue dancing Aurora Borealis if they decided to grant us as an audience. We could only do this at this time of year, without the discomfort of snowsuits and breath freezing mid-sentence, and probably only at the age I was. If I had been younger, I would have been tired. If I had been older, I would have been distracted by pubescent dramas of boys I wrote about in journals. The following summer I would retreat to my room in the basement, listening to music I thought would impress others and obsessing about my changing body.

And even though I couldn't have really known what I was doing, I look back now and recognize that I was trying to capture something in those hole-y soup cans. I was trying to control and trap something uncontainable.

So, that summer of tin cans punched through with tiny holes to let in light, I obsessed, Dad ate a lot of soup, and we stayed up late to gaze at the big-bowled milky sky. We were connected by unpolluted big prairie nights full of stars that I felt needed counting and accounting for. We were beautiful in our wonderment at the worlds so far beyond ours. We found comfort in our sameness—in our shared, dare I say inherited, need for introspection and wonder and quiet and confirmation that we were not alone.

* * *

It is the first day of spring and it has been snowing since morning. Tonight, after my son is fast asleep under a comforter featuring

Iron Man, and cuddling a plush teal *Perry the Platypus* stuffie, I step outside and look up for the stars. But it is too cloudy. Despite the snow, I know spring is coming and I think about all the jobs I'll need to do: set mousetraps with peanut butter, rake and aerate the lawn, plant pots to sit on the deck. These jobs were never mine before. And I will have to wait for summer's big-bowled prairie sky to spot the Big Dipper, the Little Dipper, Orion's Belt. There are no stars tonight to captivate me or be counted.

I've been thinking about the kind of man I want my son to become. I don't have extensive criteria: I want him to be kind, and curious, and find something to do that he loves, and to fall in love with someone who loves him back.

A few weeks ago, I spoke on a panel of women writers for International Women's Day. We sat in the upstairs of an independent bookstore on a sunny Calgary afternoon, read excerpts of our latest books, and talked about the labels "Woman Writer" and "Feminist." We talked about how young girls are captivated by their self-image in an age of social media. The discussion turned to how we can protect our daughters, how we can empower them, embolden them. I chimed in, "My most important job as a feminist is to raise my son to be a good man." And until I said it out loud in the upstairs of a bookstore to an audience of listeners, I hadn't quite articulated it. Now I know.

This marks a shift for me: I no longer think of my son as the baby that drank milk at my breast or the curious toddler who constantly discarded footwear to feel the ground beneath his feet. I no longer worry about him putting keys in sockets or choking on Cheerios. The past has been replaced by the future and by my anxiety about how I help my child become a good man.

The men I love—and have loved—in my adult life are all men I would call "good." They are observers. Quiet and contemplative. They are scientists, teachers, poets. They are the kind of people who care about ancient Rome and climate change and how a ghazal works. They know the land: they love the quiet of the forest, the cathedral-like hush of the mountains. They ask questions and don't always expect answers. The men I love and have loved look up and out at the world around them and think, "Huh. That is interesting." Sometimes the choices they make baffle me, wound me, break me. But they are men who try and make sense of the chaos.

And I am the same. In many ways, I am my father's daughter.

And this shapes how I mother my son.

I have spent much of my life trying to capture beauty, trying to hold on. I think of Heaney's lines, "Of open minds as open as a trap/ Where tongues lie coiled, as under flames lie wicks," from the poem "Whatever You Say, Say Nothing." I am okay with silence and contemplation—even when it comes with almost-unimaginable pain. I want to embrace my new life and different existence. I am not quite ready but hope I will be soon.

I never want my son to feel trapped. I want him to feel wonderment and wide-open possibilities as big as a prairie sky on a summer night.

And so as I look up at the almost-spring sky, I promise, to him and to myself, that I will keep looking up at the stars.

Rush Hour

NICHOLE QUIRING

TRAFFIC COMES TO A STANDSTILL. Her carefully-manicured nail scrapes a trail down the thick grey coat of dashboard dust. The air conditioning in the Honda Pilot, though cranked, is on the brink again. All the windows are open; a stench of fermenting sewage assaults the air. Mickey Mouse's helium voice serenades: "Oh, the buzzin' of the bees in the peppermint trees/ In the Big Rock Candy Mountains." She flips the stereo off and looks in the rear-view mirror.

She scans her face. Her eyes are underlined in dark shadows that look as if they've been stuck on with dabs of Elmer's. Her face is an expired flower brushed, lined, and glossed in synthetic colour. Veins of corrugated steel map their way through her hair, reminders of the wayward hitchhiker of youth having thumbed its way out long ago. She stops looking in the mirror and considers her body. She can't remember when she's last seen the inside of a gym. Between reviewing work accounts, potty training, and mopping the kitchen floor there is no time. Not much sex appeal in practical beige underwear these days either. The image of dimpled cellulite thighs, and the taunting pink smile branded into the skin above her panty line comes to mind.

Michael came out of that. Michael, who now weighs thirty-one pounds and measures thirty-seven inches.

She remembers being six months pregnant and entertaining Anne, her neighbour, a nurse, a mother of four, in her backyard greenhouse. She remembered bending over, her basketball-size belly low, casting a shadow across the tender seedlings reaching for the sun. Her stretched and distorted belly button in the shape of a startled "Oh."

She and Anne talked. She could still see Anne, black gum boots crunching the gravel at the bottom of the green house, hair falling down her face as she bent, dumping water from the can into the dirt. "They'll break your heart," she had said, shaking her head as she spoke, as if trying to unconvince herself. "Over and over and in ways you didn't even know it could be broken." Anne had smiled and they had continued plucking dead leaves and dampening infant plants.

Anne's pronouncement stuck to her like a burr over the next three years. She thought of how often her heart had been broken before her husband. All those failed relationships. Cakewalks compared to the way her heart could come apart now with the one a.m. checks for breath, locked windows, turned off stove, and requests for mommy kisses that cured all. Hovering, always hovering, and waiting.

She pokes her head as far out of her car window as the seatbelt allows. *What the hell is the hold up?* She sees flashing red lights and, as if on cue, hears the counterpart siren. An accident. Traffic inches forward. She presses her foot on both clutch and gas, shifts the gears and moves up. She looks at the time. She is late again. It's 5:42 p.m. She should be home making dinner. The babysitter has likely done this for Michael by now. She wonders how potty training was today. They'd mastered peeing in the toilet but number two is a whole other story. She called the paediatrician because her once-regular son had stopped going after having an accident in his underwear. Her son had begged her to get the hard, golf-ball-size lump out of the back of his underwear. It fell on the bathroom floor and, without thinking, she had bent down and picked it up with bare hands before throwing it into the toilet. She looks at her fingers now as if the incident was just moments ago, then she drums her nails on the dashboard.

At a snail's pace, she arrives at the affected intersection. A police officer directs traffic as paramedics manoeuvre a stretcher toward the ambulance. There is one car ahead of her. The officer directs them to go. The car in front of her doesn't move. *Too busy rubbernecking.* She leans on the horn and is surprised when the driver in front of her turns around and angrily flips her the bird. *Asshole.* There is a baseball bat in her trunk. She envisions getting out of the car and popping the hatch. *Batterbatterbatterbatter.* That would make her one of those crazies, one of the ones who come unhinged in traffic—the people they talk about on the six o'clock news, pissed off and beating the shit out of each other. That is not her. Besides, the baseball bat is Michael's plastic yellow t-ball bat.

She moves through the intersection only to get stuck in another jam. She is still three shops, a park, a bridge and a restaurant away from her home—twenty-six full blocks from the babysitter. She can see McDonalds now with its urine-coloured big "M" and its hungry snake-line of drive-thru patrons. Next to it stands the grocery store where she regularly shops. Her husband would laugh at her ability to map by landmarks. Like a GPS system, he'd say: "Technically, you're about two kilometres from home."

On the side of the road stand orange pylons, triangle tipped fingers pointing up to a digital sign flashing out road delays. She hears a vibrating jack hammer. They'd been re-building this damn road forever. Something about a road diet. The newspapers called it a "revolutionary" project but she wonders how revolutionary it will be if it's never completed.

A cement truck, with its hard, gestating belly, manages to pass the traffic by driving on the shoulder. A horn bellows behind her. She ignores it and wonders if she should flip the bird too.

Perspiration melds the backs of her legs to heated leather upholstery. She shifts, pulling, stretching, and ripping tender skin until the suction is severed and her legs bloom pink. Her Coach purse, cell phone and a stack of work papers sit on the passenger seat. She picks up a page and fans herself. The page has a tiny lump of dried neon Play Dough stuck to it. With her other hand she pulls the now droopy blouse away from the sticky skin of her chest. What had she been thinking this morning putting on long sleeves? That was just it, she hadn't been thinking. Michael had smeared peanut butter through his hair and she had tried to save time by cleaning him up and getting herself dressed for work—multi-tasking—which hadn't worked—because she was late dropping him off at the sitter's anyway.

He had cried to see her go.

Now here she is, in an expensive, long-sleeved blouse on the hottest day of the year. How is she ever going to get the yellow out of the armpits? She undoes the top button and looks up.

Go. Stop. She is now sitting in front of the LRT tracks. A candy-cane striped arm comes down and red lights begin to flash. Incoming train.

A stick man in grime-layered clothes draped over bones and ropes of dark, matted hair emerging from the bottom of a moss-green toque, staggers towards the tracks. She imagines he smells like pee. She watches him weave towards the tracks and feels a sudden need to bring him home and turn the garden hose on him. He begins to balance beam on the thin rungs of metal alloy neglectful of the sign next to him that reads: "Stick to the Trail, Stay off the Rail." He doesn't fall. She's transfixed by—she's not sure what—awe or envy, then a sudden anger. He makes it look easy. She wants to open the door and scream at him like the crazy, plastic bat-wielding lady she'd moments ago reassured herself she wasn't. "It's not that easy, you know!" She says fiercely, as if daring the leather-panelled walls of the car's interior to disagree.

The red lights are still alternately blinking and the arm hasn't lifted. A warning. She looks around at the other vehicles. No doors open. No movement in the shallow breathes of humid air. Should she? She pops her seatbelt, opens her door and leans halfway out.

"Hey!" She screams.

At the sound, the man turns around and staggers onto the gravel beside the track. The train rushes by.

"Jesus Christ," she inhales—less of a curse, more of a prayer.

The man stumbles away.

Choking, she undoes the second button of her shirt, pulls her leg back into the car, closes the door and does up her seatbelt.

The candy cane arm finally lifts and gives her permission to proceed. She puts her foot on the gas and slowly moves across the tracks, a quiver in her hands as she white-knuckles the steering wheel. The traffic light in front of her is red. Stop. She rubs the place on her neck where the seatbelt rubs and irritates her skin.

Something doesn't feel right. Is she PMSing? She can't even remember her last period. It was just this Saturday, Michael still asleep, that they both agreed, whispering over coffee and the standard scrambled eggs (in the old days they used to eat boiled, poached, over-easy, basted) that they were finished after one child. Babies weren't meant to be accessories like Chihuahuas or designer handbags. Besides, they were getting too old. Then Michael woke, and they were fighting over chores again.

She looks at her watch. 6:15 p.m.

She glances at the pile of paperwork sitting on the seat next to her. Six years of university education. A career. A house. A husband. A kid. She considers driving on the patch of grass to her right; it is no wider than the bath mat Michael sits on at night. Just as the cement truck had done, she too could pass all the traffic and force someone to let her in. She thinks of the man who'd flipped her the bird and of the yellow, plastic bat in her trunk and she reconsiders. Once she is past the red light and through the intersection she'll be in the thick of construction. The traffic will crawl. Two lanes down to one. Her skin itches.

The light turns green. Nobody moves. Six cars ahead of her she sees an excavator parked on the side of the road, its neck submissively bowed to the ground. Next to the excavator stands a construction worker, red hardhat perched on head, wearing jeans and an open reflector vest. His chest is bare and tanned, highlighted in hues of sunset pink and, if she was close enough, she knows she would be able to see the soft sprouted hairs coming from beneath his skin. Casually, he sucks on a cigarette and leans against the machine. His other hand—palm flat and splayed—rests on the ample hip of the backhoe, a lover caressing yellow metal. She blinks.

Her cell phone rings. She looks around. They aren't moving. She tucks a chunk of hair behind her ear and answers even though it's illegal. The babysitter: "Almonds for dessert. Michael had an allergic reaction." Instinctively, her hand moves to her heart. Reassurance. "He's fine; there was Benadryl in the medicine cabinet." A wailing question. Reassurance. "He's fine but take him to the doctor." She nods to the windshield. It's okay. Everything is okay. Relief. Frozen in the midday heat, she disconnects. *We don't have nuts in our house. We have fruit for dessert.* She looks at her watch again. 6:17 p.m. She should be home giving Michael a bath.

A large space in front of her. A honk behind her. She looks to the right. There is a spot. Go. She looks straight ahead then glances to the right again. There is an open space on the side of the road. She pulls her vehicle off to the side and onto a small patch of grass. Neutral. E-break. Keys. Silence. Door. Open. The idling stops.

"Why do you have to go Mommy?"

She can feel curious stares coming from the coloured parade of metal vehicles, puffing their plumes of disproval. She slips bare feet from patent heels and steps onto grass. Her feet sigh from the coolness. She remembers her grandmother's naked feet touching hardwood, manoeuvring their way around a clean farmhouse kitchen with the smell of fresh buns in the oven, summer dill in the air and fruit-bearing bushes in the backyard, waiting patiently to be plucked, cooked, canned and eaten. Her grandmother singing. She sang all the time. The image melts as she passes over the grass threshold and onto scorching concrete, searing the fleshy pads of her soles.

"But I want to stay with you."

She moves straight ahead in a tight black skirt and designer blouse. Her fingers reach for the third button on her shirt and she parts it gently in the same way they had parted her legs to give birth. *It's so hot.* She wipes sweat from her brow. She pulls her arms out of the sleeves and the damp silk cape flutters to the pavement below. The underwire in her bra slides and tightens around her chest, squeezing her ribs together like a tightly-laced corset. She unhooks the white undergarment and lets it drop too. She breathes.

Go. The woman walks quickly now in the direction of the babysitter's—barefoot, barelegged and bare-breasted. She flicks her short dark hair. She feels herself crumbling like the bits of jackhammered asphalt as she steps in front of construction workers, making her way down a part of the newly built Revolutionary Road.

You Didn't Take Any Pictures of Me

JEAN CROZIER

TWO WEEKS after my nineteenth birthday, I married a man who worked on the Distant Early Warning (DEW) Line, far north of any city. He worked an eight-month stint in the Arctic and then came home for two weeks. His salary was three or four times that of most urban dwellers, and the intent was that he would work away until we had developed a nice little nest egg. I thought we were on the same page—he would earn enough money to buy the bacon that I would stay home to cook, and I would be a stay-at-home mom. I wasn't old enough to know there were questions to ask: why would a previously married man with two children be interested in a starry-eyed, adolescent girl? How did he intend to support two families with only the marine electrician's training he'd received in the navy? I didn't understand that his qualifications were good enough to work in the far north or on out-of-town 'boomer' jobs but not, as I would discover, sufficient to work a job where he could come home every day, eat the pies I baked, deposit his cheques in the bank, meet the neighbours, paint the walls, and simply be present.

He quit his Arctic job as soon as we had saved enough for the down payment on a house. He found work in the city as an electrician's helper, then as replacement worker for the striking aircraft electricians ... whatever he could find. Few of his jobs paid enough to maintain one family, let alone two.

Our marriage was less than three years old when I stood, one afternoon, gazing into the refrigerator: a bag of carrots, a half quart of milk, a pound or two of potatoes, a partial bottle of ketchup.

The cupboards were as bare as the refrigerator. From the radio came Peggy Lee's voice, singing "Mr. Wonderful." Apart from the music, the house was quiet. My daughter was down for her afternoon nap and my pregnant body also needed rest. I could sometimes snatch a few moments in the afternoon, but worry typically pushed its way into my rest. That day, I'd already stared at our bankbook, wishing the figures would transform to at least two digits before the decimal point. Tonight, supper for my little girl would be mashed carrots. My husband and I would have the potatoes. There was nothing else to eat and no money to buy another morsel. I had nothing for tomorrow's meals.

The doorbell's ring pulled me from the fridge. I opened the door and saw a stranger standing outside. The man wore a wool cap and a heavy jacket that had seen several seasons: both the elbows were patched, and the pocket flap drooped.

"Your uncle asked me to bring you these." His voice was gruff.

He balanced a box on his knee. From an outside corner, where the taped edge had split open, jutted an ice-covered object.

"Here, let me put it inside for you."

He turned and stomped back to the rattle-bone truck parked at the curb.

Our address was scrawled on the box. On the upper corner, almost illegible, was my aunt and uncle's name, the ones who lived in the northern-most region of Alberta. Inside the box lay several large fish wrapped in waxed paper, maybe ten-pounders, frozen solid, pulled from one of the cold northern lakes. Even these bony jackfish would be delicious. All but one fish went into the freezer, plugged in again now that there was a reason for its coldness. Into the freezer also went my terror, removed for today, stored away for some other day, not necessary now. We would eat tonight.

The fish were a godsend.

Neither my husband nor I applied the word 'poverty' to our condition. We just didn't have any money. No one knew about our financial situation, or so we thought. I did wonder why my uncle had sent us the fish. Could he have known how desperately we needed that food? I'd never complained to anyone, certainly not to any of my relatives, but was it possible that my grandmother knew? Had she mentioned something to my aunt and uncle?

Neither Edmonton nor any other Canadian city had a food bank then. There was no place to go when a family needed food. We couldn't have collected welfare, even if we'd considered that possibility: we had purchased a house, although we were behind in the mortgage payments with their 8.5% interest, and home "ownership" disqualified us from welfare. Poverty's cause was (and often still is) misunderstood by those who have never experienced it. I was ashamed of our situation, but too young to understand the complex social reasons of poverty: how could two healthy adults be so poor? We didn't fit the pattern I'd been brought up to believe: that poorness was the result of laziness, ineptitude, poor decision-making, too many children, and just plain bad living. I don't think the term "working poor" had yet been coined.

Winter turned into summer and I planted a vegetable garden. My husband looked after the children while our neighbour and I picked saskatoons and chokecherries. I baked pork and beans without the pork and macaroni and cheese without the cheese.

The children's clothes—and mine—were hand-me-downs, they came from thrift stores, or were sewn from fabrics I found on the sale tables. Someone gave me a raincoat with worn out sleeves. I turned it inside out, fitted pattern pieces on the good parts, cut and sewed a little coat for my daughter and proudly showed off the result.

Before long another man came to the house in the middle of the day, intent on re-possessing the car we drove but for which we'd missed several payments. I didn't want to know what agreement he and my husband came to as they sat outside in the vehicle parked just down the block. There was nothing I could do. My husband was trying to sell life insurance—a commission-only job; the car was essential, the only means he had of getting to a client's home.

I'd been raised believing that "honesty is the best policy," that things would always turn out right if you went to church and if you treated people well, that a wife must always support her husband and that his wishes were paramount. To this day, my children don't know the depth of poverty from which the roots of their parents' discord grew and I have never found a way to explain it to them.

My second daughter, like my first, was born strong and healthy. She nursed well, lost none of her birth weight, and gained an ounce almost every day. I was fascinated with the perfection of this new life. She slept in a cradle we'd been given and which I placed close to my side of the bed so I could hear her breathing and get to her quickly when she awoke in the middle of the night. My babies were seldom out of my sight: they rode in a donated carriage when we took our afternoon walks, my older daughter and I exercised with the *Ed Allen Show* on television, we read stories, visited friends, played in the back yard.

My grandparents, aunts, and uncles said nothing when we could occasionally afford the gasoline to drive to the farm but I saw their disdainful looks, overt glances from the people who had provided my siblings and me with a home every summer holiday while our own mother worked. At the end of our visit, my grandparents would load up our ancient station wagon with potatoes and corn, bags of peas and beans and carrots, a loaf or two of homemade bread, and a good-bye of "Drive safe, now."

What they didn't say was, "What's she doing with that guy? He's not even feeding them. He ought to know better than to fiddle around with this life insurance stuff. Why doesn't he find a real job?" I wouldn't have known how to answer their questions anyway. If they'd asked my husband, he would likely have told them that he'd been trying to get me to make some cold calls, set up appointments so he could sell the insurance, but I didn't seem interested and how could he make the sales if he didn't have any appointments?

Two and a half months after my second child was born, we again faced no food and a host of unpaid bills. A neighbour offered to care for the children. I returned to work. My doctor told me that only time would reduce my generous milk production. We fed the baby diluted cow's milk. My engorged breasts leaked through everything for a month or two before they finally returned to their milk-less state. Each day, I took the bus home from work; my husband retrieved the children from the sitter. He spent the evenings calling on prospective clients. I bathed my little daughters and read them bedtime stories, tidied up the house, did the laundry, and managed the housework.

One night, when my husband came home, I questioned him about our eldest daughter's injured knee. "She fell again. We put a new butterfly bandage on," he shrugged. The little girl had dropped a glass milk bottle at the sitter's, then fell on it. She should have had a couple of stitches but the sitter had no way to get to a doctor and there was the matter of payment.

In the midst of winter, when the temperature dropped to minus twenty-five and thirty degrees Fahrenheit and our forty-year-old, poorly-insulated house developed frost on the windows and the corners of the bedrooms, the baby developed croup. Her lungs filled with mucous and her cough became so intense she vomited up the baby Aspirin I gave her to reduce her fever. We rolled a newspaper into a funnel and set it over the kettle to channel steam into the flannelette-shrouded carriage. The doctor found some medication samples that would work for croup. I sat with the baby all evening and her father took care of her during the day. There was no sick pay in my office and my minimum hourly wage was our only regular income.

That Christmas, the accountant I worked for agreed to close the office on Christmas Day but insisted on keeping it open the day after: "Boxing Day isn't a statutory holiday," he maintained, and we couldn't afford to have me miss even one day of pay. I forget how my husband managed to get a little spruce tree, but he brought one home and I decorated it with the few lights and baubles we'd bought on our first Christmas together, when we still had two incomes and thought we were doing well. The tree went inside the baby's playpen, safe from little fingers. I sewed new baby clothes from remnants, knitted some mittens, found a few treasures at the thrift store, wrapped them in coloured tissue paper, and set them under the little tree, along with the gifts my family had sent. But there are no photos of my little girls with Santa Claus.

None of this had been part of my dream of being the best mother ever. I was running as fast as I could but the exercise wheel that was our life just went faster and faster.

And then I became pregnant again. "For gawd's sake," complained my husband, "all I have to do is hang up my pants and you're pregnant."

By the time our third child was born, just fifteen months after her elder sister, we'd taken in my husband's son from his first marriage. What else could we do? The child's mother brought him to us, a skinny eight-year-old boy with bruises inflicted by the Army web belt his stepfather had used in punishment for some real or perceived misdemeanour. I was twenty-three years old.

My husband found a salaried job; the pay was regular, as were the hours, but there was never enough to go around. We sold our almost foreclosed-upon house and had enough to put a down payment on a newer, larger, home. We had one more child, another beautiful and healthy daughter who soon was adored by her siblings as well as her mother.

To help ends meet, I baked our own bread, grew a vegetable garden, bought the children's clothes from the end-of-season racks and used fabric remnants to make their dresses, sleepers, and diapers. All the clothes were hung to dry on the outdoor clothesline. In winter, they were brought in to be re-hung in the basement. We finally bought a dryer when our youngest child was a few months old. I stood there one day, in front of that dryer, folding flannelette diapers, counting each one, and calculating the number of diapers I'd folded since my first child was born. The answer was so depressing I immediately discarded it.

My youngest daughter was three years old in May 1969 when the prohibition against reproductive sterilization and the sale of condoms were removed from the *Criminal Code of Canada*.

In the evenings, after all the children were in bed and the supper dishes washed, I typed papers and theses for university students, for twenty-five cents a page, not much but enough to buy a bottle of milk or a hank of embroidery thread to decorate a little girl's dress. Still, I didn't want to ask what my stepson said to his teacher when she decreed that every meal should include something from each of the five food groups.

I found a job with flexible hours, evenings and weekends, and left the house four or five times a week as soon as my husband got home from work. By the time I returned at 11:00 or 11:30 p.m., everyone was in bed. The supper dishes still needed to be washed and so did the children's faces. But during those years, we were able to maintain at least a minimal degree of economic stability.

Financial precariousness wasn't totally new to me. When I was a child, my family had struggled. Even when my father was alive we didn't have much and after he passed away we had even less. One Saturday afternoon in mid-December, a few months after our father's death, a knock came at the back door. We four children were home alone. Mom had had to go back to work just a couple of months after our father died, and that morning, she was at the second of her two minimum-wage jobs. On weekdays, she woke us up at 7:00 a.m., left home at 7:30, and didn't get back until 5:30 p.m. Monday to Wednesday. Thursday and Friday she didn't get home until 10:30 p.m., and she often worked from morning until late afternoon on Saturdays.

My little brother dove under his bed, as he always did when anyone came to the house. Our older sister, at fourteen officiously in charge while our mother was elsewhere, opened the inside door, while our little sister peeked around the corner. Two men stood beyond the locked storm door, wearing heavy overcoats and dark homburgs. Each had a scarf around his neck and gloves on his hands. Between them, suspended by one man's right and the other man's left hand, was a large wooden box.

"We have a present for you," said the taller man. "Could we set it inside?"

My sister hesitated. The window began fogging up. We'd been forbidden to open the door to strangers.

"If you like, we could leave it right here. Take it inside as soon as you can, though, won't you? You don't want the cold to get at these oranges, do you?" They set the cover-less box down, turned and descended to the snowy sidewalk.

We could almost taste the Mandarins. A whole box of them, freezing outside.

"We can drag the box in, Maureen. Mom wouldn't want us to leave it out there."

The box was filled with food—a turkey, a canned ham, potatoes in a bag, canned peas and beans. A tin of Christmas pudding. A bag of red and white candies in cellophane tied with a red ribbon. On top of everything, the box of Mandarin oranges, their scent already escaping into the room. On the ends of the box, below the handhold, in red and green letters, was stamped:

"Merry Christmas
from the
Rotary Club of Edmonton."

That box would be the first my family received over the next four
or five years. They came, I believe, because we were on the list of
widows with children, women for whom the provincial government provided minimal medical and dental services but no money.

My brother emerged from under his bed after we dragged the
box through the door. Dust bunnies clung to his auburn hair. As
children, we knew nothing of the term 'poverty' or of its implica-
tions. We just knew we had no father and no money.

Neither my mother nor I expected to raise our children in utter
poverty. My guess is that when my mother met my father, a much
older man in his four-piece suit and bowler hat, she saw a desirable
alternative to the overall-clad young men in the farming community
that had been her home. Neither of them foresaw the vehicle crash
and the subsequent heart attack to which he succumbed at age
seventy-three, leaving her a young, thirty-seven-year-old widow
with four children and an out-dated teaching certificate. Likewise,
I did not anticipate raising babies in a penurious household, or
of ever wishing for one of those wooden hampers to be delivered
at Christmas. Since we weren't collecting welfare payments, and
we assumed that we wouldn't qualify for any sort of income sup-
plement, we weren't on any agency's list. Hampers went only to
those who were "on the list."

My mother and my siblings didn't deserve to be poor. Neither
did my children.

I was in junior high school when my mother rejected poverty,
when she found the time and the energy and the money to upgrade
her teaching certificate and re-enter the classroom. After years of
being poor, we were finally able to buy ham instead of Spam, a
used piano and season tickets to a concert series, and for the first
time that I knew of, my mother became close friends with men
and women who were her intellectual equals.

My youngest child was in Grade One when, fed up with raising
my children without enough money, I fled back to work and to
school, first to college then to university. By the time my youngest

child was in high school, their father and I had separated and then divorced. I built a new life.

"You need to talk to my sister, Mom," said one of my daughters recently, "she thinks the reason there's no photographs of her when she was little is because you didn't love her." I wept. By then, my daughter was married and had children of her own. She'd never asked about the lack of photographs. If she had, I would have told her that although her father had an expensive Rolliflex camera, bought during his days of high wages in the north, we'd had no money to buy film or have it developed when she was little. My photograph albums bear witness to that omission, the time when my children's lives went unrecorded. Those childhood images survive only in my memory, alongside recollections of bean stews, bill collectors, men at the door, shame, and despair.

My daughter's own daughter recently thanked her mother for always being there, at home, cooking and teaching, caring and organizing. I am happy that my daughter has succeeded so well in her self-seen role of exclusively focused homemaker. Lurking beneath my happiness, however, is an unrelenting sense of resentment, frustration that I was unable to mother my children as I'd dreamed of doing, disappointment that I hadn't been able to meet my own expectations. I am sorry that my children grew up in an emotional quagmire, and that they were caught in the war between their father and me, a battle whose roots were sown in the hardscrabble ground of poverty.

Today, I still see many children in similar circumstances. In the week before Christmas, accompanied by a strong young nephew or grandson, I join a line of volunteers. Our cars are loaded with hampers from the Christmas Bureau, cardboard boxes rather than the wooden ones we used to receive but similarly filled. We deliver hampers to 75,000 Edmontonians, about eight percent of the population. Often, a young mother comes to the door to receive her hamper, a woman who says 'thank you' but whose eyes reflect her pain and, often, the shame that I remember.

Perhaps, some day, I will be able to ask my daughters and my stepson to reconsider the years of conflict and hardship, the years when their mother worked and studied rather than baking bread and sewing clothes. Perhaps they will see that they learned the same lessons I did: that although my siblings and I may have felt paren-tally ignored, our mother's actions taught us to use our strengths and our brains. I hope my children also will find the compassion and the charity to understand.

Petro-Mama

Mothering in a Crude World

SHEENA WILSON

T HE FINGERS of my right hand freeze into a claw gripping the
steering wheel. I'm only wearing one glove. I couldn't find the
other in my rush to get him buckled into the backseat. The digital
thermostat on the dash glows blue in the pitch black of the early
morning and I read "-23 degrees Celsius: 6:53 a.m." Inside the car
the eerie silence of the dark and frozen morning is interrupted only
by the harsh and laboured sounds of his breathing. He's finally
stopped panicking, which has only seemed to constrict his airways
further. He's been shouting at me to help him.

"Mama, my neck hurts. I can't breathe."

"Breathe as deeply as you can. Calm down, bud. Screaming
and crying only make it harder for your body to get oxygen. See.
That's better. Breathe deeply."

Now that my four-year-old is so quiet, I listen anxiously to his
rapid intakes of air, calling to him repeatedly so he'll answer me
in his tiny little-boy voice so I reassure myself he hasn't passed
out from lack of oxygen. I cannot see him in my rear-view mirror.

His cheruby little body, cloaked in a grey winter coat, is slumped
over. In the darkness I search for his silhouette against the black
leather seat. But his little figure has been absorbed into the dark
cold morning behind me. The urgent need to get him to the doctor
overwhelms me. I try to focus on what I can control and listen to
the motor's hum and the groaning of the car's frozen metal body as
its internal parts grind against one another. I put the car into gear
and start backing down the driveway. Under the tires, I can hear
the crunching of snow and the breaking apart of ice as it cracks

and splits open. Inside the car, the indicator clicks rhythmically, only slightly faster than his breathing, as I turn onto a deserted roadway.

They are calling this cold snap the "Polar Vortex." Not that we aren't used to these frigid temperatures in Edmonton. The concern this time is that the cold is being caused by a shift in the jet streams. Arctic air is being pushed south. This phenomenon can create unexpected warm waves as well. These dramatic and unseasonal fluctuations in weather are, apparently, all going to be part of our new normal on an increasingly warm planet.

There are no cars on our quiet residential road at this time of the morning. I turn right. Right again. Then left. And now we are on Baseline Road, a major arterial route headed into the city. I join hundreds of commuters, but this morning I won't be going as far as them. I can faintly hear radios playing in the cars next to me. The darkness around me is broken up by the convoy of illuminated dashboards, myriad headlights and running lights. I share the road with small commuter cars, SUVs, mini-vans, and large pickup trucks. Despite the variety of makes that drivers use to indicate their class, income levels, and lifestyle—their level of cool, their brand-associated worldliness advertised by their gleaming hood ornaments—in the pre-dawn light, each vehicle looks identical when compared. Ahead of me, I notice several freight trucks slow down. I imagine they carry produce and other merchandise to the strip-mall shopping complexes and low-rise office and industrial buildings banking the north side of the road. And I look in the rear-view mirror to glimpse my ill little boy.

The rattle of his laboured breathing inside the quiet of the car juxtaposes the roar of traffic outside. Each machine resonates at a different pitch against the frozen ground, sending reverberations and emissions to bounce off commercial buildings on the right, and the facing eight-foot sound barrier wall designed to protect neighbourhoods from the noise and hopefully the pollution, not to mention the associated impact on their residential property stickers. This road will only get busier in the next hour. But this morning I'm not only worried about the flow of traffic and any potential disruptions that might slow my progress to the doctor's office, I'm also intensely aware of what all these vehicles have in common. The acrid-smelling exhaust they spit from their tailpipes is sucked up by my own car, making it harder for my boy to breathe. I think about shutting off the heat to avoid drawing into the car any more of the chemical cocktail of polyaromatic hydrocarbons and polycyclic aromatics and benzene and arsenic and formaldehyde and nitrogen oxides and carbon dioxide. But it is too cold to do that. The bitter-cold air stings the inside of my nostrils, and the caustic heady smell of burned gasoline and diesel chaffs my respiratory tract as the air moves into my healthy lungs. I feel choked. Suffocated. My chest is heavy. Is it empathy for my baby in the backseat or the oppression of the invisible particulates swirling around us in puffs of white and grey and darker-grey warmth, visible this morning only as they crystallize upon contact with the frozen black morning air outside their combustion engines, that cause me these visceral reactions?

"Are you ok Honey?" I ask.

Silence. ... but I can hear him rasping for air.

"Honey? Answer me! Honey! Are you ok?!"

I strain to see him in the review mirror. The air is choking him.

"I'm ok Mama."

He sounds quiet. And small and weak. This is what worries me: he is a robust boy who runs and dances and jokes and entertains everyone. Dashing from one spot to the next, giving quick hugs and stealing kisses from his little sister, and playing and fighting and playing some more with his older brothers. I usually have to tell him to slow down.

As we crawl toward the intersection where I'll eventually need to turn left to get to the doctor's, we are stopped at yet another light and I look off into the distance. I can see the incandescent acres of the Imperial Oil Strathcona and Suncor Energy refineries with their multiple looming red and white stacks out of which are being dissipated the flammable residues of over 320,000 barrels of refined crude a day. Huge flares go up into the morning sky. And in the foreground, squatting just on the other side of the highway, are the enormous round Enbridge tankers decorated with Canada geese flying in formation. Those tankers hold oil in various stages of refination that will eventually be burned off into the atmosphere, here or elsewhere around the world. These industries flank my regular morning commute for about thirty city blocks, some backing up onto the once scenic North Saskatchewan River. All of this is just part of the Industrial Heartland project, where we try to carve out a life for ourselves and our kids.

"Are you ok sweetie?"

"Yes Mama," he murmurs.

Left. Right. Right again. Now I'm in a commercial district of our suburb, vacant at this early hour. The quiet of the morning is a contrast to my urgency. I turn into an almost barren parking lot. It is covered in frozen snow that twinkles under the street-lights. I pull up in front of the doctor's office that opened three minutes ago. Another woman rushes from the only other car in the parking lot to the warmly lit glass-fronted doctor's office. She shields herself against the blowing wind by pulling up her hood and bending forward; she half runs, half walks, outstretched arm grabbing the metal door handle. She whips into the foyer. The sound of the door-chimes is quickly smothered by the gales blowing in from the northwest over Refinery Row. My son and I are more cumbersome in our pursuit. I'm not sure whether I should carry him or have him walk. He is limp from the lack of oxygen and tired from the effort of trying to breathe. In the end, I help him out of the car and we walk together slowly, hand-in-hand, in the -35 wind-chill. The quiet from outside has followed us into the warm enclave of the waiting room, and the sound of my son's wheezing is unmistakable. The other woman says, "Poor baby" and I briefly explain.

"Some kind of asthma attack, I think."

She smiles at him and he returns her attention with an impish look and a flirtatious grin. A glimpse of his vibrant personality peeks out, despite how terrible he feels and how hard he labours to breathe. A moment later, he crumples onto the floor of the waiting room and puts his head on the chair, meekly crying. I try to soothe him by rubbing his back and he crawls onto my knee. There is a sign on the wall that reads *A Place of Happiness*.

* * *

Inside the doctor's office, I apologize. "Sorry to come without an appointment."

The doctor smiles kindly at my comment. Distracted as he places his chilly stethoscope onto my son's warm chubby chest, a few inches below the soft spot in the centre of his collarbone. I watch my little boy's flesh pulse every time he takes a breath. I'm still tired from a sleepless night worrying and waiting. I'm also listening to his breathing to try to determine whether it has gotten better or worse since the middle of the night. I'm listening for some hope that it has, at best, and for something to alert the doctor to, at worst. Suddenly, the doctor is giving me a lot of information and instructions that I find overwhelming:

"This is a typical asthmatic wheeze ... you did the right thing ... the next two hours are critical ... we need to treat aggressively ... the triggers are five-fold: infection, allergies, cold, exercise, smoking ... we'll need to treat aggressively so that he won't have to be on bronchodilators for his whole life ... studies show that this is very effective ... a series of oral steroids and inhaled steroids ... did you get that? Two weeks for the one, four days for the other, as needed for the third."

"I'm sorry, can you repeat that again?"

He does.

"I'm sorry, there are two medications, or three?"

"Three. The two steroids—one oral and one inhaled—and the bronchodilator to be administered as needed. Got it?"

"Yes," I say and apologize again. "This is all just a bit overwhelming and I haven't had much sleep, and I couldn't decide whether to take him to the emergency room last night or not and ..." my voice trails off.

The doctor demonstrates how to use the diffuser, placing the little mask over my child's nose and mouth: "1, 2, 3, 4, 5, 6, 7, 8, 9, 10." This isn't how I thought my little guy would master his numbers: counting his own breaths.

"London Drugs is open. Go there immediately. If he isn't breathing more easily in two hours take him to Emergency at the Stollery Children's Hospital."

* * *

I bundle my son up and we head out into the cold again, bracing ourselves against the chill. His breathing has improved after the dose of bronchodilator. I buckle him into his car seat. His colour is better.

"Where are we going now Mama?"

"To get your medicine," I smile.

I'm relieved he seems to be taking an avid interest in the world around him. I feel I can stop listening so keenly to his breaths. I relax slightly and turn on the radio. A CBC interviewer is discussing the Enbridge Northern Gateway Pipeline hearings and the discontent many people have expressed about the consultation process. A lawyer for resource companies including Enbridge is talking: "Certainly from my vantage point I don't see an inherent weakness in that process . . . What the courts have actually said, very clearly, is that the balancing act between societal interests, on the one hand, and Aboriginal interests, on other, are to be decided by government."[1]

Societal versus Aboriginal? Typical! I think to myself. *Could someone please explain to me where the interests of "society" end and where other interests begin?*

Before I can hear much more about the lawyer's vision of our society that doesn't include Indigenous interests, or even my own, a phone call comes through over the car's Bluetooth, interrupting the broadcast as one concerned caller after another checks in with us. It turns out that London Drugs is, in fact, still closed, and as I drive around from pharmacy to pharmacy, trying to find one that is open, my son and I both provide updates and chat with his father, his grandparents, and with a close auntie-friend with severe asthma who can empathize. A cacophony of loving voices asks pointed questions, gives advice, and expresses concern.

"No one in the family has asthma. Why would he have asthma?"

"Is it an allergic reaction? Something he ate?"

"You should keep buying as much organic food as possible, and avoid pesticides and other chemicals."

"Have you been avoiding dairy and sugar and wheat?"

"Vitamins? Have you been giving them regularly? "

"I've heard that if you give your child too much Tylenol, they can develop asthma. Have you given him a lot of Tylenol?"

"It might not be a good idea to give him the steroids. They can't be good for him."

"Infant exposure to common house dust can cause asthma. But your house was always quite clean when he was a baby and you didn't have carpet in that place."

"Of course, don't over-sanitize or a child's immune system doesn't develop properly."

"I sent you a website that gives you a list of things you can do to help control your child's asthma."

"This can be very serious. He should always have a puffer with him. Apparently several hundred people die of asthma in Canada every year."

"I read on the Asthma Society of Canada facts and statistics pamphlet that experts are struggling to understand why prevalence rates world-wide are, on average, rising by fifty percent every decade."

* * *

Finally, we pull into the parking lot of a pharmacy that is open at this early hour.

"Is this the breathing store Mama?"

Again, I smile, trying to be reassuring. "It's the pharmacy. There isn't any such thing as a breathing store, Love."

"Are they going to help me breathe better?" my four-year-old asks.

"We'll get you some medicine here and we'll hope that it opens your airways. But we all just have to breathe the oxygen that is in the atmosphere. It is invisible but all around us."

"Too bad they don't have a breathing store Mama."

* * *

Newly equipped with a bagful of pharmaceuticals sitting in the passenger seat, some of which I've already administered to my son right inside the pharmacy, I wait to merge onto Baseline Road. I shoulder-check left in the northwesterly direction of the city. The rising sun in the east lights up distant fields of snow interrupted by the crisscrossing of Anthony Henday Drive and Baseline, eventually meeting up with Yellowhead Trail and the Trans-Canada Highway speeding towards hundreds of thousands of kilometers of networks. Over the black ribbon of asphalt, lined by newly erected transformer towers in the recently installed power-corridor, I can see the smoke stacks belching the stink of waste left over after extracting and refining that precious black-gold that drives our luxurious standard of living, that drives up the property values in our neighbourhoods, and that drives our false sense of power over the world and ourselves. There is no mistaking that we are having an effect, but it is not an impact we seem able to navigate.

I'd like to think that if I follow all the advice that I've been given this morning that I will be able to manage my son's asthma for him. I desperately want to believe that if he takes the steroids, he'll outgrow this malady. But this morning the cold air seems to be forming a blanket over the city. Far from comforting us, this ice fog is trapping particulates so they cannot rise into the atmosphere. And, as I look into the dawn, I realize that there are influences penetrating and infiltrating and dissipating and diffusing and seeping into my son's life that are far beyond my control. Despite social constructions of me as his mother, which suggest that I'm either to blame for his health or that I can manage it—by labouring to achieve increasingly high standards of domestic hygiene and by making appropriate consumer choices—I know that scouring our home and feeding him the best organic nutrient-dense foods available for consumption are feeble attempts to mitigate the fallout of what is really feeding our current political-economy. And I know that it is not only my son, but all of us, who are suffocating.

For the second time this morning, my fingers claw the steering wheel and I feel an empathetic heaviness in my chest. As my heart rate rises and finally syncs with the frantic clicking of the indicator, I merge into the steady flow of traffic. I take a deep breath to calm myself. If all goes well, tomorrow the skies will clear and the winds will shift, blowing in new directions.

NOTES

[1]*The 180 with Jim Brown.* CBC Radio One, Calgary. 31 Jan. 2014. Radio. Web. For more details about this podcast in the context of larger media-issues, see Wilson, Sheena. "Petro-Intersectionalities: Oil, Race, Gender & Class." *Fueling Culture: Energy, History, Politics.* Imre Szeman, Jennifer Wenzel, and Patricia Yaeger, eds. New York: Fordham University Press, forthcoming 2015.

Notes on the Cover Image

LAURA ENDACOTT

The cover image was provided by Laura Endacott, an artist, educator, and mother. Her interest lies in visual and conceptual representations of motherhood and in proposing fresh ideas as they relate to contemporary life. She considers her work to be part of the tradition of storytelling. Motherhood can be considered in its widest sense to include definitions of care giver, guardian, protector, and custodian, among others.

Her recent work, entitled *Phantom Vessel* (2013-2014), is both a body accessory for two and a portable boat. Designed as an extension of the body, it attaches via adjustable cotton sleeves to the participants. The sleeves are handsewn to the vessel, limiting certain movements, just as the journey of motherhood is not without its challenges and restrictions.

Both biological and symbolic mothers were invited to go on a series of walkabouts with Endacott in her metaphorical vessel and share their experiences and concerns. In concert with the concept of the maternal, this artwork also speaks to solidarity, community, and agency. Endacott's recent work considers the body as an archive, and she is interested in social life and articulations of agency using performance. Using relational aesthetics, defined as a set of social practices that create opportunities for discourse and exchange, she continues to stage performances that take the maternal out of the domestic space and into the public sphere.

Endacott is interested in the idea of the phantom as something that has been made invisible because it has been constrained to behave in certain socially-prescribed ways. By taking motherhood into public space as material culture, her artwork seeks to critique cultural myths. She feels the images of her work act as a counterpoint to traditional representations that contain culturally and historically embedded meanings. By adding fresh meaning through new images her practice seeks to subvert historical representations with a contemporary system of values.

Her large-scale sculptures, performances, and installations are part of an interdisciplinary practice. In the coming months her work will be included in a new anthology entitled *Performing Motherhood* (2014), and the Musée des maîtres et artisans du Québec will acquire several of her textile objects for their permanent collection.

She has exhibited in museums such as The Orillia Museum of Art & History (2014), Le Musée des maîtres et artisans du Québec (2009), and The Textile Museum of Canada (2000). Her work has been included in artist-run galleries as well as non-traditional spaces such as The Gladstone Hotel (Toronto), the bankonart. net (2010), along with online exhibitions such as ArtWiki: Open Data for the Arts (2012).

Contributors

Allison Akgungor is a retired community health nurse who spent much of her thirty-year career working with new mothers and families with young children. She is a mother of two and grandmother of two. Retirement enables her to pursue an interest in writing.

Janine Alcott is an adjunct at a U.S. university. She holds advanced degrees in both English and Business and has published in several peer-reviewed academic journals. Prior to teaching literature, she worked as a business manager in a high technology corporation while raising her five children.

Chris Bobel is Associate Professor and Chair of Women's and Gender Studies at the University of Massachusetts, Boston. Her research interests centre on feminist activism, gender theory and the politics of embodiment and health. She is the author of *The Paradox of Natural Mothering, New Blood: Third Wave Feminism and the Politics of Menstruation* and co-editor of *Embodied Resistance: Breaking the Rules, Challenging the Norms.*

Anne Cameron Sadava is a retired occupational therapist living in Victoria. She is a mother of three and proud grandmother of one. Since retirement, she has started to pursue her interest in writing amongst other delights.

Natasha Clark is an ex-Mormon and queer parent of four, living in Victoria, BC. An award-winning poet and writer, her work is published in anthologies and literary journals in Canada and the US. She runs a communications business and works for a book publishing company. She longs for Cortona, Italy.

Jean Crozier was born and raised in Edmonton. She married in 1959, raised four daughters and a stepson, then divorced in 1980. She obtained a Library Technology diploma (1975), and a B.Sc. (1984), while living on an acreage, working full-time, and mothering her children. Jean and her library consultancy (1981-2000) received numerous accolades, including her selection as one of Alberta's *Fifty Most Influential People* (1996). Jean remarried in 1996, then was widowed after six short but spectacularly beautiful years. Her family memoir, *No Corner Boys Here*, received the 2008 *IPPY Award*. Jean has developed and now co-teaches writing workshops.

Marita Dachsel is the author of *Glossolalia, Eliza Roxcy Snow, All Things Said & Done*, and the play *Initiation Trilogy*. Her poetry has been shortlisted for the Robert Kroetsch Award for Innovative Poetry and the ReLit Prize. She is the 2013/2014 Artist in Residence at UVic's Centre for Studies in Religion and Society.

Diana Davidson is a writer whose debut novel *Pilgrimage* was published by Brindle & Glass in 2013 and has been called a work of "frontier feminism" by *The Edmonton Journal*. Davidson's writing has been long-listed for the CBC Canada Writes creative nonfiction prize (2012) and has won the Writers' Guild of Alberta "Jon Whyte Memorial Essay Prize" (2010). Her work has appeared in *40 Below, Alberta Views, Avenue Edmonton Magazine, Little Fiction, The Winnipeg Review, Women's Words*, as well as the academic anthologies *Analyzing* Mad Men and *Spectral America*. She has a Ph.D. in literature and has taught at the University of Alberta and the University of York, UK. She was chosen as one of Edmonton's "Top 40 Under 40" by *Avenue Magazine* in late-2011. Her website is www.dianadavidson.org. Diana has one son.

Laura Endacott is a practicing Montreal artist whose research explores women's contemporary identities by focusing specifically on the subject of motherhood from aesthetic, historical, and sociological perspectives. Her art practice re-imagines maternal space. While raising two boys, she completed an M.A. SIP (Specialized Individual Programs) degree in 2010, combining Studio Art Production and Art History. Both her thesis exhibition and her written thesis explored the mother image in contemporary art. She is a part-time faculty member in the Studio Arts Department at Concordia University (Montreal).

Lynn Gidluck has three daughters. Two were adopted from China. Her third daughter was born to her once she thought her family was complete. She is currently in the final stages of writing her Ph.D. dissertation in public policy and history at the University of Regina. When she is not wearing her "mother" or "student" hats, she is a partner in a public relations agency.

Julie Gosselin is a clinical psychologist and Director of the Stepfamily Research Lab at the School of Psychology at the University of Ottawa. Her research has focused on stepfamily adjustment, gender typing in stepmothers, and risk and resilience associated with marginalized experiences of motherhood. She has also provided psychological treatment to adults, couples, and stepfamilies in community and hospital settings for over a decade, where she has developed a particular expertise in helping clients cope with multiple family transitions.

Sara Graefe is a Vancouver-based playwright and screenwriter. Her writing about motherhood has appeared in *Literary Mama*, *A Family By Any Other Name*, *The Momoir Project* blog, and on her own blog, *Gay Girls Make Great Moms* (queermommy. wordpress.com). She teaches in the Creative Writing Program at the University of British Columbia.

Kate Greenway is currently pursuing a Ph.D. in Education at York University and was recently winner of the inaugural MIRCI Gustafson Graduate Student Conference Paper Award for "The Searchings of an Adopted Daughter." Her thesis *The Brooch of Bergen-Belsen: A Journey of Historiographic Poiesis* won the

Graduate Education Major Research Prize at York for 2009. She was also a recipient of the York Alumni "Excellence in Teaching" award for 2011, and she is on the 2013 *Toronto Star* Teacher Award Honour Roll. Her interests include arts-based research, remembrance and memorialization, mother-daughter relationships, adoption search issues, as well as stained and fused glass creation.

Karen Grove was born on the family farm near Rocky Mountain House. She has lived in Edmonton since 1965. Besides being a mother, grandmother, wife, friend, and itinerant Christian, she is an enthusiastic singer, retired reference librarian, and a passionate reader, student of literature, and dog lover.

Faye Hansen lives in Edmonton, Alberta, where she is raising two grandchildren. After a career in education, she is pursuing a writing career, having recently co-authored two local history books. She often draws on her rural upbringing for inspiration. Her passions are traveling and working with a local activist group on issues of peace and social justice.

Bobbi Junior lives with her husband of over 30 years in Edmonton, AB, where she works as a communications coordinator. Bobbi writes and speaks about caregiving, drawing stories from two life altering events—a devastating accident which left her teenage daughter paralyzed, and, now, her mother's journey with dementia, a story coming out soon in her book, *The Reluctant Caregiver*. Bobbi explores this topic and more on her blog, www.bobbijunior.com.

Pam Klassen-Dueck is a resource teacher in rural Manitoba. In 2010 she completed her Master of Education degree at Brock University. Her research interests include motherhood, girlhood, Mennonite history, theories of reading, children's and adolescent literature, and arts-based educational research.

Jessica Kluthe—recently named one of Edmonton's "Top 40 Under 40"—holds an M.F.A. from the University of Victoria. Her stories have appeared in *The Malahat Review*, *Little Fiction*, and *Red*

Savina Review as well as two recent anthologies: *Eat It: Food, Sex and Women's Writing* and *40 Below: Edmonton's Winter Anthology*. Her first book, *Rosina, the Midwife*, was on *The Edmonton Journal's* best sellers list for ten weeks. "Traces," the first chapter of her book, was shortlisted for the Alberta Writers' Guild James H. Gray award. Jessica teaches full time for MacEwan University's Bachelor of Communication Studies program.

Fiona Tinwei Lam is the author of two poetry books, *Intimate Distances* and *Enter the Chrysanthemum*, and the children's book, *The Rainbow Rocket*. Her poetry, fiction, and nonfiction appear in over twenty anthologies, including *The Best Canadian Poetry 2010*, *In Fine Form: An Anthology of Canadian Form Poetry*, and *Force Field: An Anthology of 77 BC Women Poets*. Along with Cathy Stonehouse and Shannon Cowan, she co-edited the literary nonfiction anthology *Double Lives: Writing and Motherhood*. She also edited *The Bright Well: Contemporary Canadian Poetry about Facing Cancer*.

Martha Marinara teaches writing at the University of Central Florida and has published most recently in *Massachusetts Review*, *Xavier Review*, *Clockhouse Review*, *Broken Bridge Review*, and *Lost Coast Review*. In 2000, she won the Central Florida United Arts Award for poetry. Her first novel, *Street Angels*, was published in 2006.

Sandra McEnhill holds a Master's degree in Social Work from the University of Calgary. She is the mother of three beautiful, spirited young women who are her inspiration for creative musings on mothering, separation and healing.

Naomi McIlwraith hails from Edmonton, Alberta, and earned her M.A. in English from the University of Alberta. Emerging from her cross-disciplinary study of *nêhiyawêwin*, the Plains Cree language, the poems in her collection *kiyâm* express her deep appreciation for her rich family history. A poet, essayist, teacher, editor, mentor, canoeist, and lover of all things just and green and riparian and lacustrine, Naomi is one of three authors who collaborated on *The Beginning of Print Culture in Athabasca Country: A Facsimile*

Edition and Translation of a Prayer Book in Cree Syllabics by Father Émile *Grouard, OMI.* Naomi's favourite words are "imagine" and "tawâw."

Melissa Morelli Lacroix, originally from Saskatchewan, is a writer and mother who lives and works in Edmonton. She has degrees in writing from Lancaster University and the University of Alberta. Her work has been published in Canada, the UK, and the U.S. Her first book of poetry, *A Most Beautiful Deception* (University of Alberta Press, 2014), further explores, among other things, food/body obsession.

P. R. (Piper) Newton is a Canadian author with two books currently available—*Shattered Embrace* and *And Then My Uterus Fell Out*. Her writing has been described as insightful, brutally honest, and emotional, and draws on her background in psychology and as a mother through birth and adoption. Piper is a proud geek mom to two boys, and is obsessed with *Doctor Who*, chocolate, and travel. http://prnewton.com

Sonia Nijjar graduated from the University of Alberta with a degree in Political Science and Creative Writing. She left Alberta to pursue a J.D. at Osgoode Hall Law School, where she will graduate in June, 2014. As a first-generation Indo-Canadian with an interest in creative non-fiction, she thinks endlessly about the gendered and cultured identities that have shaped her experience living in the Canadian diaspora. Sometimes, she finds time to write about it. She is grateful to all of her creative writing professors for instilling confidence and alleviating the fear that comes when we tell stories with truth.

Susan Olding is the author of *Pathologies: A Life in Essays*, winner of the Creative Nonfiction Collective's Readers' Choice Award for 2010. Her writing has appeared widely in literary journals, magazines, and anthologies across Canada and the United States, including *Event*, *The L.A. Review of Books*, *The Malahat Review*, and the *Utne Reader*, and has won a National Magazine Award, two Edna Awards, and many others.

Beth Osnes, Ph.D., is an assistant professor of theatre at the University of Colorado. She is featured in the award-winning documentary, *Mother: Caring for 7 Billion* (www.motherthefilm. com). Her book, *Theatre for Women's Participation in Sustainable Development* was published by Routledge in 2014.

Nichole Quiring is the mother of a pre-schooler and two stepdaughters. She has taught creative writing and penned various articles for a variety of publications. Nichole is currently employed with the Writers' Guild of Alberta. She became serious about her own creative writing four years ago when she began her first novel, *Wynter's Game* (working title).

Garrett Riggs lives in Florida with his sons; his fiction and nonfiction have been published in *Bright Lights Film Journal*, *The Popcorn Farm*, *The International Journal of the Humanities*, *Cineaste*, and *Tampa Review*.

M. Elizabeth (Betsy) Sargent, author of *Conversations about Writing: Eavesdropping, Inkshedding, and Joining In*, teaches writing at the University of Alberta; an earlier nonfiction piece about her aging parents, "Maintenance," won the Cécile E. Mactaggart Travel Award for Narrative Writing. She's proud that the sisters in "Our Dead Fish" have grown into strong women and expert writers: Hannah publishes on travel, integrative health, and food politics; Molly publishes on nonviolent action.

Robin Silbergleid is the author of the chapbook *Pas de Deux: Prose and Other Poems* (Basilisk Press, 2006), as well as *Frida Kahlo, My Sister* (Finishing Line Press) and the memoir *Texas Girl* (Demeter Press), both forthcoming in 2014. She lives in East Lansing, Michigan, where she directs the Creative Writing Program at Michigan State University and raises her two children.

Nancy Slukynski is a mother to three children all under the age of six. Aside from a mother, she is wife, daughter, sister, aunt, friend, writer, reader, listener, adventurer, hiker, and cooking enthusiast. A graduate of the University of Alberta, she also studied at the

University of Leeds (England) and Uppsala Universitet (Sweden). Based on her international experiences in Western Europe, Ukraine, South Korea, and the United States, she created and directed Dovetail Canada, an employee relocation support service. She currently lives with her family in northern Alberta.

Ann Sutherland lives and writes in Edmonton, Alberta. Her work has been published in anthologies, newspapers, and magazines, and has been broadcast on CBC Radio. She is married and is the mother of two adult sons.

Leslie Vryenhoek is a St. John's-based writer and editor whose poetry, fiction, and memoir have appeared across Canada and internationally. She is the author of *Scrabble Lessons* (fiction) and *Gulf* (poetry), published by Oolichan, and founding director of Piper's Frith: Writing at Kilmory. Leslie also works for Women in Informal Employment: Globalizing and Organizing (wiego.org), a research network that works to improve the lives and livelihoods of working poor women.

Stephanie Werner's nonfiction, prose, and poetry work has been published in literary journals, the *Women's Words Anthology,* and is forthcoming in *Our Canada Magazine.* She has a B.A. in English Literature and Creative Writing from Concordia University, and a B.Ed. from the University of Calgary. She is currently working on a poetry collection, a novel, and is a mother of three girls.

Kat Wiebe works as a wellness mentor in a Mental Health Capacity Building Project and as a pre-natal educator. She's been previously published in the 2009 Seal Press Anthology *Ask Me About My Divorce,* Mothering Magazine (on-line), and *Island Parent.* She is the author of *Willow Creek Summer* (Coteau Books, 2000).

Janice Williamson is Professor of English and Film Studies at the University of Alberta and a public intellectual committed to social justice. She mothers a teenage daughter. She has lectured widely and published essays on Canadian women's cultural work, mothering, adoption, trauma narratives, shopping malls, peace, and social justice. Most recently, she is the editor of *Omar Khadr, Oh Canada* (MQUP, 2012) and the co-editor of *Women's Words* (University of Alberta Extension, 2013). Her memoir *Crybaby!* (NeWest Press, 1998) explores family photography, memory, and trauma. Her essay "The Turquoise Sea" won a 2010 Canadian National Magazine Award. She has also published a collection of interviews, *Sounding Differences: Conversations with Seventeen Canadian Women Writers* (UTP, 1993)—a *Books in Canada* Best Book of the Year, and was principal editor of *Up and Doing: Canadian Women and Peace* (Women's Press, 1989).

Sheena Wilson is a professor of literature, culture and writing studies at Campus Saint-Jean, University of Alberta. Her research involves an interdisciplinary approach to cultural representations of human and civil rights abuses, as well as women's literature, film, and media. She is currently researching petrocultures: the socio-culture aspects of oil and energy in Canada and the world today. Her books include *Writing After the Gaze: Rupture of the Historical* (2007), *Joy Kogawa: Essays on Her Works* (2011), and *Sighting Oil* (2012). She is Director of the Bilingual Writing Centre (University of Alberta), editor-in-chief of the bilingual online journal *Imaginations: Journal of Cross Cultural Image Studies*, and co-director of the Petrocultures Research Group. Her homepage is sheenawilson.ca. Sheena has four children ranging in age from one to thirteen years: a stepson, two young boys, and a baby girl.